Seven Arrows

SEVEN ARROWS

Hyemeyohsts Storm

BALLANTINE BOOKS • NEW YORK

 Published in the United States by Ballantine Books, a division of Random House, Inc., New York, and simultaneously in Canada by Ballantine Books of Canada, Ltd., Toronto, Canada.

Library of Congress Catalog Card Number: 77-184216

ISBN 0-345-27757-0

This edition published by arrangement with Harper and Row, Publishers

Manufactured in the United States of America

First Ballantine Books Edition: September 1973
Seventh Printing: April 1978

The symbolic shield on the cover is designed by Hyemeyohsts Storm and painted by Karen Harris.

This book is lovingly dedicated to

Mary Ann Storm

Veronica Storm

Michelle Storm

Rocky Storm

Antonette Storm

There are some magical people I wish to thank for being so beautiful. They are:

Sandra Storm, *Medicine Song*

Robin and Tony Ridington, *Sun Bow Drum*

Douglas Latimer, *Guiding Wolf*

Harry and Linda MacCormack, *Lodge Builders*

Robert and Connie Sayre, *Arrow Makers*

Sid and Karen Harris, *Coyote and Painting Wolf*

Everet Frost and Faith Wylding

Neil Kleinman

and THE CANADIAN COUNCIL

Contents

The Pipe

You are about to begin an adventure of the People, the Plains Indian People. You probably have known of these People only by their whiteman names, as the Cheyenne, the Crow and the Sioux. Here you will learn to know of them as they were truly known among the People, as the Painted Arrow, the Little Black Eagle, and the Brother People.

The story of these People has at its center and all around it the story of the Medicine Wheel. The Medicine Wheel is the very Way of Life of the People. It is an Understanding of the Universe. It is the Way given to the Peace Chiefs, our Teachers, and by them to us. The Medicine Wheel is everything of the People.

The Medicine Wheel is the Living Flame of the Lodges, and the Great Shield of Truth written in the Sign of the Water. It is the Heart and Mind. It is the Song of the Earth. It is the Star-Fire and the Painted Drum seen only in the Eyes of Children. It is the Red Pipe of the Buffalo Gift smoked in the Sacred Mountains, and it is the Four Arrows of the People's Lodge. It is our Sun Dance.

The Medicine Wheel Way begins with the Touching of our Brothers and Sisters. Next it speaks to us of the Touching of the world around us, the animals, trees, grasses and all other living things. Finally it Teaches us to Sing the Song of the World, and in this Way to become Whole People.

Come sit with me, and let us smoke the Pipe of Peace in Understanding. Let us Touch. Let us, each to the other, be a Gift as is the Buffalo. Let us be Meat to Nourish each other, that we all may Grow. Sit here with me, each of you as you are in your own Perceiving of yourself, as Mouse, Wolf, Coyote, Weasel, Fox, or Prairie Bird. Let me See through your Eyes. Let us Teach each other here in this Great Lodge of the People, this Sun Dance, of each of the Ways on this Great Medicine Wheel, our Earth.

The Circle

Dear Reader:

If you and I were sitting in a circle of people on the prairie, and if I were then to place a painted drum or an eagle feather in the middle of this circle, each of us would perceive these objects differently. Our vision of them would vary according to our individual positions in the circle, each of which would be unique.

Our personal perceptions of these objects would also depend upon much more than just the different positions from which we looked upon them. For example, one or more of us might suffer from color blindness, or from weak eyesight. Either of these two physical differences would influence our perceptions of the objects.

There are levels upon levels of perspectives we must consider when we try to understand our individual perceptions of things, or when we try to relate our own perceptions to those of our brothers and sisters. Every single one of our previous experiences in life will affect in some way the mental perspective from which we see the world around us.

Because of this, a particular object or event may appear fearful to you at the same time that it gives pleasure to me, or appears completely uninteresting to a third person. All things that we perceive stimulate our individual imaginations in different ways, which in turn causes us to create our own unique interpretations of them. Love, hate, fear, confusion, happiness, envy, and all the other emotions we feel, act upon us to paint our perceptions of things in different colors.

If the thing I were to place within our circle should be an abstraction, such as an idea, a feeling, or a philosophy, our perceptions of it would then be even more complicated than if the object had been a tangible thing. And further, the number of different perceptions of it would become greater and greater as more and more people were added to our circle. The perception of any object, either tangible or abstract, is ultimately made a thousand times more complicated whenever it is viewed within the circle of *an entire People as a whole.* The understanding of this truth is the first lesson of the Medicine Wheel, and it is a vital part of Sun Dance Teaching.

The Medicine Wheel

In many ways this Circle, the Medicine Wheel, can best be understood if you think of it as a mirror in which everything is reflected. "The Universe is the Mirror of the People," the old Teachers tell us, "and each person is a Mirror to every other person."

Any idea, person or object can be a Medicine Wheel, a Mirror, for man. The tiniest flower can be such a Mirror, as can a wolf, a story, a touch, a religion or a mountain top. For example, one person alone on a mountain top at night might feel fear. Another might feel calm and peaceful. Still another might feel lonely, and a fourth person might feel nothing at all. In each case the mountain top would be the same, but it would be perceived differently as it reflected the feelings of the different people who experienced it. This book, *Seven Arrows,* is such a Mirror. It is a Medicine Wheel, just as you are.

Here is a drawing of a simple Medicine Wheel. Among the People, the Teachers usually constructed it from small stones or pebbles, which they would place like this before them upon the ground.

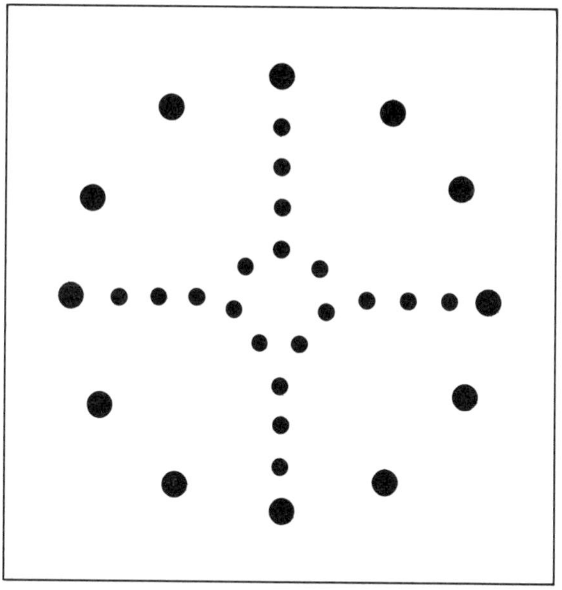

Each one of these tiny stones within the Medicine Wheel represents one of the many things of the Universe. One of them represents you, and another represents me. Others hold within them our mothers, fathers, sisters, brothers, and our friends. Still others symbolize hawks, buffalo, elks and wolves. There are also stones which represent religions, governments, philosophies, and even entire nations. All things are contained within the Medicine Wheel, and all things are equal within it. The Medicine Wheel is the Total Universe.

Our Teachers tell us that all things within this Universe Wheel know of their Harmony with every other thing, and know how to *Give-Away* one to the other, except man. Of all the Universe's creatures, it is we alone who do not begin our lives with knowledge of this great Harmony.

All the things of the Universe Wheel have spirit and life, including the rivers, rocks, earth, sky, plants and animals. But it is only man, of all the Beings on the Wheel, who is a determiner. Our determining spirit can be made whole only through the learning of our harmony with all our brothers and sisters, and with all the other spirits of the Universe. To do this we must learn to seek and to perceive. We must do this to find our place within the Medicine Wheel. To determine this place we must learn to *Give-Away.*

The *Vision Quest,* or perceiving quest, is the way we must begin this search. We must all follow our Vision Quest to discover ourselves, to learn how we perceive of ourselves, and to find our relationship with the world around us.

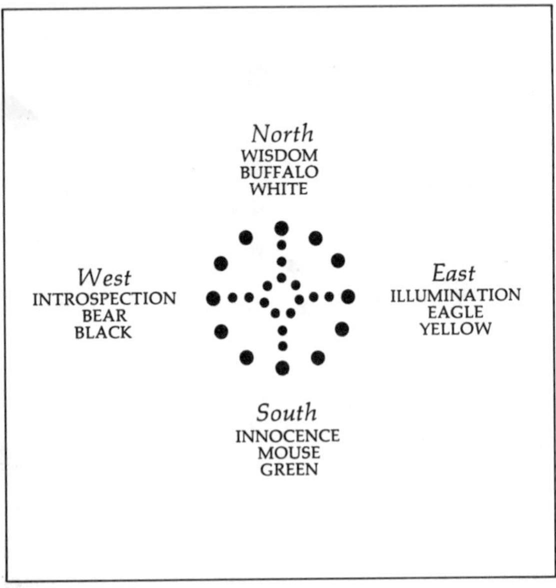

The Powers

Among the People, a child's first Teaching is of the Four Great Powers of the Medicine Wheel.

To the North on the Medicine Wheel is found Wisdom. The Color of the Wisdom of the North is White, and its Medicine Animal is the Buffalo. The South is represented by the Sign of the Mouse, and its Medicine Color is Green. The South is the place of Innocence and Trust, and for perceiving closely our nature of heart. In the West is the Sign of the Bear. The West is the Looks-Within Place, which speaks of the Introspective nature of man. The Color of this Place is Black. The East is marked by the Sign of the Eagle. It is the Place of Illumination, where we can see things clearly far and wide. Its Color is the Gold of the Morning Star.

At birth, each of us is given a particular Beginning Place within these Four Great Directions on the Medicine Wheel. This Starting Place gives us our first way of perceiving things, which will then be our easiest and most natural way throughout our lives.

But any person who perceives from only one of these Four Great Directions will remain just a partial man. For example, a man who possesses only the Gift of the North will be wise. But he will be a cold man, a man without feeling. And the man who lives only in the East will have the clear, far sighted vision of the Eagle, but he will never be close to things. This man will feel separated, high above life, and will never understand or believe that he can be touched by anything.

A man or woman who perceives only from the West will go over the same thought again and again in their mind, and will always be undecided. And if a person has only the Gift of the South, he will see everything with the eyes of a Mouse. He will be too close to the ground and too near sighted to see anything except whatever is right in front of him, touching his whiskers.

There are many people who have two or three of these Gifts, but these people still are not Whole. A man might be a Bear person from the East, or an Eagle person of the South. The first of these men would have the Gift of seeing Introspectively within Illumination, but he would lack the Gifts of Touching and Wisdom. The second would be able to see clearly and far, like the Eagle, within Trust and Innocence. But he would still not know of the things of the North, nor of the Looks-Within Place.

In this same way, a person might also be a Golden Bear of the North, or a Black Eagle of the South. But none of these people would yet be Whole. After each of us has learned of our Beginning Gift, our First Place on the Medicine

Wheel, we then must Grow by Seeking Understanding in each of the Four Great Ways. Only in this way can we become Full, capable of Balance and Decision in what we do. *Seven Arrows* speaks of this Growing and Seeking.

The Touching

To Touch and Feel is to Experience. Many people live out their entire lives without ever really Touching or being Touched by anything. These people live within a world of mind and imagination that may move them sometimes to joy, tears, happiness or sorrow. But these people never really Touch. They do not live and become one with life.

The Sun Dancer believes that each person is a unique Living Medicine Wheel, powerful beyond imagination, that has been limited and placed upon this earth to Touch, Experience and Learn. The Six Grandfathers Taught me that each man, woman, and child at one time was a Living Power that existed somewhere in time and space. These Powers were without form, but they were aware. They were alive. Each Power possessed boundless energy and beauty. These living Medicine Wheels were capable of nearly anything. They were beautiful and perfect in all ways except one. They had no understanding of limitation, no experience of substance. These Beings were total energy of the Mind, without Body or Heart. They were placed upon this earth that they might Learn the things of the Heart through Touching.

According to the Teachers, there is only one thing that all people possess equally. This is their loneliness. No two people on the face of this earth are alike in any one thing except for their loneliness. This is the cause of our Growing, but it is also the cause of our wars. Love, hate, greed and generosity are all rooted within our loneliness, within our desire to be needed and loved.

The only way that we can overcome our loneliness is through Touching. It is only in this way that we can learn to be Total Beings. God is a presence of this Total. *Heamavihio,* the Breath of Wisdom, and *Miaheyyun,* Total Understanding, are but two of the words in the Cheyenne language which express this Wholeness.

Medicines

This brings us back again to the Medicines. Each of us has as his personal Medicine a particular animal reflection. The characteristics of this reflection are determined by the nature of the animal itself, and also by the location of our individual Beginning Place on the Medicine Wheel. These two things, our Medicine Animal and our Beginning Place on the Medicine Wheel, together are the Beginning Gift to each of us from *Miaheyyun.*

For example, there are Eagle People, Elk People, Bear People, Wolf People, Pheasant People, Otter People, Buffalo People, Mice People, Rock People, Cloud People, and as many other kinds of People as there are kinds of living beings on this earth. And within each of these different kinds of People, there are the other differences of the Four Great Directions. Thus an Elk Person might be born a White Elk of the North, a Green Elk of the South, a Black Elk of the West, or a Yellow Elk of the East, depending upon the Direction of their Beginning Gift.

It would be impossible for me to tell you here of all the different Medicines, but I will speak to you of one of them, the Mouse. Mice live all their lives next to the ground, building their nests and gathering their food among the roots of the tall grass and bushes of the prairie. Because of this, Mice never see things at a distance. Everything they can see is right in front of them, where they can sniff at it with their noses and Touch it with their whiskers. Their lives are spent in Touching things in this way, and in gathering seeds and berries to eat.

But since it is really people that we are talking about, the Medicines must be understood within the ways of people. A Mouse Person would be one who saw everything close up, and whose vision would be limited to the immediate world around him. He would be a gatherer of things. He might gather facts, information, material objects, or even ideas. But because he could not see far enough to connect his world with that of the great prairie of the world around him, he would never be able to use or understand all that he saw and gathered.

If a Mouse Person were to be born into the North, his Beginning Gift would be the Gift of the Mind. His Name might be White Mouse. He would be a wise Mouse Person, but he would not yet be Whole. To become Whole, he would first have to seek the South, the place of Heart, and find the Marriage of this Gift with his Beginning Gift. Then he would have to visit and have Intercourse with the things of the East, Illumination, and travel to the Looks-Within place of the West. He would be able to Grow and become a Full Person only by doing all of these things, which would give him an understanding of his own Nature.

In this way he would become able to make his decisions within the Balance of the Four Directions. A person with the Beginning Gift of the Mind must always try to include his Heart in his decisions. When he does this, he begins to turn upon the Medicine Wheel. A man can live out his entire life without ever finding more than what was already within him as his Beginning Gift, but if he wishes to Grow he must become a Seeker and Seek for himself the other Ways.

When you have done this yourself, and when you have reached a full Understanding of the different Medicines of men, you will never feel surprised or threatened by the actions or decisions of your Brothers and Sisters. This Understanding is held within the meaning of the Shields carried by the People, which were Mirrors of their Medicines.

The Shields

To Understand the Sun Dance, we must first gain an Understanding of the Shields. My Father, whose Name was Hyemeyohsts and who gave his Name to me, was a Shield Maker and my Teacher. Hyemeyohsts taught me the construction of many Personal Shields. He also taught me the construction, Painting and Medicine Ways of the other Shields: the Men's Shields, Women's Shields, Children's Shields, Peace Shields, and the Sacred Shields. This was Hyemeyohst's Gift to me, as it was his Gift from his Fathers and from the Medicine Power, the Great Spirit. It is *Miaheyyun's* Gift to all of us, in order that we might learn and become Sun Dancers together.

There were originally Twelve Sacred Shields. At the time of the annual Renewal these Twelve Sacred Shields were brought together, and placed inside the Twelve Forked Poles which formed the outer circle of the Sun Dance Lodge, the People's Lodge. But these Sacred Shields were never together except at Renewal time. They were never kept by any one Tribe, but were passed on from one People to another.

If a man or woman in their lifetime aspired to high honor, they might seek to be the Keeper of one of these Sacred Shields. At any one time there could only be Twelve of these Keepers of the Shields of Light. These people were the most powerful and respected among all the People. They were Healers, Diviners, and Teachers. It was they who carried the Sacred Shields from camp to camp, and from Tribe to Tribe. I once asked my Father, Hyemeyohsts, about these Shields. He answered, "Over the Earth there are Twelve Great Tribes. Two of these Peoples are the Indian People. The Other Ten are the Other Peoples of the Earth. These Twelve Peoples are the Sacred Shields."

The Chief's Shields are tied to the Sacred Shields, in that they each tell a part of the Story of the Sacred Shields. There are Forty-Four of these Chief's Shields. Because the Chiefs were Peace Chiefs, and because their Shields were used for Teaching about the Sacred Shields and the Sun Dance Way, their Shields were also known as Peace Shields or Teaching Shields.

Among the People, every person possessed a Shield of one kind or another. One of the most important things to understand about these Shields is that they were never intended to give physical protection in battle. They were not made to turn away arrows or bullets, or for people to hide behind. Usually they were much too thin and fragile for this. Sometimes they were made from the tough hides of bears or buffalo bulls, but more often they were covered only with the soft skins of deer, antelope, coyote, otter, weasel, or even mice. They were then hung with eagle plumes, cedar pouches, tassels of animal fur, and many other things. They were also painted with various symbolic figures.

In the case of the Personal Shields, all of these different things represented the individual Medicines and Clan Signs of the men who carried them. These Signs told who the man was, what he sought to be, and what his loves, fears and dreams were. Almost everything about him was written there, reflected in the Mirror of his Shield.

The Personal Shields of Men were first constructed and given to them after their Vision Quest. On their return from the Quest, they would tell four chosen Spiritual Fathers of their experiences. Sometimes these experiences might actually have included true visions, but more often the Seeker would simply have had normal experiences and thoughts. His Fathers would then interpret these experiences, whatever they might have been, in terms of what they reflected of the Seeker's character and Medicines. They would then give him a Name which symbolically represented these things, and would construct for him a Shield that visually reflected the same symbolic meanings.

These Shields were carried by the men among the People in order that anyone they met might know them. Even when they rested in their lodges, their Shields were always kept outside where all could see them. They might be hung up by the lodge door, or up by the smoke hole, or on a tripod near the lodge, according to each person's own Medicine Way. But they were always kept outside, where the People might see and learn from them.

The women also carried their Medicine Signs in ways to be seen, usually as symbolic designs woven with porcupine quills or beads on their dresses or belts. The Woman's Belt was usually the most important of her Shields. Many times it was her only Shield, since not all of the different Peoples had both Dress and Belt Shields. These Belts were totally symbolic in design. Usually they contained the symbols of the

Brotherhood Societies the women lived among, such as the Kit Fox, Rattling Hoof, Crazy Dog, Coyote, or Painted Spear Societies. Added to these Signs were those of the woman's Spiritual Family, her blood family, and those of her personal Medicines, or Name.

The woman's Spiritual Clan relatives were called her Clan Fathers, Clan Mothers, Clan Uncles, and Clan Brothers and Sisters. It was to these people that she had her closest ties and responsibilities. Her Clan Fathers, Mothers and Uncles reciprocated these responsibilities to their Spiritual Children. Because of this, intermarriages between different Peoples caused the tradition of the Shields to spread widely. The Brotherhood of the Shields grew and became very powerful among the People. It was a time of great peace and Spiritual Renewal. It was the time of the Medicine Wheel, the Sun Dance.

Names

You have learned that Names always had symbolic meaning among the People, and were the Reflections of the People's individual Medicines. Within *Seven Arrows* you will meet many different People. Their Names will tell you much about them. They will tell you of their Medicines, and of their Ways of Perceiving.

One of these Reflections you will meet will be Day Woman. Translated within the People's tongue, Day Woman means Woman of the Sun, or Truth. This Name is also the Sign of Sun Dancing, or the Seeking of Harmony.

You will also meet a person called Hawk. The Hawk is the Little Brother of the Eagle. This person's Medicine Sign means that he was born with the Gift of Seeing both at a Distance and Closely. Of course, this should be interpreted symbolically rather than literally. Hawk's Gift was the ability to perceive clearly and broadly the things of the Mind, the Heart and of the Way of the People, the Sun Dance Way. Red Hawk was this man's Color. Red symbolizes Fire. Fire represents the Living Spirit of the People, and it also tells us that Hawk Perceives with the Illumination of the Golden East.

Within the Story of *Seven Arrows,* Night Bear's Name and his Way of Perceiving are also explained. As you learn of these things, you may also find your own Name.

The Stories

There are many old Stories told within *Seven Arrows.* These Stories were used among the People to Teach the meaning of the Sun Dance Way. They were themselves a Way of Understanding among the People, and also between different Peoples. Because the People did not have a written language, these Stories were memorized and passed down in one way through countless generations.

The Stories are about both animals and people. You will find Stories about Mice, Wolves, Raccoons, Otters and Buffalo. *These Stories are almost entirely allegorical in form, and everything in them should be read symbolically.* Every story can be symbolically unfolded for you through your own Medicines, Reflections and Seekings. As you do this, you will learn to See through the eyes of your Brothers and Sisters, and to share their Perceptions.

Questioning is one of the most vital paths to understanding these Stories, which will Teach you of the Sun Dance Way. When you question, the Medicine Wheel is turned for you. These Stories are magical Teachers in this way. They are Flowers of Truth whose petals can be unfolded by the Seeker without end.

These Stories were meant to be told, not

written. In this way the Teachers, whether speaking verbally or in sign language, were able to give inflections to particular words to reflect their symbolic content. For example, the word "year" holds many different meanings. It reflects the concept of a cycle, which is symbolically represented by a circle, which in turn symbolizes the Medicine Wheel and the Universe. Similarly, the word "way" can mean simply a path or direction, but it can also mean an entire philosophy of life, a religion, or a Way of Perceiving.

Within *Seven Arrows*, and particularly within the old Stories, the words to which the Teller would have given inflections are capitalized. *These words are symbolic Teachers, and it is very important that you approach them symbolically rather than literally.* These capitalized words may sometimes seem inconsistent, but do not be confused by this. The Coyote is known among the People as a gentle trickster, and his Way is a part of Sun Dance Learning.

I want you, my Brothers and Sisters, to know that I too am still learning about the Way of the People. The Understanding of this Way is not found just through the memorization of Stories and Symbols. It is a Living, Growing Thing that comes from Touching and Experiencing within each of the Four Great Directions.

The Sun Dance Way itself is a Living Thing. It is always Growing and Turning within the People. It is not to be learned by studying archaic rituals or traditions, but by Seeking Understanding and then allowing it to Grow within your own Heart and Mind. Within *Seven Arrows* there are many ancient Stories taught to me by my Fathers and Grandfathers. But there are also new Stories that I have written from within my own Understanding and Experience. They are there as Teachings from which you can Learn, and which you can Build upon in your own Way. This Turning and Growing is called the Building of the Thunder Bow.

Seven Arrows itself, from beginning to end, is a Teaching Story. It is a Story of the Sun Dance Way, constructed in the same manner in which I was taught by my Fathers to tell Stories. It is a complete Medicine Wheel all by itself. Read the book with a friend, wife, or loved one, or best of all, with children. You too are a Medicine Wheel, and the magic of your Perceiving will be unfolded.

Hyemeyohsts

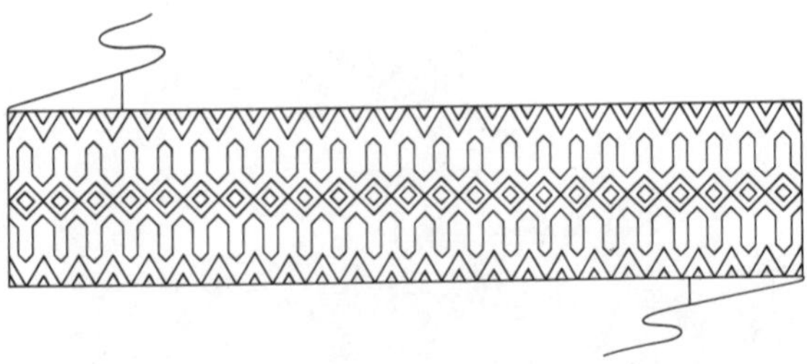

The Medicine Wheel Circle is the Universe. It is change, life, death, birth and learning. This Great Circle is the lodge of our bodies, our minds, and our hearts. It is the cycle of all things that exist. The Circle is our Way of Touching, and of experiencing Harmony with every other thing around us. And for those who seek Understanding, the Circle is their Mirror. This Circle is the Flowering Tree.

When we experience the Flowering Tree, we hear the lightning flash within our darkness. Then we see the thunder within this illumination. The one speaks quietly to us, and the other sings to us of our learning. Together they become one song. This song they sing is the Song of the Coyote, the gentle trickster of learning.

As the Coyote sings, his song is echoed by many other Coyotes. These songs, the Teachers tell us, are the songs of the many Reflections that live within all of us.

For example, within every man there is the Reflection of a Woman, and within every woman there is the Reflection of a Man. Within every man and woman there is also the Reflection of an Old Man, an Old Woman, a Little Boy, and a Little Girl.

From my Grandfathers I learned an old Story about the Coyote which speaks to us of these Reflections. I will now tell you this old Story, which is also a new Story.

It seems that at One time the People were Living Scattered Out all Over the World, and Each of them had Heard about a very Powerful Person who Lived in the River. It was Said that this Person could Settle any Problem, no matter what it was.

Because no one really Wanted to Admit to Anyone Else that they Possessed Problems, Everybody had to Sneak Down to the River Alone when they Wished to Hear this Powerful Person Speak. And Everybody did Sneak Down to the River to Hear the Powerful Person, but No One ever Spoke to Anyone Else About it.

Then One Day a Little Boy and a Little Girl Returned from the River. The Little Boy and the Little Girl began to Talk to Everyone About their Journey.

"It was a very Strange thing," the Children said.

"What was it that was so very Strange?" the People asked as they Gathered Around the Children, Pretending they did not Know.

"Have you not Seen what is at the River?" the Children asked.

"No," the People All answered. "What was it that you Saw there?"

"Have All of you not Sneaked Down to the River, just as we Did?" the Children asked in Surprise.

"Who ever Said such a silly thing?" the People asked Angrily.

"We did," the Children answered, Becoming Frightened.

"Never say such an Awful thing again," the People told them Accusingly.

The Children Became even more Frightened. They Perceived that they were Strangers even to their Own Mothers and Fathers.

This Caused All the People to Move Away, Leaving the Little Boy and the Little Girl Alone Upon the Prairie. That Night they were all Alone and Frightened. They Cried, because Everything seemed to be so Terrible.

"Calm yourselves, my Children," a Gentle Voice suddenly said to them. The Children Looked to See who had Spoken.

"Who are you?" the Children asked.

"It is me, Old Man Coyote," the Voice said. As he Spoke, Old Man Coyote Entered the Children's Lodge and Set Down a Bundle of Firewood Beside them:

"And it is me, Old Woman Coyote," another Voice said to them Softly. She Sat Down and Began to Turn an Arrow Within her Bow to Make them a Fire.

Soon there was a Warm Fire and there was Light Within their Lodge. Sitting Across the Fire from them were an Old Man and an Old Woman.

"Who are you? the Children asked. They were now Feeling better.

"We are your Grandfather and your Grandmother," the Old Woman answered, Offering the Children some Buffalo Meat.

"And we are Also the Powerful Person at the River," the Old Man added, Offering the Children some Sweet Foods.

"But we Saw Only ourselves when we Visited the River," the Little Boy and the Little Girl said Together.

"Yes, that is True," the Old Woman and the Old Man answered Together.

"I do not Understand this," the Little Girl said.

"How very Strange," the Little Boy said.

"The People have All Visited the River as you Did," the Old Woman began.

"And they All Saw Only themselves, just as you Did." The Old Man Finished the words.

"How very Strange," the Little Girl said.

"I do not Understand," the Little Boy said.

"They too Thought it Strange," the Old Man answered.

"And they too did not Understand," the Old Woman answered.

"Were you also their Reflections, as you were ours?" the Little Girl asked Excitedly.

"And they did not Trust their Eyes," the Little Boy said with Excitement.

"Yes," the Old Man said, "you are Right. Now you must Find the People and Offer them these Gifts."

"What are these Gifts?" the Little Girl asked.

"They are these Two Coyote Robes," the Old Woman answered. "Tell them to Put them On and they will not be Hungry any more."

And so the Children Did this. They Found the People the Next Day and Offered them the Two Coyote Robes.

"What are these for?" the People asked. "There are Thousands upon Thousands of these Coyote Robes to be had," they laughed. "What we Need to Satisfy our Hunger are Buffalo, not these silly Robes."

"Put them On," the Two Children Coaxed the People. And as they Coaxed the People to Put On the Coyote Robes, they Spoke to them of their Vision. But this only made the People Laugh even Harder.

Within this Camp there Lived Two Kind People. One was a Man and the Other was a Woman. They were Living Together in the Same Lodge. These Two Kind People Loved the Little Girl and the Little Boy, and Wished to Care for them. They Both Stepped Into the Circle of People and Put their Arms Around the Two Children, Adopting them.

"I will Wear One of the Robes," the Man said to the Little Girl.

"And I too will Wear One of the Robes," the Woman said to the Little Boy.

The Children Gave their Robes to the Man and the Woman who had Adopted them, and the Man and Woman Put them On.

"There are Buffalo to the North and to the South," the Man said to the People, because now he could See them.

"And there are Buffalo to the West and to the East," the Woman said, because now she too could See them.

The People All Became Excited, because Suddenly they too could See the Buffalo.

"Let us Hunt them in the North," some of the People said.

"No," Others Quickly Shouted. "The Buffalo are much Fatter in the South."

"No! No!" still Others argued. "They are Bigger in the West."

"No! No!" the Rest of the People said Angrily. "The Best Ones of All are to the East."

"Please! Please! Do not Fight Among yourselves," the Man, Woman, Little Boy and Little Girl Pleaded. "You are Only Tricking yourselves. Put On the Coyote Robes and you will Understand."

But the People were very Angry, and they would not Come Together in a Circle to Counsel.

"Kill these Trouble Makers," the People shouted. And they Rushed in All Together Upon these Four who were Sitting in the Middle of the Camp Circle. But when they Reached the Center of the Camp Circle, they Discovered that the Little Boy and the Little Girl had Become a Flowering Forked Tree. They Quickly Looked for the Man and the Woman who had Adopted the Two Children, but All they Found of them were their Tracks. They were the Tracks of Two Mountain Lions. These Tracks were Leading to the North.

The People were so Angry they Struck at the Flowering Tree.

"Let us Follow the Two Lions and Kill them," the People then Decided Together. They Followed the Tracks to the North to Find them. They Ran and Ran, until Suddenly the Tracks of the Two Lions Became the Tracks of Four Lions. These Led the People in a Great Circle Back to the Flowering Tree.

The People Sat Down Together Around the Tree because they were so Tired, and they Began to Talk to One Another.

"Why are we Doing this?" Some of them asked the Others.

"We do not really Wish to Hurt or Kill Anything," said some Others.

"Then why were you Running?" asked Still Others.

"We were Only Following you," those Spoken To said in Amazement. And they All Began to Laugh.

Then the People All Heard Singing, and they Looked Up. There, Sitting in the North, they Saw a White Coyote and he was Singing. They Also Looked to the South, and Sitting there was a Green Coyote. She too was Singing. Then they Looked to the West, and Sitting there was a Black Coyote and he was Singing. Finally they Looked to the East, and Sitting there was a Gold Coyote and she was Singing.

The People Sat there Quietly All Together and Learned these Four Beautiful Songs. They were the Songs of Four Lions. Then the People Looked All Around and Saw that Each of them was Wearing a Coyote Robe. They put their Arms Around Each Other and Began to Dance Toward the Flowering Tree Together in a Great Circle. The People were Happy.

This Story we have just heard has now become a portion of our awareness, or understanding. Stories are like paths, or Ways. Whenever we hear a Story, it is as if we were physically walking down a particular path that it has created for us. Everything we perceive upon this path or around it becomes part of our experience, both individually and collectively.

This particular story has within it many Mirrors which Reflect certain realities that exist in all of us. Each one of these little Mirrors, when we look into it as a whole thing, or Wheel, can be a Teacher for us. So that you may understand this more fully, let us now experience the Story once more in a new way. Let us open our eyes wide as we walk down its path a second time, so that we may look into some of its Mirrors and see the many images that are Reflected there for us.

This is a Story that has been told to us about the Trickster of Learning. It seems there are times in each of our lives when we are not in balance with our brothers and sisters. We are unable to communicate with ourselves or with the world we live in. And yet each one of us knows of the powerful person who lives within us, and who can settle any problem, no matter what it is. This powerful person is our spirit. But we never really want to admit to anyone, or even to ourselves, that we actually have a problem. So every one of us sneaks down many times to the river inside ourselves. This river is the spirit of the power of the universe. But when we go there to hear the powerful person, we usually are afraid to speak about it.

That is, until one day the little boy and the little girl within each of us speaks to us about it. This little boy and this little girl begin to make themselves known in our minds.

"It is a very strange thing," these children say inside our own hearts and minds.

"What is it that is so very strange?" we ask, not wanting to admit to anyone else, or even to the two children inside ourselves, that we know

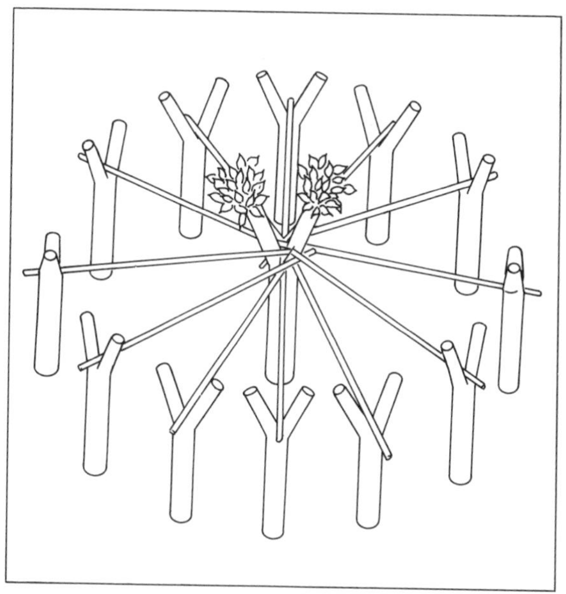

what they are talking about.

But of course the children within us speak again, asking us, "Have you never seen what is at the river?"

And we reply, "No."

And even though we know, we ask, "What was it that you saw?"

We do this because we do not want anyone else to know that we have often sneaked down to the river, like the children.

Of course these children within us are surprised, and they ask us again, "Have all of you not sneaked down to the river, just as we did?"

"Who ever said such a silly thing?" we answer ourselves angrily.

"Ourselves," the children say inside us. They are now becoming frightened.

"Never say such an awful thing again," we say to ourselves accusingly.

And, as you remember from the Story, this makes the little girl and the little boy inside us very afraid. But it also teaches us something. It teaches us that we cannot trust ourselves, because the mother and father that are within us are not able to communicate with the little boy and the little girl that are also within us. They are strangers to each other.

And so we move away, putting those things out of our mind. We leave the little boy and the little girl within us there alone upon the prairie, which symbolizes everyday life.

Within our time of night, which here symbolizes introspection, fear, and blindness, we know the children within us are crying, and that they are alone and frightened. During one of these nights, while we are feeling lonely and afraid and wondering why everything seems so terrible, we hear a voice speaking inside us.

The voice tells us to calm ourselves. We hear the voice say to the children inside us, "Calm yourselves, my children." And we, like the children, look to see who it is that has spoken.

"Who are you?" we hear the children ask.

"It is me, Old Man Coyote," we hear the voice answer the children.

"And it is me, Old Woman Coyote," we hear a softer voice inside us say.

Then we feel her turn an arrow in us, a teaching arrow within the bow that is our tension, to make the fire.

Soon inside us there is a bright fire. This fire represents the living spirit, either of a person or of a whole people. It is warm within us, and this fire illuminates the darkness that is in the lodges of our minds. Sitting within our illumination, this warm and living spirit of the people, are the old man and the old woman. And these ancient ways speak to us, offering some food of the spirit to the two children inside us.

"Every man and every woman is the Sun Dance Lodge and the Living Circle of the Flowering Tree. We, the grandparents, Dance around you. There are six of us grandfathers. We are the Power of the North, the Growing of the South, the Changing of the West, the Rebirth of the East, the Law of the Universe and its Mirror, the Law of the Earth. And there also are six of us grandmothers. We are the Marriages of these Teaching Ways. We twelve Dance together in One Lodge. We are also the powerful person at the river inside you."

Then we hear the children say, "But we saw only ourselves when we visited the river which flows inside us."

"That is true," the old Marriage of Teaching and the old Teacher of Marriage answer together.

"I do not understand this," the little boy says inside us.

"How very strange," the little girl says inside us.

And we hear the old woman and the old man say, "All of the people come to the river, and they too perceive only themselves, as you do."

"How very strange," we hear the little boy say.

"I do not understand," we hear the little girl say.

"They too perceive only themselves, and they too think it strange," we hear the old man within us answer.

"Are you then the reflection of what they are?" we hear the little girl ask excitedly.

"And they do not believe in themselves," we hear the little boy say inside us.

"You must find the People and offer them these Gifts of Understanding that you now see inside yourself," we hear the old man say.

"But what are these Gifts?" we hear the little girl say.

"They are the Understandings which you now perceive inside yourself, and which you must *Give-Away* to the People so that they may also perceive. Then they will no longer be starving for these Ways of Learning," the old Woman said.

Within their new Illumination, the children find the People and offer them these Coyote Robes of Understanding.

"What are these things for?" the people ask. "There are thousands upon thousands of these Trickster Coyotes. Their robes are everywhere, and they are much too flimsy to wear. Just hearing the howling of all those tricksters is enough," and they laugh.

The two children coax the people to put the robes on, telling them of their beautiful Vision, but the People laugh even harder. But within the camp of people there is a man and a woman who were living together in one body. These two people love the little boy and the little girl that are inside them, and wish to care for them. They show all the people around them that they care for the two children within them. The woman asks the little boy for his robe, and the man within that woman then asks the little girl for her robe.

The children inside this Medicine Woman give the man and woman their robes to put on.

"These are our Gifts in Wisdom, and in Trust and Innocence," the man says to the People because now he can perceive them.

"And they are also our Gifts within Introspection and Illumination," the woman says, because now she has Given Birth to them and can perceive them.

The People become excited by this Illumination.

"Let us hunt these Gifts of Wisdom," some of the People say.

"No," others quickly shout. "These Gifts of Trust and Innocence are more healing."

"No! No!" still others of the People argue. "There are bigger Gifts of Introspection to the West."

"No! No!" the rest of the People reply angrily. "The best Gifts of all are to be found to the East, within Illumination."

"Please! Please! Do not fight among yourselves," the man, woman, little boy and little girl plead. These four represent the Circle of the People. "You are only tricking yourselves. Make this Teaching part of yourselves, and you will see that you are all out of Balance."

But the People are very angry, and they will not come together in a Circle to talk with one another.

"Kill the troublemakers," the People all shout. Then they all rush together. But when they reach the center of their Circle they discover only the Twin Reflections of themselves, the Flowering Forked Tree. The People are so angry with themselves that they strike at this Flowering Tree.

Then they quickly begin to pursue the man and woman who are the symbols of the Teachers among the people. They discover for the first time the spirit and meaning of what these Teachers represent. The Signs of these Teachers are the tracks of the Lion, the symbol of Balance. These signs Teach of the North, the place of Wisdom.

"Let us follow the Signs of these Two Balances and kill them," the People decide together in their blind anger. Not realizing that they have been Tricked into doing something together as a Whole People, they all run off together in the direction of Wisdom.

They run and run until they perceive the signs of Four Balances, and discover that they have run in a Great Circle and have come back to themselves. Even though the People are angry, they have been Tricked into coming together as a Whole People. And because they are now a Whole People, they are able to discover their Balance within the Ways of the Four Directions.

All the People then sit down around the Flowering Tree because they are so tired, and as soon as they have done this they begin to communicate with each other.

"Why are we doing this?" one asks the other.

"We do not want to hurt or kill anything," others say.

"Then why were you running?" ask still others.

"We were only following you," those who now are communicating say in amazement.

All the People begin to laugh.

Then they hear sounds of Harmony, and they look up, wanting to perceive it.

There, sitting within Wisdom, is a Wise Coyote-Teacher. He is singing, and he is in Harmony with the People. Next the People perceive within Trust and Innocence, and sitting there is a Trusting Coyote-Teacher. She too is within Harmony. Then they perceive within Introspection, and sitting there is an Introspective Coyote-Teacher. He also is within Harmony. Finally they perceive within Illumination, and there they see an Illuminated Coyote-Teacher sitting within Harmony.

The People all sit there quietly together, and learn these Four Harmonies of Balance.

Each of the People can now perceive each other, and they realize that they are all Teachers.

They put their arms around each other and care for each other, and they adopt each other. Then they begin to Dance toward the Flowering Tree together in a Great Circle. Now they are Sun Dancing together for the first time as a Whole People. But still more important, they now are able to Sun Dance with their own selves as well. Each person's Way of Perceiving has been changed.

As we learn we always change, and so does our perceiving. This changed perception then becomes a new Teacher inside each of us.

Often our first Teacher is our own heart. This Teaching Voice is spoken of by the old Sun Dance Teachers as the Chief. Within the Stories, or Mirrors, this Teacher may be symbolized by the Old Man, the Old Woman, the Little Boy, the Little Girl, the Contrary, the Spirit, or by *Vihio,* the Knowledgeable Fool. These Seven Symbols, or Teaching Arrows, are a tiny portion of the Great Mirror. When you have learned to place these Seven pieces of Mirror together within yourself, you will discover that there are Seven more. Their Reflections will go on and on forever.

Four of these same Seven Arrows are symbolized by the Four Directions. They are the North, South, West and the East. As you remember, these symbolize Wisdom, Trust and Innocence, Introspection and Illumination. These are known as the Four Ways. The Mother Earth is the Fifth Mirror. The Sky, with its Moon, Sun and Stars, is the Sixth Mirror. The Seventh of these Arrows is the Spirit. Among the People, this Spirit is spoken of as the Universal Harmony which holds all things together. All of us, as Perceivers of the Mirrors, are the Eighth Arrow.

Now what we shall do, all of us together, is to Look into another one of these Teaching Mirrors. The Name of this Mirror is the Singing Stone.

The young man you will see in this Mirror is yourself. If you are a woman, then you should change the symbol of the young man to that of a young woman.

"Sand blows endlessly into the rivers, yet they never fill up," Fire Dog said quietly.

The young man who sat across from him watched their tiny fire and moved uncomfortably.

"Whirlwinds great and small bring the sand.

The small ones dance for our eyes, but the great ones are so vast that we can only feel a part of them. We experience them as the prairie wind," Fire Dog went on without looking up. "And so it is with our understanding."

"But why has the Power chosen to Teach us in this Way?" the young man asked. "If the Power is so all knowing, why then does he not just speak to us in a simple way that we can all understand?"

The fire illuminated Fire Dog's white braids. The old man sat quietly and unmoving. The young man watched him intently.

"There is a smile within your eyes, little brother," Fire Dog said softly, "because you think my silence is Trickery from the South."

"You understood my question, did you not?" the young man asked. "I did not wish my question to stake you down, but I have wondered for a long time about this. How is it that we are Taught by the Power in this manner?"

"Place your hand over the fire, Black Elk, and feel of its heat," the old man answered.

The young man placed his hand over the fire. He felt the heat grow within it, until he was forced to pull his hand away again. Then Fire Dog spoke once more.

"All that you feel and see, and the flowers these things open in your mind, are your answers," Fire Dog said, raising his voice. "The fire is life. It is warm, glowing with color, surrounded by the night, yet speaking of the day. It is promising, painful, dangerous, harmonious, visible at this moment, then moving into invisibility, alive, consuming, changing and finally disappearing into death. We ourselves are another fire upon this earth. We are part fire, and part dream. We are the physical mirroring of Miaheyyun, the Total Universe, upon this earth, our Mother. We are here to experience. We are a movement of a hand within millions of seasons, a wink of touching within millions and millions of sun fires. And we speak with the Mirroring of the Sun."

"And the whirlwind?" Black Elk asked. "Is this the Teaching Voice? If it is, I have found it silent, for it has taught me nothing."

"The wind is the Spirit of these things," Fire Dog answered, looking up. "The force of the natural things of this world are brought together within the whirlwind. Each tiny grain of sand is separate from the next, but they are all one thing within the whirlwind. Some people bite their own lips in anger when the whirlwind blows sand into their eyes. Others stand in awe or fear of these tiny swirls of wind and sand. Children run among them, and a few learn from them. We too are of this earth, and we too are brought together within these whirlwinds, these turning wheels. These teachers speak loudly to those of us who listen."

"Your Teaching is painted over my eyes," Black Elk said as he added more wood to the fire. "But I am torn with confusion. If these voices speak so loudly, how is it that I cannot hear them?"

"A Shield speaks softly, yet it can reflect for you many of the ways within these whirlwinds that you may hear them sing. Would you have a Shield painted for you?" asked Fire Dog.

"Yes," answered the Youngman. "What is this Story?"

"It is the Story of the Singing Stone," Fire Dog began.

One Day a Youngman of the People Approached his Grandfather and Sat with him.

"Grandfather," the Youngman said, "I Hear that somewhere there Exists a Singing Stone, and that when it is Found, it will Hold great Medicine for its Finder. Is this True?"

"It is True," answered the Grandfather. "Go to the North and you will Find it."

At the Next Sunrise the Youngman Began his Journey to the North. It was his First Day. He had not Gone Far Before he Saw what Appeared to be Smoke in the Distance.

"It is a Fire!" the Youngman thought. "I will be Burned!" He was very Afraid.

But he was Determined to Go On. That Evening he Saw that the Smoke was the Rainbow Mist of the Sacred Mountains. That Night he Rested.

His Second Day he Walked Among the Pines of the Sacred Mountains until he Came Into a Broad Circle that was Green and Bright with the Sun. The Pines completely Circled this wonderful Place except to the East, which was Left Open. The Youngman Walked with the Sun all that Day to Cross this Place. That Night he Slept.

His Third Day the Youngman Came to a very beautiful Lake. Everything of the World was Mirrored in this Lake. The Flowers, Trees, Beings of the Prairie, Lodges of the People, the Mountains, the Day and Night Sky and the Sun were All Reflected there. This was the Medicine Lake. He Drank the Sweet Water from the Lake and Refreshed himself. Then he Rested.

His Fourth Day the Youngman Saw his Grandfather Sitting Upon a Stone Waiting for him.

"Welcome, Grandson," his Grandfather said.

The Old Man's Hair was White, and his Braids Touched the Ground. The Old Man Fed his Grandson Buffalo Meat, Roots and Berries of the Prairie, and Other wonderful Tasting Food. After the Youngman had Finished his Meal, his Grandfather Offered him a Gift.

"Here are my Braids," the Grandfather said, Cutting his Braids and Offering Them to the Youngman.

But the Youngman could not Keep the Braids Upon his Own Head, even when he Tried to Tie Them there.

"Your Braids will not Stay Upon my Head," the Youngman said.

"Then Tie Them to your Waist," the Grandfather answered.

The Youngman did this. Then he said, "I have Come for the Singing Stone."

"The Singing Stone is not to the North," the Grandfather answered. "It is to the South."

The Youngman Returned to his Camp and he Rested. This was the End of his First Day. The Next Morning he Began his Journey South.

His First Day he Met a Mother Fox and her Kit Foxes. They Played with the Youngman and Walked with Him.

"Where are you Going?" the Kit Foxes asked him.

"I am Going to Find the Singing Stone," the Youngman answered. "Can you Help me?"

"Yes!" the Kit Foxes answered. "Follow the River and you will Find the Singing Stone."

That Night the Youngman Slept.

His Second Day the Youngman Met a Turtle. The Turtle Walked with him All that Day and Sang him Four Songs.

That Night he Rested.

His Third Day the Youngman was Walking Along the River and suddenly Found that he could Go no Further.

"Now what will I Do?" the Youngman asked Himself.

"I will Help you," answered Coyote. "Just Follow me."

Now the Youngman could See Coyote, and he Followed him Onto the Prairie. But soon the Trails Coyote Led the Youngman Upon Crossed and Recrossed and Ran Off in Every Direction.

"You have Tricked me!" the Youngman exclaimed.

"No," answered Coyote, "I have not Tricked you. The River is right Over There." The Youngman Looked, and he Saw that it was. That Night the Youngman Slept.

His Fourth Day the Youngman Set Out again. He soon Became Confused and Discouraged.

"Nowhere can I See the Singing Stone!" the Youngman said, "All that I can See Here are the Mountains, Prairie, Sky, Sun, Trees and Beings of this Place." He Became very Angry.

Then the Youngman Heard a Voice saying,

"Look at Me!" It was a beautiful Many Colored Dragonfly. It was Balanced Above the Moving Waters of the River.

And the Youngman Leaned Far Out Over the River to See his beautiful Brother more Closely.

"See how beautiful I am," said the Dragonfly. His Wings Reflected the Sun from Above, and also All that was Upon the Face of the Water.

The Youngman was Held within Wonder at the beauty he Saw Reflected there. Then he Lost his Balance and Fell into the River. He became Afraid and thought he would Drown.

"You have Tricked me!" he cried Angrily.

"No, little Brother," answered Dragonfly. "I have not Tricked you. You have only Fallen into the River. The Singing Stone is not to the South, it is to the West."

The Youngman Returned to the Camp and Rested. This was the End of his Second Day. The Next Day he Began his Journey West.

His First Day Walking West the Youngman Met a She Dog and her Puppies. They Walked with him All that Day. The Youngman Played with the Puppies and Found Comfort with Them. That Night he Rested.

His Second Day he Found a Place of Sweet Grass. It Took him One Full Day to Cross it, and that Night he Slept.

His Third Day he Met a Great Elk with Lightning Painted on his Shoulders and in his Horns. He Walked with the Youngman All that Day, and Sang him Four Songs. That Night the Youngman Rested.

His Fourth Day the Youngman Saw a Mouse, and the Mouse Saw the Youngman. The Mouse Began to Run and the Youngman Chased him All Day. He Chased the Mouse into a Cave. The Cave Became Smaller and Smaller until it was only Big Enough for the Mouse. The Mouse Stopped, Turned Around and Spoke to the Youngman.

"Why are you Chasing me?" asked the Mouse.

"I am Seeking the Singing Stone," the Youngman answered.

"This is a Mouse Cave," the Mouse said to the Youngman, "The Singing Stone is not to the West, it is to the East."

This was the End of the Youngman's Third Day and he Went Back to the Camp and Rested. The Next Morning was the Beginning of his Journey East.

His First Day he had not Walked very Far before he Saw a beautiful Lodge in the Distance. An Old Woman met him at that Lodge and Fed him a great Meal which they Ate Together.

"What is this wonderful Lodge, Grandmother?" the Youngman asked.

"This is the Lodge of Gambling, Grandson," answered the Old Woman. He Rested that Night with the Old Woman.

His Second Day after he Left that Lodge he Saw Another Lodge in the Distance. It was even more beautiful than the First, and it was Glowing Brightly. It was Painted with All the Colors.

Mahko, the Grandfather-Little Boy, Came Out and Greeted the Youngman.

"Welcome my Grandson," Mahko said, Taking the Youngman into his Lodge. "I have been Expecting you. Here, Come Sit with me and Eat this fine Buffalo Meat. It is my Gift to you."

After they had Eaten, the Youngman asked Mahko about the Painted Lodge.

"This is the Lodge of the Painted Arrows, the Sacred Arrows," Mahko answered.

The Youngman Slept there that Night.

His Third Day, the Youngman Came to a very Wide River. He Looked Up and Down its Banks for a Place to Cross, but he could Find None. Then he Listened Closely to his Own Heartbeat, and he Felt his Heart say, "There is Always a Place for Children to Cross the River." So he Crossed, and as he Did So the Water never Came Above his Knees. That Night he Rested.

His Fourth Day, the Youngman Sat Upon a Hill. He Saw in the Distance a Strange Camp. He Got to his Feet and Walked Toward the Camp. He Became very Afraid because the Paintings and Signs of the Lodges were Strange to him, and he could not Recognize them. The Closer he Came to the Lodges, the more he Felt the Bow of Tension Pulled within him: But he was Determined to Go On.

He Stepped into the Circle of Lodges. Then his Sisters, Mothers, Brothers, Fathers, Grandmothers, Grandfathers, Uncles, Aunts, and all his Relatives Came Out to Greet him, saying, "Welcome to our Counsel Fire, Singing Stone."

"And that cuts it off," Fire Dog said as he reached for his Pipe.

Everything you have just read within this Story, the Singing Stone, is a portion of the Teaching of the Flowering Tree. Now let us listen together, and we shall unfold some of the petals of this Flower.

The young woman in the Story you have just read goes to one of her grandmothers and asks her about the Singing Stone. This grandmother is a symbol of one of the Six Directions, the North, South, West, East, and the Sky and the Earth. And she is, of course, also a symbol of the Teacher inside the young woman. The young woman begins to speak with this Teacher, which is herself.

"Go to the north," the grandmother tells the young woman in the Story. The Teaching here is that we must first look for those things that we seek within Wisdom.

The Story then speaks of the young woman's sunrise and her First Day. Both of these symbols represent mean new Illumination, new beginning, or new questioning.

The fire in the story represents the Spirit of the People. It is also a symbol of the East.

Evening means the time of rest and dreams. It is also the entrance to the Introspective Way of the West.

Rainbows and rainbow mist symbolize the myths that we create here upon the earth.

On the young woman's Second Day, she walks across the place of the pines. This place of the pines, and the broad circle within it, are symbolic of that special place within each of us that is the lodge of all of our feelings, thoughts, fantasies and dreams.

On her Third Day, the woman comes to a very beautiful lake. This lake is a symbol of the Mirror of Totality, or Wholeness. Some people perceive this Totality to be God, but this is only one of many Reflections within this Mirror.

On the woman's Fourth Day, she meets her own Reflection, the grandmother, again. The meal the young woman eats with her Teacher is the food of learning, or information.

The grandmother's braids are symbols of experience. The fact that her braids touch the ground means that her experience touches the Natural Law of the Mother Earth. Her white braids represent experience within Wisdom.

This is the end of the young woman's first day. Within this day there have been four symbolic days representing the Four Great Directions, or the Medicine Wheel. The young woman in this Story has now visited each of these four directions within Wisdom, in order to find Balance within the Way of the North. This understanding can be shown with a simple drawing.

As you can See, above the greater Wheel there is a smaller Wheel to the North, in the Place of Wisdom. This Place of Wisdom is also Balanced within the Four Great Directions.

The young woman in the Story enters the Lodge of Wisdom by first experiencing the Place of the South within Wisdom. That is her First Day, her First Illumination. On her Second Day she visits the West, and on her Third Day

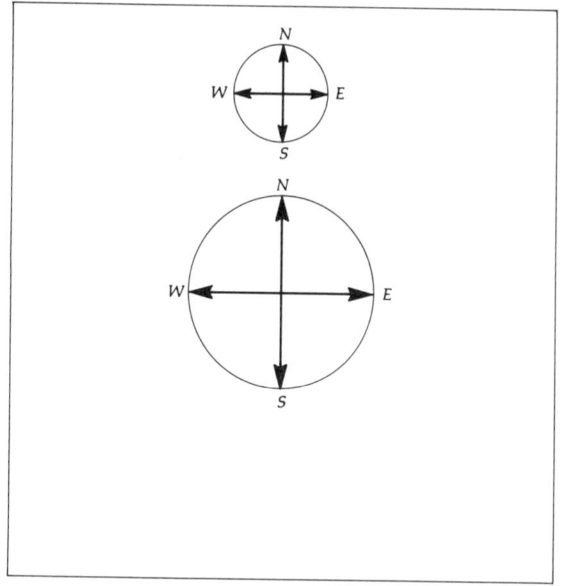

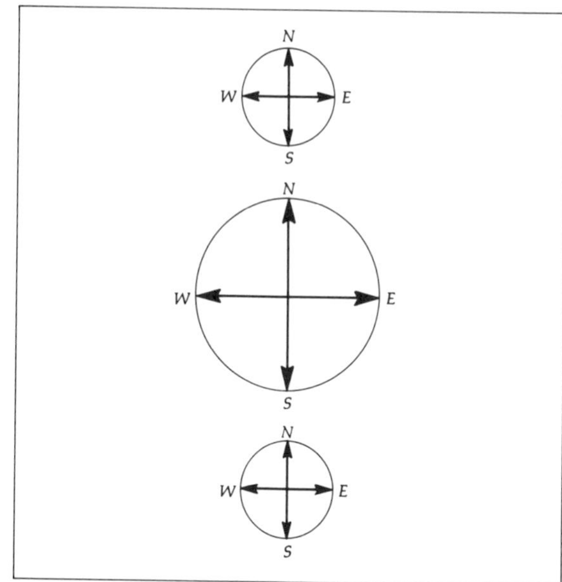

she visits the North. On her Fourth and Final Day within Wisdom she visits the East, the Place of Illumination.

She has had full Intercourse with the North and is Illuminated by visiting all of its Four Directions, and experiencing their Balance.

The next morning in the Story is the young woman's Second Day within the Sun Dance Way. The Mother Fox and her Kit Foxes in the Story are symbolic of her peer group.

The Turtle she meets on her Second Day is symbolic of the Traditions of the Earth. The Four Harmonies, or Songs, the Turtle sings to her Reflect the Four Directions, and also Four of the many Harmonies that exist within Tradition. One of these Harmonies is the reality that a man and a woman must come into intercourse with each other in order to have children.

On her Third Day, a Coyote leads her from the river to the prairie. The prairie is a symbol of everyday life, and the river is a symbol of the Spirit of Life.

The Coyote, as you have learned, is symbolic of the Gentle Trickster. He represents all those things that trick us into learning.

On the young woman's Fourth Day she meets the Dragonfly. The Dragonfly is symbolic of the many things in our life that hypnotize us, or cause us to fixate upon something.

Even as we unfold some of the Teachings within this Story, you may possibly become fixated upon one particular understanding of a symbol that Reflects many meanings. It is for you to move these symbols within your own experience so that you may learn.

This is the end of the woman's Second Day. As you can see, her Second Circle upon the Medicine Mirror Wheel is in the South. The South, her Place of Trust and Innocence, is also Balanced now within the Four Great Directions.

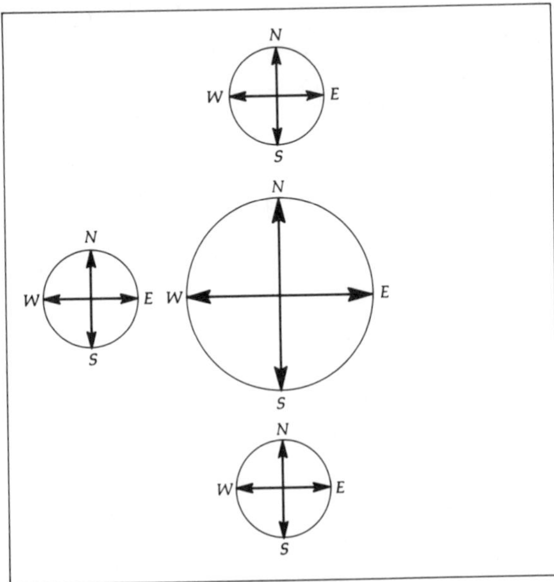

On her Third Day the young woman meets a He Dog and his Puppies. This He Dog and his Puppies are the symbol of Philosophy. The Dog also represents the servants among the People.

Sweet Grass is burned for incense. It is the Earth symbol or Mother symbol. Within the Story the Sweet Grass is braided, meaning that these things of the Earth are within our experience.

The Lightning Elk is the symbol of Illumination within Introspection, and also of death and the power of rebirth. The Horns of the Elk symbolize lightning.

The Mouse, as you remember, perceives only whatever is very close to it. The Teaching here is that when we look too closely within our Introspection, we may sit too much within the circle of ourselves to perceive anything clearly. To perceive the Circle of the West, we must first move outside of it.

Now, as you can see, the young woman has visited the Third Circle of her Vision Quest. This Circle is within the West, and it is also Balanced within the Four Directions.

The East is the young woman's Fourth and Final Way. It is the Place of New Questioning, or Illumination. Whenever we experience the Illumination of the East, we will always have new questions.

The Lodge of Gambling represents the many gambles within the realities of our daily lives.

The Lodge of the Sacred Arrows is the Lodge of the Great Mirrors. It is the Heart of the People, and the Song of the Sundance Way Itself. The Lodge of the Sacred Arrows is also the Lodge of the Common Fire of the People.

Within each of our own Separate Lodges, deep within ourselves, there is also part of this same Great Medicine Fire of the People. The question we are always asking ourselves is, "who am I," or "who is this living spirit, this fire?" The questioning of this mystery is the beginning of our search for Understanding of our Fire of Self, and it is a Circle that always leads us back to the Great Medicine Fire, the Lodge of the Sacred Arrows.

This Great Fire and this Lodge are Songs that are Reflected within the Sound of the Drum inside the many Colored Rainbows that have been Painted on the Sacred Arrows. These Rainbows are the Myths within the Sacred Mountains, and they are Mirrored for you in *Seven Arrows.* As we experience *Seven Arrows,* we will come into Understanding of the Fire within us through the Balance of the Four Great Directions.

And we now hear this Drum clearly within us. It speaks of our crossing the Great River. And we too now sit upon the hill in our Vision Quest, like the young woman in the Story of Singing Stone. Both she and we are beginning our Vision Quest, the Quest to Perceive Ourselves within the Harmony of the Four Balances.

And will we not also Perceive our own Camps to be Strange, as this Young woman does? Why will this be so? And why will we be unable to Recognize our People? Why will the Symbols and Signs that are Painted upon the Lodges of the People appear so Strange to us? Will it be because they have suddenly changed, or will it be because it is our own Perception that has changed?

Seven Arrows is a Mirror of this Teaching Way. It will Reflect your Learning within the Great Medicine Wheel.

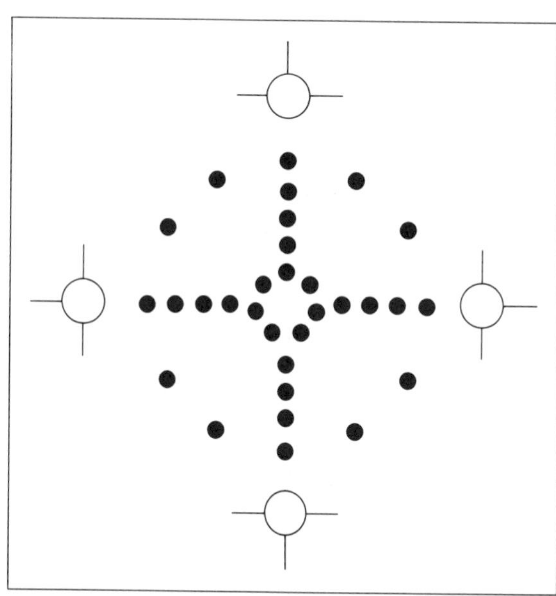

Nine Moons had begun Crescent, become Full, and had Passed. Winter Man had been Lazy with his Cold and there had been many Days of Sunshine. The Wings of Thunderbird Stirred the Air and brought the Gentle Southern Breeze to the Camp of White Shield.

Day Woman stopped her work at the edge of the creek and untied her braids, letting the gentle Medicine of the south bathe her face and hair.

The camp circle was waking up. The voices of children beginning to play mingled with the excited barking of the camp dogs, happy to see their young masters. The camp crier was making his round of the lodges, crying the news of the night.

Day Woman returned to her work, secure within the familiar sounds and scenes. She only half listened to the crier singing his news to the camp. She began to daydream about her little sister, Morning Star Woman. The doeskin she was working on would be whiter and softer than any she had ever made and it would soon become the most beautiful dress in the whole camp. In her dream, she could already see Morning Star Woman smiling shyly for all her admirers and spinning around for everyone to see the new dress. It was a magical morning, one made for the daydreams of a young woman. The sun danced and sparkled on the water in the creek, helping her dream to grow.

Her whole family would be there to see the

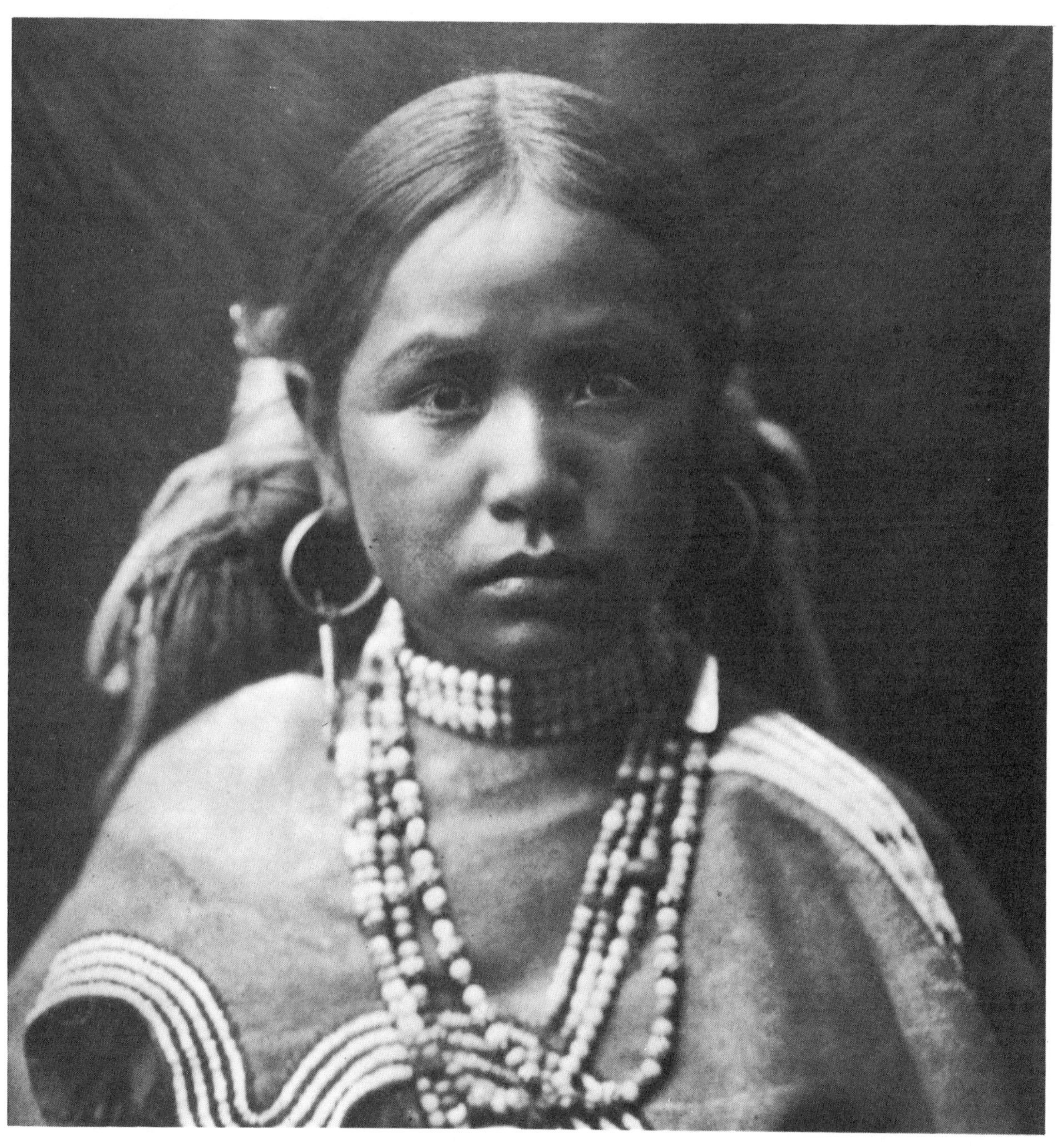

new dress. Day Woman saw herself braiding her baby sister's hair while she tied the last feathered plume in it. Morning Star Woman wiggled in excitement to be outside showing off her new dress.

"Hold still, little rabbit, or you will wriggle right out of your new dress and we will have to begin all over again," Day Woman laughed in her dream.

Finally the last touch was finished and the little girl was released. She ran for the lodge door, stopped and added her own small touches to her appearance, and then walked outside for the world to see her.

Lame Bear and Standing Eagle, two of her uncles, saw her first. Lame Bear stalked around Morning Star Woman, snapping the string of the bow he had been working on.

"By the Power, Standing Eagle, we have a Spirit Woman here!" he said, pretending to be overcome by Morning Star Woman's beauty.

Day Woman smiled with the perfect success of her dream. Good, tall, Lame Bear, her favorite uncle, would have spoken in just that way, and kindly, round-tummied Standing Eagle would have joined in the pretending with a little more reserve, but just as enthusiastically as her other uncle.

"Day Woman! Day Woman!" someone called.

The girl let the dream dim quietly as she looked up and saw her best friend, Prairie Rose, running towards her. Her friend's excitement made her get to her feet.

"What is it? Is something wrong?" she asked as Prairie Rose reached her, grabbing her hand.

"Come on!" Prairie Rose said, dragging her friend after her. "Have you not heard the crier? Dancing Water has returned to the camp! She is in Flying Cloud's lodge, and she had her baby last night!"

The two girls ran for the camp, the fringe on their dresses flying, showing their knees. They slowed down at the edge of the camp and walked hurriedly toward Flying Cloud's lodge.

Day Woman was excited and pleased by the news of her aunt's return to the camp, but she was unable to fight down the uneasiness that touched her stomach. They had visited not long ago when their camps had been together on the Powder River. The five miles that had separated the two camps then had been an easy walking distance, and Prairie Rose and she had visited Dancing Water almost every day. Now Dancing Water had come so suddenly to their camp, and the possible reasons for her abrupt arrival crowded into Day Woman's mind.

There was no joy upon the faces of the people outside Flying Cloud's lodge. Both girls were silent as they approached. Suddenly their thoughts were interrupted by the muffled thunder of pony's hoofs, as the warriors of the camp galloped past Flying Cloud's lodge. A young warrior named Stinging Eyes was mounted in front of the lodge, holding Flying Cloud's war pony. Flying Cloud ran from the lodge, bow in hand, leaped upon the waiting horse, and both men raced off after the other riders. Prairie Rose ran to watch the party of men as they disappeared over the hills, and was nearly knocked down by Lame Bear's horse as he rode by after the others at a full gallop.

Day Woman turned to enter the lodge.

"The Wars! The Wars! Has the whole world gone mad?"

It was Standing Eagle speaking. The group of men with him lounged in the shade, some of them busy repairing their camp equipment. A camp dog snapped at what it believed to be a fly. Whining and growling, the dog bit at its tail and began to run in circles.

"Look at that dog," Standing Eagle continued. "All of us are like that dog. The poor fool still does not understand that it has bitten a bee and been stung. It runs in circles just as we do."

Falls Down called the dog to him and began to soothe the animal.

"It is all right, old fellow," he said, rubbing the dog's jaw. "You will live and so will we. We will not let that old man scare us. We will. . . ."

"Scare us!" Standing Eagle roared, jumping to his feet. "You young fool, do you not realize that our whole world is falling to pieces? That the People are being exterminated like rabid camp dogs?"

"How do you know?" Falls Down struck back. "All we know is that there have been two or three camps ravaged by packs of mad wolves. These unnatural white wolves can be fought and beaten. All we have heard of their power has been just hearsay. How do you know that the stories we have heard have not been stretched out of shape? Have you seen any of these broken camps? Were all the People truly murdered as we heard, or were the stories of this only the whinings of frightened women?"

"The stories we heard were from no frightened women, my brother." It was Grey Owl who answered, getting to his feet. His dark, handsome face gave no sign of the fury that was in his heart. Falls Down's words and actions seemed to be typical of all young men in the last few years and Grey Owl hated them. He walked to a pole that supported a rack of drying meat and leaned against it. Taking a piece for himself, he threw the remainder to Falls Down. The two young men ate in silence. Grey Owl let much of the anger die inside him as he ate.

The man who had carried word of the broken camps to them had been his clan brother. Their two camps had come together on the Medicine Wheel River for the Sun Dance, Grey Owl's first.

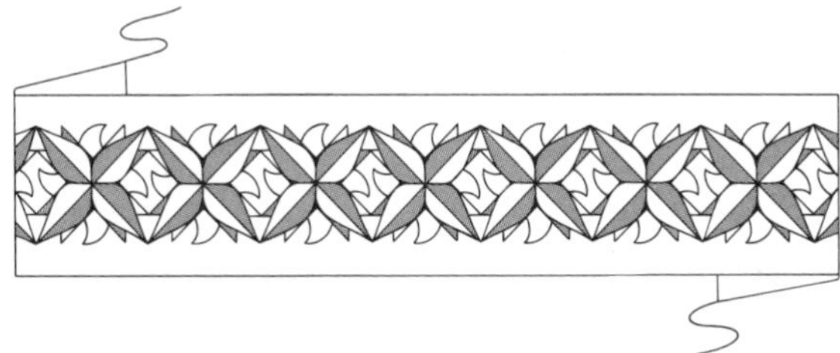

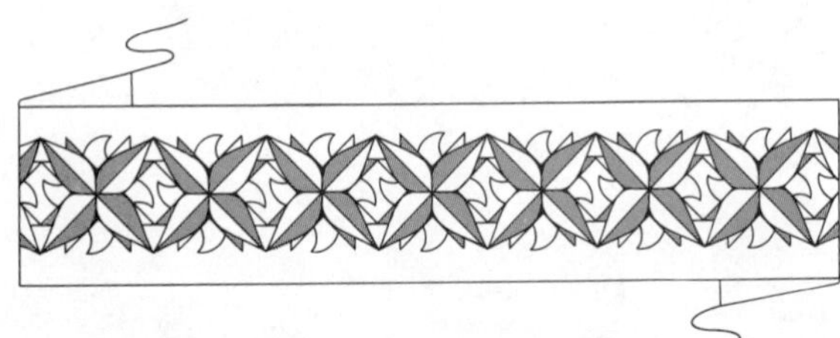

It was the eleventh moon and the summer sun was hot. Grey Owl lounged in the shade of an arbor that he and his father had made near the lodge, and watched his mother embroidering his Sun Dance belt with porcupine quills. All the lodges had been put up in a common circle along with those of the Sioux, the Brother People. He lazily watched a few Sioux women, latecomers who were just now putting up their lodge. A pretty girl was tending their children and talking to Prairie Rose.

"Who are those people, Mother?" Grey Owl asked, indicating the direction with his eyes.

"That is the lodge of Painted Elk," she answered without looking up. "He is your clan uncle, and the girl you are so interested in is Morning Song, his daughter."

"*Zahuah,* Mother!" Grey Owl bleated, shuffling nervously, "That thought is a ragged feather."

"Ragged feather thought?" his mother laughed, "You remember what you said when she went for water at the river?"

"I remember," Grey Owl answered, getting to his feet and leaning his arm against the arbor, hoping the subject was ended.

"By the thunder, Mother, where is my father? I thought we were to hunt together this morning."

"White Shield left before the sun was up, long before you stopped your dreaming."

"*Zahuah,* Mother!" Grey Owl whined, "Owls

sit on your head! Why did you let me sleep?"

"My sleepy son, I tried to wake you. . . ." Their conversation was interrupted by the arrival of Painted Elk and his family.

Grey Owl turned to look at the visitors. Prairie Rose was pulling Morning Song along by her hand. She was laughing and pointing to her brother. Morning Song was trying her best to maintain her gait and keep her balance with the little girl tugging at her.

Morning Song was even more beautiful than Grey Owl had thought, and he felt a tension grow inside of him that was totally new in his experience. "By the Power!" he thought, "Why did I sleep so late this morning instead of going hunting!"

"Peace, my sister. I wish to borrow my nephew from your camp. He will hunt with his uncle if he wishes," Painted Elk said as he approached the shade.

"All I have seen here all morning is a lazy green lizard. You may have to cuff him awake to get him to go hunting with you," Grey Owl's mother answered as she hugged Painted Elk's wife.

A few minutes later, Grey Owl led his horse to Painted Elk's lodge. A young man the same age as Grey Owl was standing beneath the arbor and was tying four quivers of arrows to his horse. Another horse that was tied to the arbor snorted and pulled nervously against its reins. A painted and quilled robe was draped over the horse's back, and an ornamented sheath with a strange weapon in it was also tied there. Even though Grey Owl had never seen a thunder stick before, he recognized it by the stories he had heard of them. The carved wooden butt of the thunder iron was

decorated and tied with hawk feathers. It was beautiful.

The three of them rode in silence together onto the broad, rolling prairie. While they rode, Grey Owl studied his companions. Painted Elk was almost as lean and tall as his son, but more muscular. Hung loosely from his back was his Shield, on which was painted a black bear with elk signs over the bear's eyes. The seeker band that cut diagonally across the Shield was painted in rainbow colors, with four white eagle feathers at its middle. Painted below the band was the symbol of the water, his Clan Sign.

Painted Elk's son turned in his saddle toward Grey Owl, and began to speak to him in sign language.

I am your Clan brother, he signed. *This will be my first Sun Dance. Will it also be yours?*

Yes, it will be, Grey Owl quickly signed back. *I am called Grey Owl.*

And I am called Lame Buffalo, he signed with a broad smile.

What is the meaning of the four white eagle plumes upon your father's Shield? Grey Owl asked.

These were given to him at the Sun Dance by White Wolf. I think that White Wolf's tongue is that of the Little Black Eagle, the Crow. My father was given these signs to seek wisdom within his Medicines, Lame Buffalo answered.

What are his Medicines? Grey Owl asked. *Does he know them all yet?*

My father knows of three. They are the Grey Stands Alone Wolf, the Orphaned Yellow Buffalo Calf, and the Red Robed Bat, Lame Buffalo answered, then turned to his father and said something in his own tongue.

Painted Elk rode on for a moment in silence. Grey Owl was just about to ask Lame Buffalo what he had said, when suddenly Painted Elk stopped his horse and dismounted. The two young men looked around quickly and then they also dismounted.

The older man made signs for the young men to sit with him. He pointed to where an eagle was feeding upon the carcass of an antelope. Four or five she-wolves were lying near the half-eaten animal, some of them suckling their pups. *Do you see that bird?* Painted Elk signed. *That eagle will stuff himself until he cannot fly up from the ground. That is Vihio, surely a knowledgeable fool. Very few of the creatures of this world see as much and as far as he does, but he foolishly comes down to blindness and gorges himself. What have you to say about the meaning of this Way of the Eagle?*

Their talk was all with sign language, so that each could understand and take part in it.

Lame Buffalo signed first. *This foolish thing seems to be a common weakness among all People.*

Grey Owl said nothing, wanting a little more time to think before answering.

You have asked about my Medicine Ways, Painted Elk signed to Grey Owl. *When Lame Buffalo spoke to me just now, he was asking about the name I had been given by the same old man who had given me the four white eagle plumes. The name he gave me was Lame Eagle. This means one who is lame in what he wants to do, because of his way of gorging himself too full to fly.*

Painted Elk had hardly finished his signing before he broke out in laughter. Grey Owl and Lame Buffalo were laughing as hard as he. Painted Elk began again.

I will seek my colors in this Sun Dance. It will be

your first, and I will be dancing with you. I have asked White Wolf of the Little Black Eagle People to paint me and also to paint both of you. He will be here soon and we will have the Give-Away. I already have asked White Shield's approval to Give-Away for you too, Grey Owl. I will Give-Away this horse, my robe, my tobacco pouch, and this iron that speaks.

When he had finished signing, he mounted his horse, kicked him into a run, and yelled in Cheyenne to Grey Owl, "Come, little green lizard, or I will cuff your ears."

That evening nearly all the young men of the camp played arrow and hoop games. The women visited together and tended their children, letting their daughters watch and cheer at the games and, of course, meet young men.

Morning Song was watching with Dancing Water, Grey Owl's cousin. Grey Owl had per-

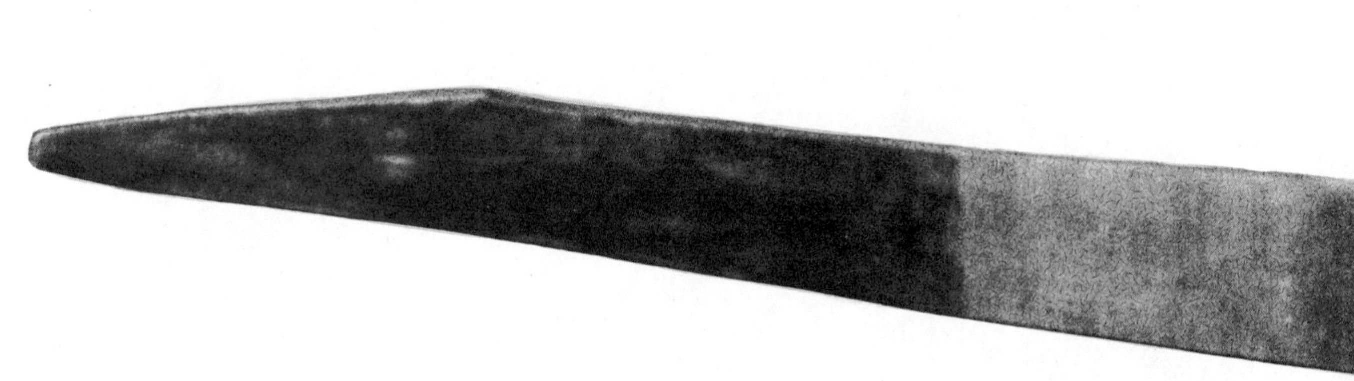

formed pitifully at arrow throwing and was being teased unmercifully by Stiff Arm. Grey Owl was as tight as a bowstring because of the teasing, and because he had noticed the presence of Morning Song. He had also noticed that at each chance Stiff Arm got, he went and stood next to Morning Song. For some reason Grey Owl burned inside when he saw this, which made him all the more clumsy. It was not long before Lame Buffalo joined in Stiff Arm's teasing of Grey Owl. Grey Owl grinned, but it hurt his face to do it.

Finally his turn came again during the hoop game, and he was determined to prove himself. He took careful aim, pulling the bowstring taut, but just a second before the hoop was rolled the string broke. Lame Buffalo doubled over with laughter. Morning Song was laughing and so was Dancing Water. In fact, everyone was. Grey Owl's patience was at an end. His wooden smile disappeared and he reached for another bow, jerking it from a young Sioux's hand who stood next to him. He fitted an arrow into the bow, pulled it half-way back, and took one step backwards. But luck was not with him. Turtle, his faithful dog, was lying stretched out on the ground just behind him. When Grey Owl stepped back to shoot, it was squarely onto his dog. The dog yelped and squirmed from under his foot. Grey Owl went down into a heap of angry boy, dog, and bow. He was humiliated, and he avoided the laughing eyes of Lame Buffalo and Morning Song.

In the days that followed, Stiff Arm grew intolerable. He became fast friends with Lame Buffalo. Lame Buffalo had taught Stiff Arm some of his language, and whenever Grey Owl found himself with them in small groups of

boys, the two would look at him, say a few words in Sioux, and laugh.

One morning, while Grey Owl hunted with his father, they came upon a small herd of buffalo. As soon as they sighted the riders, the buffalo ran and scattered into ravines. Grey Owl rode by himself into one of the ravines and suddenly came upon a second herd. He rode straight into their middle, scattering them. The herd milled frantically around and tried to climb the steep banks. Many failed in the attempt, and retreated to run in other directions. Grey Owl picked out a two-year-old bull, and set out to bring him down.

He failed to notice that he had also been joined in the chase by Lame Buffalo, Stiff Arm and his own father. The other riders smashed into the herd, driving their arrows into the buffalo nearest them. Lame Buffalo was about to bring down a fat cow when suddenly his horse collided with Grey Owl's, who still had not seen him. Grey Owl's horse was knocked to the ground, spilling him from the saddle. Lame Buffalo's horse, staggered by the blow, lost its footing for a second and then righted itself with a quick jump. Barely keeping his seat, Lame Buffalo turned his horse to regain control and to see what had happened. He could dimly see Grey Owl through the dust and frenzied animals. Grey Owl had caught his horse and was trying to mount, but the horse jerked and bucked, trying to run. Grey Owl had his back to the bull he had wounded and did not see it start to charge him. Lame Buffalo kicked his horse into a run, putting himself between the bull and Grey Owl. The bull hit Lame Buffalo's horse, snapping ribs and spilling him into the dirt.

Grey Owl had remounted and saw Lame Buffalo's wounded horse trying to get up. When the bull charged again, Lame Buffalo was still trying to get to his feet. Grey Owl never moved. Everything seemed to be happening in a dream, with the bull charging, Lame Buffalo running, and then the sudden appearance of White Shield, who jerked Lame Buffalo to safety on the back of his own horse.

That evening Grey Owl sat by his mother, fuming.

"What happened?" his mother asked. "Lame Buffalo seems to have broken his leg."

"Lame Buffalo! Lame Buffalo! That mouse-minded fool. . . . *Zahuah,* Mother, forget it!"

"Forget it!" His father had entered the lodge almost spitting the words at his son. "Forget it! He saved your life. He put his horse between you and the buffalo bull. He. . . ."

"He what?" cut in Grey Owl. "*Mahka-Zaughan,* no! I never knew!"

The boy jumped to his feet and ran into the night. His mother jumped up and started to run after him.

"Leave him alone!" White Shield said, throwing the lodge flap back and leaving. Grey Owl's mother sat down and began to cry.

Grey Owl had run from the lodge, his mind and heart a blinding confusion of pain and sorrow. A double and triple shame was his, because he had shamed himself, his parents, and his People. The tears in his eyes blinded him just enough that he did not see the three young people who were walking towards him. They were Morning Song, Dancing Water, and Stiff Arm.

"Hello, Grey Owl," Morning Song said.

Her gentle voice cut into Grey Owl's brain

like crippled lightning. He jerked his eyes from the ground and saw Stiff Arm. Stiff Arm grinned and said something he didn't hear. Grey Owl's mind exploded with hate and he grabbed for his knife. Morning Song screamed as the two young men locked themselves in a death struggle. Stiff Arm slipped and fell to the ground. Grey Owl kicked his knife from his hand and stood over him.

"Please, oh please, do not harm him!" someone pleaded. It was Bear Woman. The girl grabbed Grey Owl's arm and was crying. "Please, my beautiful cousin, do not harm him!" she begged, looking into his eyes. "Your jealousy is for nothing! Morning Song has slept with him and they were not of one song! Please listen to me!" she begged. "Morning Song loves you!"

Grey Owl's knife was scarcely a half-inch from Stiff Arm's throat.

"I . . . I am sorry, my cousin," Stiff Arm's voice wavered. "Forgive me."

"I cannot kill you, Stiff Arm," Grey Owl said through tears. "You must also forgive me." His knife fell from his hand as he stood up.

The next morning Stiff Arm, Grey Owl and Lame Buffalo were called to the council.

"None of you three have walked within the People's Way." The speaker was Grey Mouse. Grey Mouse was the youngest of the Pledgers, and a Dog Soldier. "Today we have all learned because of your actions. You are our brothers and we are your brothers. What are your pledges?"

Stiff Arm spoke first. "I have never loved Grey Owl, but I promise this day to understand him. I have acted shamefully and as a child. I also pledge postponement of my marriage for

one year to collect robes for the family of White Shield. And I pledge my life to protect that of Grey Owl." There was not a sound in the camp, even the dogs were still.

Grey Owl spoke second. "I was driven to madness with jealousy, like a rabid mouse. I too have never loved my cousin Stiff Arm. I pledge all of my power that I receive in this Sun Dance to Lame Buffalo and Stiff Arm. And I pledge the care and protection of every child of Lame Buffalo's until each child is a grown man or woman. And then I pledge him my bow. From this day forward, I pledge myself a Dog Soldier to the Brother People, and also to my own People, the Painted Arrows."

The pledging was translated into sign language for Lame Buffalo. After the young men had finished their speech, Lame Buffalo spoke.

"I too acted as a child. And I pledge this Sun Dance to my brothers the Cheyennes, the Painted Arrow People. And I pledge myself a Dog Soldier for both the People."

There was a feast later that same day for the People. Stiff Arm, Lame Buffalo, and Grey Owl were inseparable. A few days before the Sun Dance, Lame Buffalo married Dancing Water.

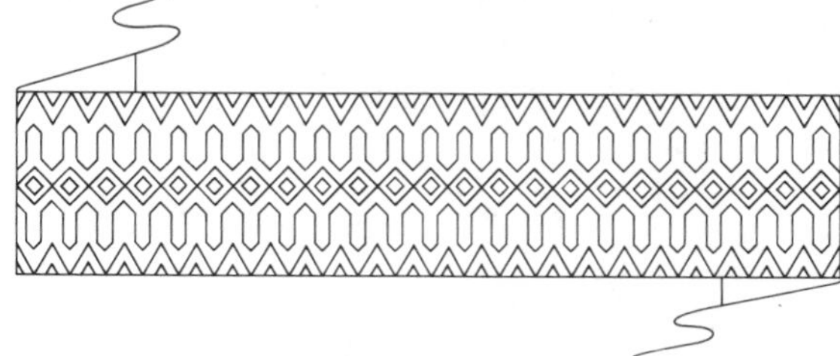

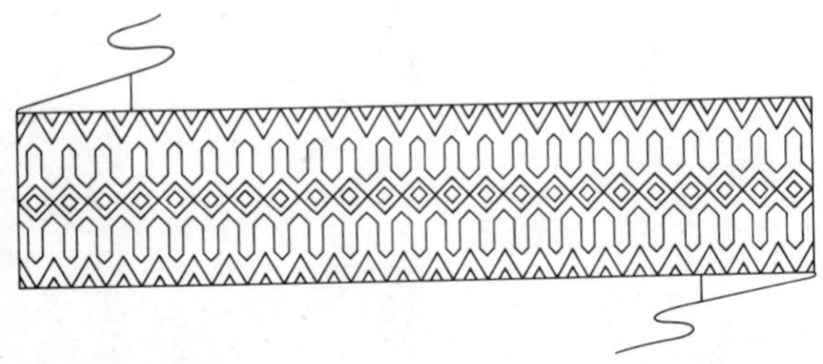

"The man you speak of as being a woman, Falls Down, is my brother and one of the bravest men I have ever known," Grey Owl said after he had finished his meat. "And I will cut out your tongue, my little brother, if you ever speak in such a way about my brother again."

"What is your brother's name?" asked Stands in Timber.

"His Beginning Name was Lame Buffalo," answered Grey Owl, "But you know him now as Four Bears."

"Four Bears?" said Falls Down, "The husband of Dancing Water? The Peace Chief? Is this the same man?"

"Yes," answered Standing Eagle, "the same man."

There was a long silence as no one seemed to know what to say. Curious Antelope finally broke the silence.

"We must find out about the foreigners. I am told that their wars are fought not for the honor of touching the enemy, but to kill. It is my thought that we must send someone to the camps of the Brother People, perhaps to the lodge of Four Bears, from whom our news of these strange beings has come."

"Whoever goes will not be able to return until the third season," added Runs Above.

"Count me as one of them," said Falls Down, excitedly, "I would like to meet one of these strange beings."

Runs Above gave his sign of approval and

allegiance by throwing his bow a short distance through the air, toward the sun. "There is my bow. My father and mother are camped to the north, probably near the Brother People, and it would be good to see them."

Falls Down followed suit and bounced his bow near the bow of Runs Above.

"Why do you not throw your bow with theirs, Grey Owl?" asked Standing Eagle. "Our brother, Runs Above, may find himself a strong-minded young woman who will pull him around by his ears, and Falls Down is too young to be alone."

"My fear is not the meeting of a woman, Standing Eagle," Runs Above laughed. "I am afraid those Brother People will see my great stomach and will use me as their dancing drum."

"All right, I will go with you to save you from becoming their drum," said Grey Owl, as he rose to his feet. "It is settled."

Grey Owl entered his lodge and slumped into his backrest. He reached for the rope he had been braiding, tying it to his foot and twisting the leather.

A young man entered the lodge and sat across from Grey Owl. The skin of the lodge was rolled up on its poles. The young man turned his backrest to one side, settled his hands behind his head, and stared lazily into the sunset.

"The Man of the Shield of Light spoke to us today," Hawk said from his comfortable position. "These were his words."

Of all the Creator's Creations, only Man is Illuminated through Mind, through Wisdom, and through his Gift of Thought. He will Perfect and Bring into Realization those things that Man Wishes, the things of the North. In the North are Found the Tools of both Building and Destruction. The Power Placed the Woman to the North, my

Son. Her Hair is White and she will Never Grow Old. She, my Son, is what Man must Marry—this Concept, the Being of Wisdom. Your Children with her are the Reality of Gifts from the North. But there is the Winter Man of the North also. Winter Man Spreads his Coldness of Heart over all the Land, and has the Power to Destroy. Man has Used Winter Man and his Destruction. He has Used this Wisdom far more than he has the Marriage, my Son. The Man who Realizes Only the North is not a Full Man. He has not Visited the South.

In the South, the Power Placed a Man. His Hair is Green. The South is the Hardest Way to Walk. All must Walk this Way of Trust and Innocence in Brotherhood. Gifts of Another Spirit are Found here. And there also is a Marriage here, my Son. It is with the Sister of the South. Only he can Offer her in Marriage, and Always only through Brotherhood. The Gift of the Reality here is the Touching Within Love. Many have Sought The Way of the South Within the Wisdom of Love. It is a Way, but this Seeker's Way can be One that is not of Feeling. This Seeker may not Know the Song that is Sung by the Marriage of the South. The Drum Beat of this Way can be a Myth Reality for the Seeker, because it is more of the Mind than it is of the Heart. To Find the Touching of this Give-Away, the Seeker must Walk this Way. This First Teacher is the Way of this Growing into Fullness. Myth now can Become Reality for the Seeker Within this Marriage Way. The Children of this Marriage can now Bring Reality to the Seeker. You must Visit this Way in total Trust, my Son.

The Place of the East is the Way of total Illumination, but this is True only if a Man has Visited the North and Married, has Visited the South, and has also been Given the Sister there for Marriage. Man is able to See Far when he Visits the East, my Son. The East Begins the New Day for Man, and Lights his Way to the West and Paints its Colors there. For all the Colors are the Children of these Marriages.

The West is the Place of Looking-Within. When One Looks-Within, he is able to Recognize the Stars that Guide him in his Times of Darkness. There is the Northern Star, the Southern Star, and the Morning Star of the East. This is the Way of the People. This is the Great Medicine Wheel, the Universe Dance.

"The Medicine Chief spoke within these Ways," said the young man, turning to Grey Owl. "He spoke of those Medicine Colors that I see right now in the sunset. Do you suppose he has walked all these Ways?"

Grey Owl jerked the braid on his rope tighter, and spoke sharply. "I do not know, Hawk. I do not know. But I do know this. These Peace Chiefs talk of realities, but what about the realities that rage among us? The Peace Chiefs' Ways are dead!"

"Dead?" broke in Hawk, "How are they dead?"

Grey Owl stopped his work momentarily and looked at the boy across from him. Hawk was a beautiful boy, a boy who would gladden the hearts of any People. But it seemed to Grey Owl that the boy was doomed to disappointment and hardship, because of the wars and the new Way. Four Bears had described to Grey Owl the grisly scenes of those ravaged camps, and the overwhelming power of the men who had done it.

"The Medicine Power has sent us new teachers, Hawk," Grey Owl began slowly. "Teachers who have everything! Teachers who have power! Teachers who make us appear puny! Medicine Colors, *Aaiah!* How can Medicine Colors stop the killing?"

Grey Owl threw Hawk a bow and a quiver of arrows and added, "Learn to use these, or you will die! What does your Medicine Chief have to say concerning these things?"

Hawk touched neither the bow nor the quiver. He waited for a moment, got to his feet, and left through the side of the lodge. Grey Owl never looked up.

"Was that Hawk I saw leaving the lodge?" Day Woman asked as she drew near the lodge opening. Prairie Rose and Morning Song were with her.

"Yes, it was," answered Grey Owl. "He visited with me for a while."

"Everything is ready for you when you leave in the morning," Morning Song said as she sat down. The two girls sat on each side of her and resumed some quilling they had begun on a robe. Morning Song looked wistfully at Grey Owl. "There is no possibility of my going, is there?"

"No," Grey Owl quickly answered. "Travel has become too dangerous now. You will be much safer here."

"Still, there will be one young woman accompanying you on the journey," said Morning Song. "Lame Winged Woman is going."

"What?" asked Grey Owl. "Why is she going?"

"Our camp will be moving and Lame Winged Woman wants to join her mother and father in the camp of Four Bears," Prairie Rose answered.

The next morning their party set out. Falls Down and Runs Above rode together, swapping stories and keeping to the rear. Behind Grey Owl rode Lame Winged Woman. The horse she was riding was being taken as a gift

to Painted Elk. As the days passed the girl became more friendly with Grey Owl, and before long they were sharing one bed.

Two weeks after they had left, Grey Owl saw camp smoke ahead of them and signalled for a halt. Grey Owl and Falls Down left their horses and set out on foot to investigate. Recognizing the camp as that of the Brother People, Grey Owl signed for Runs Above to bring up their horses. They were about to mount when they were suddenly surrounded by many warriors.

"Where did they all come from?" Falls Down asked Grey Owl in astonishment.

Grey Owl, feeling he had been made a fool of, was ashamed. "They were hidden, naturally," he said, spitting his answer. He made the sign for peace and told his captors he and his friends wished to visit their camp.

One of the warriors made the sign for them to dismount and walk to the camp.

"Tell them we are trying to find the camp of Painted Elk and Four Bears," Grey Owl told Lame Winged Woman, who was of Four Bears' People. "Ask them if they have heard where he is camped."

"The young man said that he will show you the camp of Painted Elk," Lame Winged Woman translated.

Grey Owl felt uneasy. The camp they were being herded towards was very small, containing no more than fifteen lodges. Horses were tethered outside each lodge, and weapons were hung from each one. No one came out to greet them. There were no playing children. The camp was completely silent. As they drew nearer, Grey Owl recognized a Shield that hung from one of the lodges. It was Painted Elk's.

What has happened here? Grey Owl signed to his uncle after they were seated. *Where is Four Bears, my brother?*

Painted Elk began to sign. *Our camp was struck by People of the Brotherhood and the Shield. Foreigners rode with them and they were many. All that you see here is what is left of our great camp. A hundred of us are gone, many of them women and children. They were killed for their hair. The whitemen offer valuable goods for the hair cut from their heads. Your brother is still alive, and is taking his turn as guard. Dancing Water is also alive. Your brother Stiff Arm and his family are dead. I saw him fall in front of his lodge, felled by a thunder stick.*

Killed for their hair? Grey Owl asked, unable to believe his ears. *Do you mean that their braids were taken, but not as in our way of touching the enemy?*

No, Painted Elk replied. *The scalp and hair are both taken with a knife. The whiteman will not trade unless this is shown as proof of death.*

I have never heard of such insanity, Grey Owl signed. *What does it mean?*

Painted Elk began again. *The Power has been kind to your People, Grey Owl. The mountains and prairies have protected your ears and lives. Twenty-four moons have passed since we saw our first camps murdered. Four Bears was sent to your People with this news, so that you might protect yourselves from the terror finding you.*

Many of the People did not believe his story, signed Grey Owl. *Only this season did our council become aware of the danger. We have had many tales brought to our camp concerning the whiteman and his power. I have believed the stories even though I have seen nothing. Because of*

my love and trust for Four Bears, I believed.

There are many people who still know nothing of this, signed Painted Elk, *or who refuse to believe what they have heard. Yet the stories are very old. Many of us have heard them all our lives, although until recently we had seen little proof of them. Now the whiteman's Way is already travelled by many of the Brotherhood. The Sun Dance has been dying among us for years. Fewer and fewer still carry the Shields. What you have heard to now of the whiteman's power is nothing. They have monster iron horses, and even something tied between trees that speaks for them. They have great, puffing monsters that crawl the rivers and that are masters over them.*

Grey Owl blinked in disbelief. *It is hard for me to believe this, Painted Elk,* he signed.

I know, signed Painted Elk. *It is hard to believe even when one witnesses it. But there are unimaginable numbers of these whitemen, and their Gifts make our world seem puny.*

Just fourteen suns ago I told one of the young men in our camp, a boy called Hawk, that these new teachers made us look puny. But I was speaking of the power of their new weapons, their thunder sticks. If I had told him what you have just told me, he would only have laughed, Grey Owl signed.

Just then Four Bears entered his father's lodge and gripped the arm of Grey Owl. He sat down and began to eat a piece of dry meat, offering some to Grey Owl.

Has my father told you the news? he signed.

Yes, answered Grey Owl, *he has told me everything. I will hurry back to my camp and tell my People. Your father and his People should ride with me because it will be hard to convince them. The camp here is small and it is a journey of only fourteen suns from here to our camp.*

Yes, signed Painted Elk, *that was our plan.*

You tell me the Brotherhood and the Shield are dying, signed Grey Owl. *How can this be?*

Many of the People of the Brotherhood, signed Four Bears, *so many that you would not believe, have thrown away their Medicine Bundles and Shields. Already among many of the Peoples, children are no longer taught about the Shield and the Brotherhood. Whitemen in black robes, and others, move among the People and teach about a new Way, the Way of Geessis. This Geessis appears to be a new Power, one which loves death and rewards mightily those who kill. Because of this, the camps of the whitemen are rewarded most.* Four Bears unrolled a robe, exposing knives, brightly colored cloth, beads, and many other new things for Grey Owl to see.

Grey Owl could hardly believe his eyes. He touched and examined everything closely. *Many of these things appear beautiful to me,* he signed, *but I am also confused with them. What are their uses?*

Those are beads more beautiful and precious than porcupine quills, signed Painted Elk. *That which you hold in your hands is cloth. And this!* He unrolled the most beautiful robe Grey Owl had ever seen. *This is a robe that the color will not rub off from, and it is very warm. It is called a "ba kit" in the language of the whiteman.*

"Ba kit?" Grey Owl repeated the word. He had never heard a whiteman's word spoken before and he repeated it again, feeling the sound on his tongue.

Four Bears began his explanation again. *What you see here, my brother, is nothing. Many of the people in the camp have traded pelts for greater things. And you must know that there are people in this camp, where you now sit, who now carry no Shield and have turned from the People's Way.*

Only because they are afraid to live with the whiteman do they still live among us.

At that moment, Falls Down burst into the lodge excitedly, holding a strange shiny device.

"This thing I have is a trap!" Falls Down explained, hardly able to contain himself. "And it is mine! These people have many of them. I traded my robe for this one!" His eyes lit upon the treasure in the robe. He fell on his knees and began to touch everything. "Look! Look, my cousin!" Falls Down said even more excitedly. "By the Power, these people are the richest people in the whole universe!" Falls Down ran from the lodge with his trap.

Grey Owl immediately translated for Four Bears what Falls Down had said.

You see, signed Four Bears, *already he is changed. It is no surprise that our young men are leaving us. Many have already gone. Come, my brother, I wish you to see more.* Four Bears and Painted Elk led Grey Owl from the lodge. They walked to where a fire was burning in the center of the camp. As Grey Owl neared the place, he noticed that the men around the fire were talking loudly and jostling each other. Four young women were with the men. Three were dancing in the nude. The other was fast asleep on a whiteman's brightly colored robe near the fire.

What is this? signed Grey Owl. *Have your children gone mad?*

Yes, they have, Four Bears answered. *They are crazy on stinging water. This is the last of it, thank the Power! This is more deadly than all the other whitemen's things combined. Some have even killed their brothers and sisters while they were crazy with it.*

Killed? signed Grey Owl. *Has there been a Renewal?*

There has been no Renewal in this camp, my brother, answered Four Bears. *The last Sun Dance I saw was the one with your People, long ago.*

Grey Owl returned to Four Bear's lodge. He was almost asleep when the attack came.

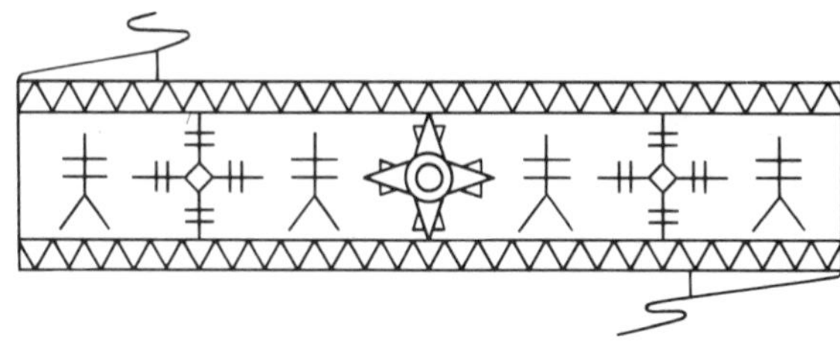

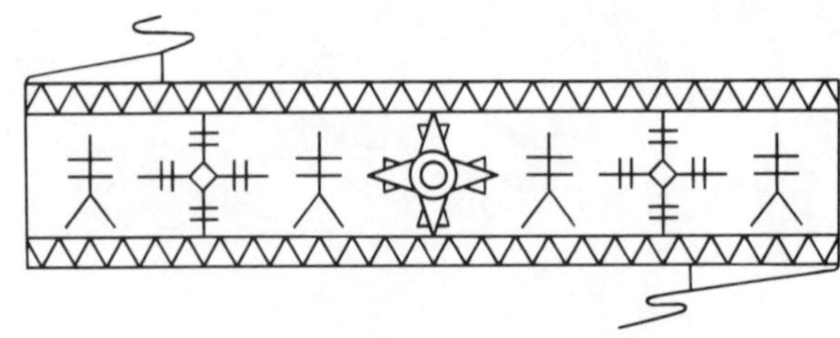

Day Woman and Prairie Rose entered Flying Cloud's lodge and hugged Dancing Water. Both girls peeked at the newborn baby before sitting down next to Dancing Water. Two Sioux women were working on buckskins, their eyes so full of tears that they could hardly work. Day Woman saw the tears in Dancing Water's eyes and looked down at her hands.

"You must know quickly," said Dancing Water through her tears. "Grey Owl, Painted Elk, Four Bears, and many more are all dead." Day Woman was crying hard herself now, but still she could not help but see the brightly colored material that Dancing Water dried her eyes with.

Early the next morning the men returned. Day Woman was awakened by the barking of the camp dogs. She slipped on her dress and stepped from the lodge just as Lame Bear dismounted.

"I will put your horse in hobbles for you," she said, walking to Lame Bear's horse.

"No," Lame Bear answered, his voice tired. "Picket him in front of the lodge and leave the weapons tied."

As Day Woman busied herself making her uncle's meal, she noticed his haggard face but said nothing, waiting for him to talk.

"We will have to move soon," he finally said as he began to eat. "The people who murdered your brothers and uncles were not whitemen, Day Woman." His voice was full of emotion. "We have known, we all have known, for a very long time. The Brotherhood is dead. The men of the Shield are no more. The Way of the Medicine Wheel that bound us together in the Brotherhood is truly dead."

"The Way is not dead!" the Medicine Chief said as he entered the lodge. He was a big man, over six feet tall, with broad shoulders and muscular arms, a man of about forty winters. Hawk followed the man into the lodge and sat with him across from Lame Bear. Reaching for more bowls, Day Woman set them before the men. Lame Bear was silent, not looking at his guests.

"Wars," continued the Peace Chief, "have been with man for so long that man has forgotten when they began. I am amazed to hear you speak this way, Lame Bear. The very Power that has made our Way possible has been in those of the People who have held fast to the Ways of the Shield."

"What," Lame Bear exploded, "has the Great Spirit been so horribly blind and deaf then? Or has our Way been only the foolish Way of children? By the Power, man! Look around you! Look what the Power has given to the whiteman! The gifts to these men overwhelm the mind! And they are a People of war! They despise peace! Yet still the Power given them by the Universe is a far greater Medicine than ours! Their gifts of wealth and power are a living proof!"

"Is the love of the universe reflected only in material gifts?" the Chief answered quickly. "Lame Bear, I do not claim to understand these men, but if their Way is one of war and death, then they cannot be a full people. And remember, my brother, their gifts are ours too. And one day we will find peace and live together. And we will grow."

"Grow!" Lame Bear barked, holding his head with both hands. "Did you hear him, Day Woman? He said grow!" Lame Bear laughed almost hysterically. "Will Grey Owl grow? Or the others who have died? Will there be anyone left alive to grow, other than the whitemen? I have dreamed, Man of the Shield, and in my dreams it has all been made clear to me. I asked to understand. And do you know what has been told to me? The whitemen are determined to destroy all People whose Ways do not reflect their own. They have set the People one against the other and will kill whichever is left when the wars have ended. And know this! The universe has given them even the Power to have talking leaves. Go away, Man of the Shield. I am weary. I want to sleep. Even the Power of talking leaves," he mumbled as he lay down.

Deep sorrow etched the eyes of the Peace Chief as he rose to leave. Day Woman and Hawk followed him from the lodge. He sat down under the shade of the lodge arbor and rubbed his forehead hard, as if trying to erase some thought.

"Is it true?" asked Day Woman timidly, addressing the Chief. "Do they really have leaves that talk?"

The Peace Chief raised his head and stared quietly at the distant mountains. They stood out sharply above the green landscape. "Yes," he said gently, turning to Day Woman, "they do."

"Great Father," said Hawk, looking straight into the eyes of the chief, "if they have these wonderful gifts, than why do they kill?"

"That, my son, is one of the riddles of men," answered the Chief. "Would you listen to a Story concerning men?"

"A Story?" asked Day Woman excitedly, "Great Shield, please let me run for my sister, Prairie Rose, so that she too may hear it."

"Bring as many of my children who will listen as you can!" smiled the Chief as Day

Woman flew to find her friend.

Soon half a dozen children were clustered around the Story-Teller. He lit his Pipe and began:

Once there was a Mouse.

Squinting his eyes, he touched his nose to the nose of a little girl near him.

He was a Busy Mouse, Searching Everywhere, Touching his Whiskers to the Grass, and Looking. He was Busy as all Mice are, Busy with Mice things. But Once in a while he would Hear an odd Sound. He would Lift his Head, Squinting hard to See, his Whiskers Wiggling in the Air, and he would Wonder. One Day he Scurried up to a fellow Mouse and asked him, "Do you Hear a Roaring in your Ears, my Brother?"

"No, no," answered the Other Mouse, not Lifting his Busy Nose from the Ground. "I Hear Nothing. I am Busy now. Talk to me Later."

He asked Another Mouse the same Question and the Mouse Looked at him Strangely. "Are you Foolish in your Head? What Sound?" he asked and Slipped into a Hole in a Fallen Cottonwood Tree.

The little Mouse shrugged his Whiskers and Busied himself again, Determined to Forget the Whole Matter. But there was that Roaring again. It was faint, very faint, but it was there! One Day, he Decided to investigate the Sound just a little. Leaving the Other Busy Mice, he Scurried a little Way away and Listened again. There It was! He was Listening hard when suddenly, Someone said Hello.

"Hello, little Brother," the Voice said, and Mouse almost Jumped right Out of his Skin. He Arched his Back and Tail and was about to Run.

"Hello," again said the Voice. "It is I, Brother Raccoon." And sure enough, It was! "What are you Doing Here all by yourself, little Brother?" asked the Raccoon. The Mouse blushed, and put

his Nose almost to the Ground. "I Hear a Roaring in my Ears and I am Investigating it," he answered timidly.

"A Roaring in your Ears?" replied the Raccoon as he Sat Down with him. "What you Hear, little Brother, is the River."

"The River?" Mouse asked curiously. "What is a River?"

"Walk with me and I will Show you the River," Raccoon said.

Little Mouse was terribly Afraid, but he was Determined to Find Out Once and for All about the Roaring. "I can Return to my Work," he thought, "after this thing is Settled, and possibly this thing may Aid me in All my Busy Examining and Collecting. And my Brothers All said it was Nothing. I will Show them. I will Ask Raccoon to Return with me and I will have Proof."

"All right Raccoon, my Brother," said Mouse. "Lead on to the River. I will Walk with you."

"Get me another brand from the fire, my son," the Chief said to Hawk. "And we will talk more about this Mouse."

Hawk ran for the brand and brought it to the Chief. Lighting his Pipe, the Chief looked up at the little girl nearest him. "And what will happen to little Mouse?" he asked, grabbing the end of her nose. She blushed and looked down at her hands.

"He will fall into the river," she answered in a voice almost too small to be heard.

"*Aai ya hey!*" the Chief said, gripping his Pipe. "Did Seven Arrows visit you and whisper the Story in your ear?"

"No," she giggled. "Grandfather told me the beginning."

"That is exactly what will happen," the Chief smiled. "But let us talk about it before we continue."

Hawk squirmed in his impatience. What did this have to do with the Power and the riddle he had asked? He looked at a group of boys who were playing the hoop game nearby, and he wished he could join them. "If nothing more interesting happens soon," he thought, "I will go play with them."

Just then Bull Looks Back's wife stuck her head out of her lodge and called. Two of the children sitting in the group got up and ran to their lodge.

"As you already know," began the Chief, "we were discussing the riddle of men. Men are like little Mouse. They are so busy with the things of this world that they are unable to perceive things at any distance. They scrutinize some things very carefully, and only brush others over lightly with their whiskers. But all of these things must be close to them. The roaring that they hear in their ears is life, the river. This great sound in their ears is the sound of the Spirit. The lesson is timely, Hawk, because the cries of mankind now are everywhere, but men are too busy with their little Mouse lives to hear. Some deny the presence of these sounds, others do not hear them at all, and still others, my son, hear them so clearly that it is a screaming in their hearts. Little Mouse heard the sounds and went a short distance from the world of Mice to investigate them."

"And met Raccoon," Hawk added. "Is the Raccoon the Great Spirit?"

"In a manner of speaking he is, little brother, but he is also the things that man will discover, if he seeks them, that will lead him to the Great River. The Raccoon can also be a man, or men."

"Men?" said Day Woman. "What kind of men?"

"Men," continued the Chief, "who know of the Medicine River. Men who have experienced and are familiar with life. The Raccoon washes his food in this Medicine. These types of men are unique, my children."

"Now, let us continue the Story," the Chief began again, glancing quickly at Hawk. "That is, if you wish."

Hawk looked fleetingly towards the hoop game and turned his eyes back to the Teacher. "Yes, please continue," he said, settling himself in place.

The man turned his smiling face to the mountains, clapped his hands together, and began.

Little Mouse Walked with Raccoon. His little Heart was Pounding in his Breast. The Raccoon was Taking him upon Strange Paths and little Mouse Smelled the Scent of many things that had Gone by this Way. Many times he became so Frightened he almost Turned Back. Finally, they Came to the River! It was Huge and Breathtaking, Deep and Clear in Places, and Murky in Others. Little Mouse was unable to See Across it because it was so Great. It Roared, Sang, Cried, and Thundered on its Course. Little Mouse Saw Great and Little Pieces of the World Carried Along on its Surface.

"It is Powerful!" little Mouse said, Fumbling for Words.

"It is a Great thing," answered the Raccoon, "but here, let me Introduce you to a Friend."

In a Smoother, Shallower Place was a Lily Pad, Bright and Green. Sitting upon it was a Frog, almost as Green as the Pad it sat on. The Frog's White Belly stood out Clearly.

"Hello, little Brother," said the Frog. "Welcome to the River."

"I must Leave you Now," cut in Raccoon, "but do not Fear, little Brother, for Frog will Care for you Now." And Raccoon Left, Looking along the River Bank for Food that he might Wash and Eat.

Little Mouse Approached the Water and

Looked into it. He saw a Frightened Mouse Reflected there.

"Who are you?" little Mouse asked the Reflection. "Are you not Afraid being that Far out into the Great River?"

"No," answered the Frog, "I am not Afraid. I have been Given the Gift from Birth to Live both Above and Within the River. When Winter Man Comes and Freezes this Medicine, I cannot be Seen. But all the while Thunderbird Flies, I am here. To Visit me, One must Come when the World is Green. I, my Brother, am the Keeper of the Water.

"Amazing!" little Mouse said at last, again Fumbling for Words.

"Would you like to have some Medicine Power?" Frog asked.

"Medicine Power? Me?" asked little Mouse. "Yes, yes! If it is Possible."

"Then Crouch as Low as you Can, and then Jump as High as you are Able! You will have your Medicine!" Frog said.

Little Mouse did as he was Instructed. He Crouched as Low as he Could and Jumped. And when he did, his Eyes Saw the Sacred Mountains.

"Like those over there," the Chief said, pointing to the distant mountains. Then he went on.

Little Mouse could hardly Believe his Eyes. But there They were! But then he Fell back to Earth, and he Landed in the River!

The Chief laughed and looked at the little girl.

Little Mouse became Frightened and Scrambled back to the Bank. He was Wet and Frightened nearly to Death.

"You have Tricked me," little Mouse Screamed at the Frog!"

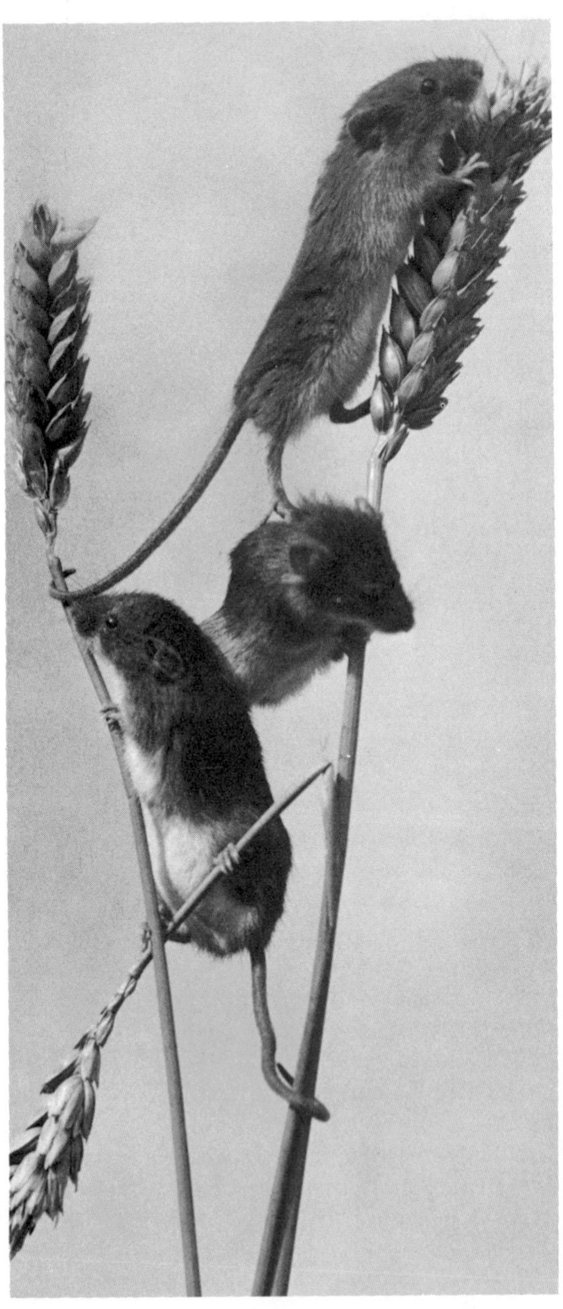

"Wait," said the Frog. "You are not Harmed. Do not let your Fear and Anger Blind you. What did you See?"

"I," Mouse stammered, "I, I Saw the Sacred Mountains!"

"And you have a New Name!" Frog said. "It is Jumping Mouse."

"Thank you. Thank you," Jumping Mouse said, and Thanked him again. "I want to Return to my People and Tell them of this thing that has Happened to me."

"Go. Go then," Frog said. "Return to your People. It is Easy to Find them. Keep the Sound of the Medicine River to the Back of your Head. Go Opposite to the Sound and you will Find your Brother Mice."

Jumping Mouse Returned to the World of the Mice. But he Found Disappointment. No One would Listen to him. And because he was Wet, and had no Way of explaining it because there had been no Rain, many of the other Mice were Afraid of him. They believed he had been Spat from the Mouth of Another Animal that had Tried to Eat him. And they all Knew that if he had not been Food for the One who Wanted him, then he must also be Poison for them.

Jumping Mouse Lived again among his People, but he could not Forget his Vision of the Sacred Mountains.

The Medicine Chief reached again for his Pipe, and Hawk ran for a new brand from the fire to light it for him.

"Is this Story about the Green of the South?" asked Hawk as he sat down. "I remember you talked before about the Man of the South and his Sister. Is this Man the Frog?"

"Yes," the Chief answered. He blew a long puff in the air. "The South is the place of innocence. Men who walk there must walk with a heart of trust."

"Your own Shield is bordered with lodges of green," Day Woman said, pointing to a Shield that hung a few lodges away.

"Those marks are Signs of the Mirroring, just as when Jumping Mouse looked into the river and saw his Reflection," said the Chief.

"But," Hawk added quickly, "that Sign you have upon your Shield is the Medicine Wheel, the Sun Dance. How is it then also the Mirroring?"

"The Medicine Wheel, my children," said the Chief, "is the Mirroring of the Great Spirit, the Universe, among men. We are all the Medicine River. And the Universe is the Medicine River that man is Mirrored upon, my children. And we in our turn see the Medicines of men Mirrored in the Universe."

"Then who is the Frog?" Hawk asked. "I am confused. I do not understand."

"Nor I," Day Woman chimed in.

"Do not make this matter complicated for yourselves," the Chief said. "Little Mouse heard the roaring in his ears and sought to solve its mystery. He met Raccoon and was taken to see the Medicine River, which represents Life. He saw himself Mirrored there in Life.

All of us are so Mirrored, my children, but many men have not visited the Great River and have not witnessed it. Some have followed Raccoon to the River, seen their Reflection, but become frightened and retreated among the mice again. But the lesson is always there for those who seek it. It is in the place of the South. The place of trust."

"Will you explain more to us about the Raccoon?" asked Day Woman.

"No, little Day Woman, because it is for you to visit this place yourself. The Raccoon and the Frog will then become clear to you."

The Chief immediately began the Story again.

The Memory Burned in the Mind and Heart of Jumping Mouse, and One Day he Went to the Edge of the River Place . . .

"Come with me, children," the Peace Chief said, getting to his feet. They walked through the camp, and past it to the river. Even though it was a warm, almost a hot day, many of the People were still busy about the camp.

A group of young men were riding into the camp laughing and teasing with one another. When they rode past Hawk and Day Woman they turned their teasing to the boy and girl. As they rode by, one of the young men slipped from his horse and walked up to the Medicine Chief.

"Good Father," he said, not looking at the Chief, "You are invited to the lodge of my parents for the evening meal. Medicine Crow, my grandfather, has been made well from sickness. The Medicine Power has healed him. My father told me to tell you these things, and also that he will sponsor a dance and Give-Away to the People in thanksgiving tonight."

"A dance!" squeaked Day Woman and Prairie Rose, almost together. "We must prepare," the girls explained to the Chief, and then they were off, running hand in hand to their lodge.

"Well, it appears that now only we three are left," said the Chief.

As they began to walk again, a girl the same age as Singing Flower ran up and grabbed her hand, said something, and left to play. Singing Flower hesitated for a moment and then ran off to join her.

"This," explained the Chief after he and Hawk had reached the brush and trees along the river, "is where Jumping Mouse began. Do

you see those lodges of our People? Those, my son, we will pretend are the Sacred Mountains. Lie down here upon your stomach and see how a Mouse would perceive the Prairie."

Hawk lay on his stomach and looked. The expanse of Prairie appeared to him as a measureless sea of grass. The Chief helped Hawk back to his feet and found them a cool place to sit. There he began the Story again.

Jumping Mouse went to the Edge of the Place of Mice and Looked out onto the Prairie. He Looked up for Eagles. The Sky was Full of many Spots, each One an Eagle. But he was Determined to Go to the Sacred Mountains. He Gathered All of his Courage and Ran just as Fast as he Could onto the Prairie. His little Heart Pounded with Excitement and Fear.

He Ran until he Came to a Stand of Sage. He was Resting and trying to Catch his Breath when he Saw an Old Mouse. The Patch of Sage Old Mouse Lived in was a Haven for Mice. Seeds were Plentiful and there was Nesting Material and many things to be Busy with.

"Hello," said Old Mouse. "Welcome."

Jumping Mouse was Amazed. Such a Place and such a Mouse. "You are Truly a great Mouse," Jumping Mouse said with all the Respect he could Find. "This is Truly a Wonderful Place. And the Eagles cannot See you here, either," Jumping Mouse said.

"Yes," said Old Mouse, "and One can See All the Beings of the Prairie here: the Buffalo, Antelope, Rabbit, and Coyote. One can See them All from here and Know their Names."

"That is Marvelous," Jumping Mouse said. "Can you also See the River and the Great Mountains?"

"Yes and No," Old Mouse Said with

Conviction. "I Know there is the Great River. But I am Afraid that the Great Mountains are only a Myth. Forget your Passion to See Them and Stay here with me. There is Everything you Want here, and it is a Good Place to Be."

"How can he Say such a thing?" Thought Jumping Mouse. "The Medicine of the Sacred Mountains is Nothing One can Forget."

"Thank you very much for the Meal you have Shared with me, Old Mouse, and also for sharing your Great Home," Jumping Mouse said. "But I must Seek the Mountains."

"You are a Foolish Mouse to Leave here. There is Danger on the Prairie! Just Look up there!" Old Mouse said, with even more Conviction. "See all those Spots! They are Eagles, and they will Catch you!"

It was hard for Jumping Mouse to Leave, but he Gathered his Determination and Ran hard Again. The Ground was Rough. But he Arched his Tail and Ran with All his Might. He could Feel the Shadows of the Spots upon his Back as he Ran. All those Spots! Finally he Ran into a Stand of Chokecherries. Jumping Mouse could hardly Believe his Eyes. It was Cool there and very Spacious. There was Water, Cherries and Seeds to Eat, Grasses to Gather for Nests, Holes to be Explored and many, many Other Busy Things to do. And there were a great many things to Gather.

He was Investigating his New Domain when he Heard very Heavy Breathing. He Quickly Investigated the Sound and Discovered its Source. It was a Great Mound of Hair with Black Horns. It was a Great Buffalo. Jumping Mouse could hardly Believe the Greatness of the Being he Saw Lying there before him. He was so large that Jumping Mouse could have Crawled into One of

his Great Horns. "Such a Magnificent Being," Thought Jumping Mouse, and he Crept Closer.

"Hello, my Brother," said the Buffalo. "Thank you for Visiting me."

"Hello, Great Being," said Jumping Mouse. "Why are you Lying here?"

"I am Sick and I am Dying," the Buffalo said, "And my Medicine has Told me that only the Eye of a Mouse can Heal me. But little Brother, there is no such Thing as a Mouse."

Jumping Mouse was Shocked. "One of my Eyes!" he Thought, "One of my Tiny Eyes." He Scurried back into the Stand of Chokecherries. But the Breathing came Harder and Slower.

"He will Die," Thought Jumping Mouse, "If I do not Give him my Eye. He is too Great a Being to Let Die."

He Went Back to where the Buffalo Lay and Spoke. "I am a Mouse," he said with a Shaky Voice. "And you, my Brother, are a Great Being. I cannot Let you Die. I have Two Eyes, so you may have One of them."

The minute he had Said it, Jumping Mouse's Eye Flew Out of his Head and the Buffalo was Made Whole. The Buffalo Jumped to his Feet, Shaking Jumping Mouse's Whole World.

"Thank you, my little Brother," said the Buffalo. "I Know of your Quest for the Sacred Mountains and of your Visit to the River. You have Given me Life so that I may Give-Away to the People. I will be your Brother Forever. Run under my Belly and I will Take you right to the Foot of the Sacred Mountains, and you need not Fear the Spots. The Eagles cannot See you while you Run under Me. All they will See will be the Back of a Buffalo. I am of the Prairie and I will Fall on you if I Try to Go up the Mountains."

Little Mouse Ran under the Buffalo, Secure and

Hidden from the Spots, but with only One Eye it was Frightening. The Buffalo's Great Hooves Shook the Whole World each time he took a Step. Finally they Came to a Place and Buffalo Stopped.

"This is Where I must Leave you, little Brother," said the Buffalo.

"Thank you very much," said Jumping Mouse. "But you Know, it was very Frightening Running under you with only One Eye. I was Constantly in Fear of your Great Earth-Shaking Hooves."

"Your Fear was for Nothing," said Buffalo. "For my Way of Walking is the Sun Dance Way, and I Always Know where my Hooves will Fall. I now must Return to the Prairie, my Brother. You can Always Find me there."

"Come with me, Hawk," the Chief said. "Let us walk to those pines on that hill."

"Tell me," said Hawk, "What is the meaning within this Teaching?"

The Chief walked in silence until he was almost to the top of the hill. A coyote jumped from behind a small rock and ran over the top of the hill, but not before stopping once and looking back at the two men.

The smell of the campfires and cooking food drifted up from the camp below. The voices of children laughing at their play blended with the sounds of the wind in the pines and the songbirds of the prairie.

"When you experience this seeking," the Chief began, "You will meet the Old Mice of the world. They can name for you the beings of the Prairie, but they have neither touched nor known them. These people have received a great Gift, but they spend their lives hidden within the sage. They have not yet run out on to the Prairie, the everyday world. Like Jumping Mouse, they fear the spots the most.

"But remember, my son, that Mice see clearly only that which is very near to them. To those people who perceive in this way, the sky will always be full of spots because of their nearsightedness. And of course in their fear they will always perceive them as Eagles," the Chief chuckled.

"But Jumping Mouse does not stay, he runs. As you already know, the Buffalo is the great Spirit's greatest Gift to the People. He is the Spirit of Giving. Jumping Mouse Gives-Away one of his own eyes, one of his Mouse's ways of perceiving, and heals the Buffalo."

"Why must he Give-Away an eye to heal the Buffalo?" Hawk asked.

"Because this kind of person, this Mouse, must give up one of his Mouse ways of seeing things in order that he may grow. People never are forced to do these things, Hawk. The Buffalo

did not even know Jumping Mouse was a Mouse. He could have just stayed hidden like the Old Mouse."

"What would have happened if he had let the Buffalo die?" asked Hawk.

"He would have had to live with the stink of the rotting flesh, my son. Or he would have had to retreat to the place of Old Mouse. And if he had decided to live there instead of moving and growing, then he would have experienced thirst. The chokecherries he would have eaten would have made him thirst mightily for water.

"Believe me, Hawk, many men have reached these places. Some choose to live with the stink, and others, refusing to leave the Old Mouse's place, thirst constantly. Still others run endlessly under the great Buffalo. These are probably the most powerful of men, but no doubt the worst. They have the Power, but they speak always from fear. Fear of the great hooves of the Spirit, and of course the fear of the spots, the high Eagles, the unknown."

"Is there yet more, Shield Man?" Hawk asked.

"Yes, there is," answered the Teacher. "But do you wish to eat first?"

"No," said Hawk quickly, "I can eat later. Please finish the Story."

The Man of the Shield smiled and let his eyes rest on the camp below him.

Jumping Mouse Immediately Began to Investigate his New Surroundings. There were even more things here than in the Other Places, Busier things, and an Abundance of Seeds and Other things Mice Like. In his Investigation of these things, Suddenly he Ran upon a Gray Wolf who was Sitting there doing absolutely Nothing.

"Hello, Brother Wolf," Jumping Mouse said.

The Wolf's Ears Came Alert and his Eyes Shone. "Wolf! Wolf! Yes, that is what I am, I am a Wolf!" But then his mind Dimmed again and it was not long before he Sat Quietly again, completely without Memory as to who he was. Each time Jumping Mouse Reminded him who he was, he became Excited with the News, but soon would Forget again.

"Such a Great Being," thought Jumping Mouse, "but he has no Memory."

Jumping Mouse Went to the Center of this New Place and was Quiet. He Listened for a very long time to the Beating of his Heart. Then Suddenly he Made up his Mind. He Scurried back to where the Wolf Sat and he Spoke.

"Brother Wolf," Jumping Mouse said. . . .

"Wolf! Wolf," said the Wolf. . . .

"Please, Brother Wolf," said Jumping Mouse, "Please Listen to me. I Know what will Heal you. It is One of my Eyes. And I Want to Give it to you. You are a Greater Being than I. I am only a Mouse. Please Take it."

When Jumping Mouse Stopped Speaking his Eye Flew out of his Head and the Wolf was made Whole.

Tears Fell down the Cheeks of Wolf, but his little Brother could not See them, for Now he was Blind.

"You are a Great Brother," said the Wolf, "for Now I have my Memory. But Now you are Blind. I am the Guide into the Sacred Mountains. I will Take you there. There is a Great Medicine Lake there. The most Beautiful Lake in the World. All the World is Reflected there. The People, the Lodges of the People, and All the Beings of the Prairies and Skies."

"Please Take me there," Jumping Mouse said.

The Wolf Guided him through the Pines to the

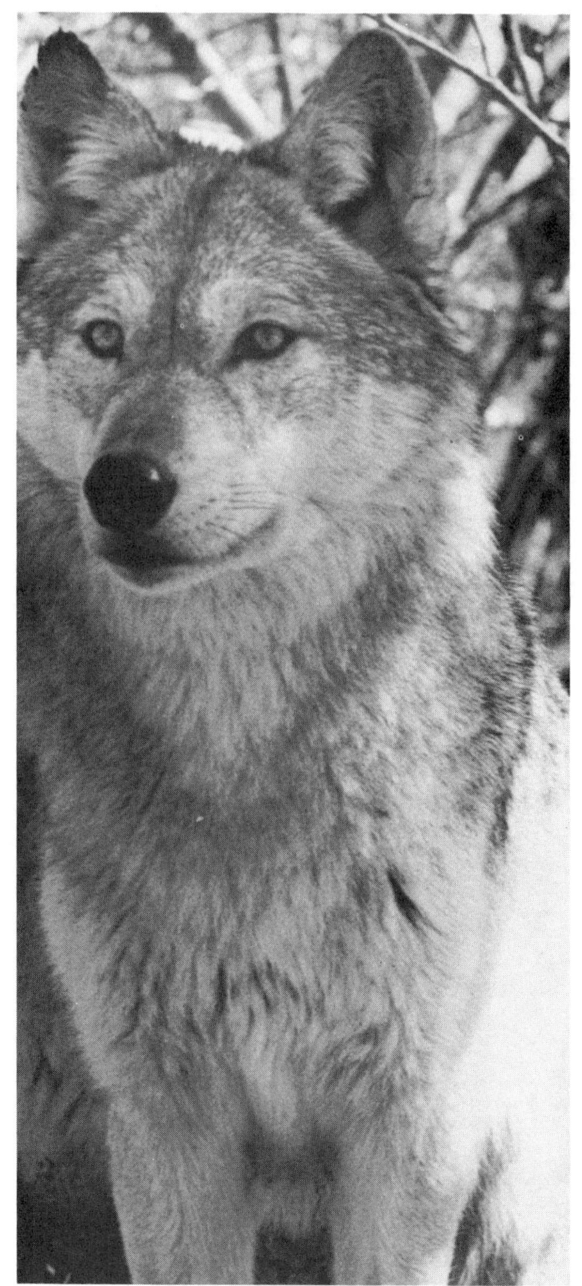

Medicine Lake. Jumping Mouse Drank the Water from the Lake. The Wolf Described the Beauty to him.

"I must Leave you here," said Wolf, "for I must Return so that I may Guide Others, but I will Remain with you as long as you Like."

"Thank you, my Brother," said Jumping Mouse. "But although I am Frightened to be Alone, I Know you must Go so that you may Show Others the Way to this Place."

Jumping Mouse Sat there Trembling in Fear. It was no use Running, for he was Blind, but he Knew an Eagle would Find him Here. He Felt a Shadow on his Back and Heard the Sound that Eagles Make. He Braced himself for the Shock. And the Eagle Hit! Jumping Mouse went to Sleep.

Then he Woke Up. The surprise of being Alive was Great, but Now he could See! Everything was Blurry, but the Colors were

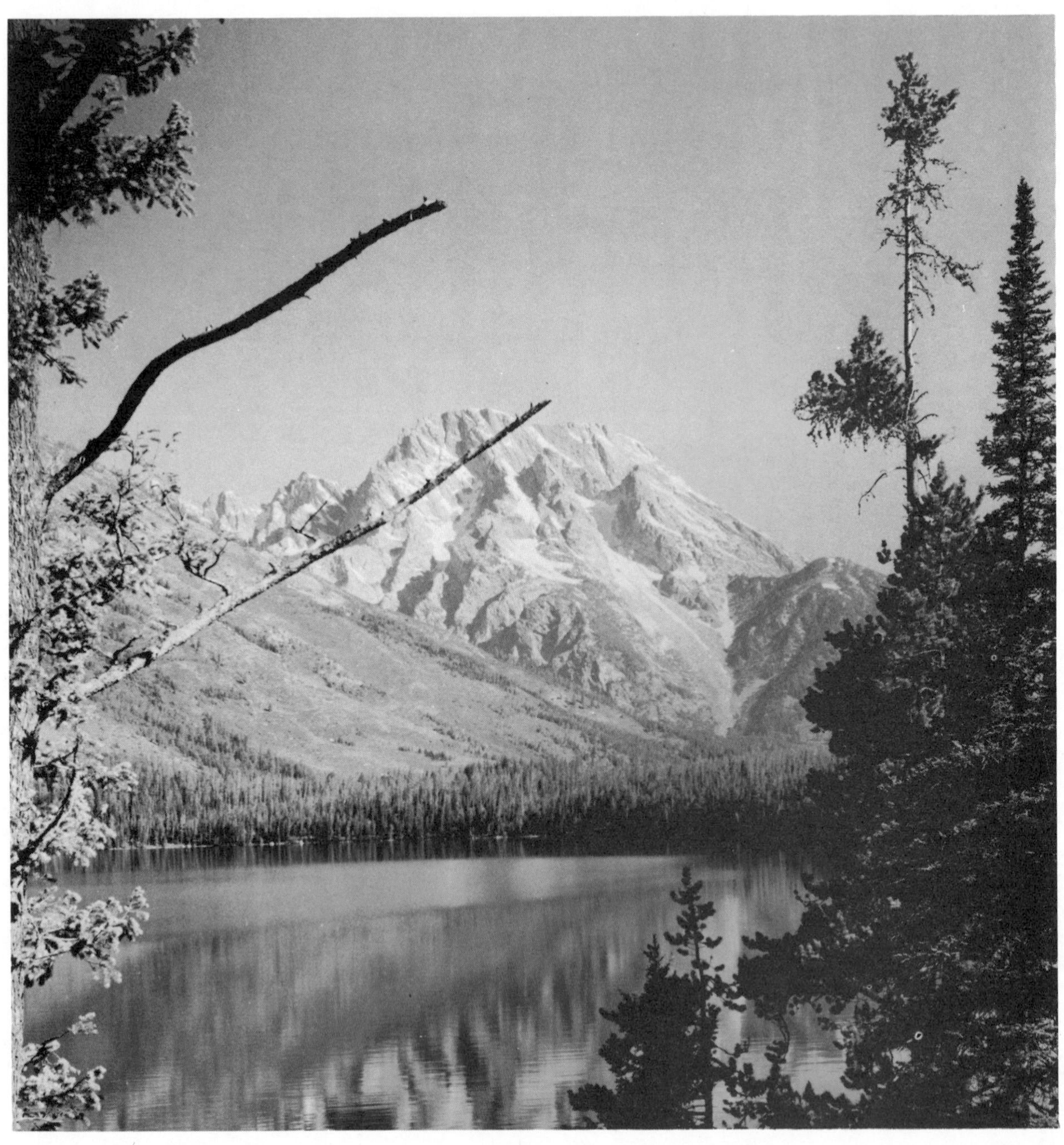

Beautiful.

"I can See! I can See!" said Jumping Mouse over again and again.

A Blurry Shape Came toward Jumping Mouse. Jumping Mouse Squinted hard but the Shape Remained a Blur.

"Hello, Brother," a Voice said. "Do you Want some Medicine?"

"Some Medicine for me?" asked Jumping Mouse. "Yes! Yes!"

"Then Crouch down as Low as you Can," the Voice said, "and Jump as High as you Can."

Jumping Mouse did as he was Instructed. He Crouched as Low as he Could and Jumped! The Wind Caught him and Carried him Higher.

"Do not be Afraid," the Voice called to him. "Hang on to the Wind and Trust!"

Jumping Mouse did. He Closed his Eyes and Hung on to the Wind and it Carried him Higher and Higher. Jumping Mouse Opened his Eyes and they were Clear, and the Higher he Went the Clearer they Became. Jumping Mouse Saw his Old Friend upon a Lily Pad on the Beautiful Medicine Lake. It was the Frog.

"You have a New Name," Called the Frog. "You are Eagle!"

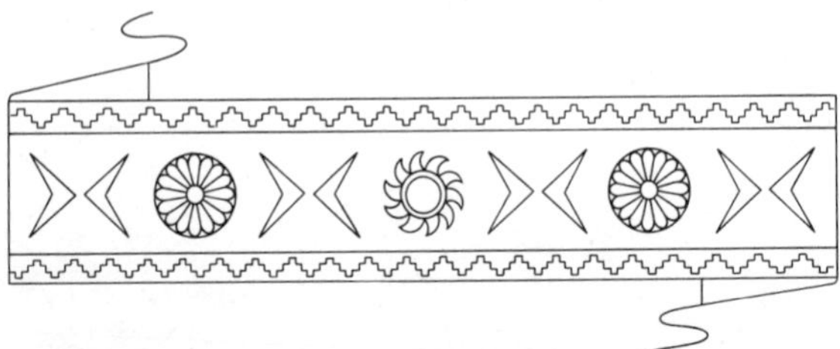

Everyone turned out for the dance that evening with the exception of the Dog Soldiers, who were the night guard for the camp. Hawk danced near Day Woman. She was wearing her best buckskin dress and quilled belt. The white eagle plumes that were tied in her black hair stood out sharply, floating with the motion of each step she took. She was more beautiful than he had ever seen her before. The dress she was wearing was cut in the Arapaho style, and molded itself to her breasts and hips. She saw him looking at her and smiled. Each time she caught him at it, Hawk would spin and dance low so that she would not see him blush.

Then twelve of the best and oldest singers picked up their hand drums and walked to the middle of the dancing ground. It was time for the Round Dance. It would be for the women to choose their partners, and Hawk, hoping in the same thought that Day Woman would pick him and yet that she would not, wondered what to do. Day Woman came toward him. Hawk pretended to fix his ankle rattles. He saw her moccasins come up to him and stop. He looked up, and she was smiling as she held out her hand to him. They went to the circle of dancers and found their places. Hawk felt her arm circle his waist and hold him. His hand followed the quilled belt around her waist and stopped on her hip. Hawk was stiff when the circle began to move, but soon he relaxed to Day Woman's rhythm. She pressed hard against him as they danced and he held her waist tightly.

"Medicine Crow was sick and now is well," the crier called. "The Medicine, *Miaheyyun,* has made him well. And in thanksgiving his children wish to Give-Away."

"Why do we Give-Away, great Teacher?" asked Singing Flower as she tugged at the Peace Chief's shirt.

"Because the great Spirit gives us so very much," said the Chief. "Because the Power is so very rich, it has taught the People to give to one another." The Chief was on his haunches when he answered the little girl, and he picked her up and held her when he had answered. He danced out into the stream of dancers with Singing Flower and spun around with her.

The sudden appearance of horsemen riding into camp stopped the drums and singing. The dancers stood where they were, waiting to see what news they brought.

Holds His Braids slid from the back of his pony and ran up to Standing Eagle.

"We have been riding for fifteen days," Holds His Braids began. "Pony Soldiers are killing everyone. They are very strong, and they are searching everywhere for the camps of the People. You must be prepared!"

"Are they coming here?" Standing Eagle asked.

"Yes!" Holds His Braids answered. "They are on their way!"

Some of the women began to cry and run for their lodges. The dancing stopped immediately and a council was held.

"We are only a small village," Lame Bear said. "We must join the rest of our People as soon as possible at Sand Creek."

"No!" Medicine Rock broke in. "That is what the soldiers will expect. Why do we not instead send the Dog Soldiers to warn the people at Sand Creek? And we in this village can join with our Arapaho brothers, the Throw Away Boy People. There are also the Medicine Song Bird People, our Kiowa Brothers of the Shield, camped not too far from them. Together we will be strong."

"What do you have to say, Holds His Braids? You have been away from the camp, what is the news?" Ten Bears asked.

"They are everywhere! The Pony Soldiers are everywhere! North, south, east, and west. There is a Sioux Brother of the Shield. His name is Sitting Bull. I have news that he is calling the Brotherhood of the Shield together. But I have also heard and seen with my own eyes those who will not honor the Shields."

"We know nothing!" Lame Bear said, standing up. "We are like rabbits caught in a flood. There is no place to run. There is no help! We must join the People at Sand Creek. I know our brothers there still honor the Shields. Only last year we danced together with them in the Great Medicine Lodge. They cannot have changed in just one year. Let us go to them!"

"Does anyone else wish to speak?" Standing Eagle asked. There was silence. "Then it is settled. We will move tomorrow for Sand Creek."

Spotted Calf had remained seated on his horse. Hawk watched him kick his mount and thread his way through the crowd that was rapidly breaking up. He was coming toward him and Day Woman.

Handsome, popular Spotted Calf was Hawk's brother and best friend, but in the last few years, Spotted Calf had become bigger, luckier, better looking, and stronger than Hawk. Hawk now found himself uneasy around his childhood friend.

When they had been younger, Spotted Calf and Hawk had been part of a group of boys which had always been looking for adventure. Hawk suddenly remembered a time when they had decided to explore a group of caves the men had found while hunting. One of the caves had been large enough for the men to enter on horseback, and a warrior who had ridden into it for a quick look had seen a human skeleton. This had made the mystery of the caves grow larger and larger among the boys of the camp. The bravest group of boys, which of course had been Hawk and his friends, had decided to explore the caves first.

Just as they had been leaving the camp to look for the caves, Holds Him Fast had called out to them.

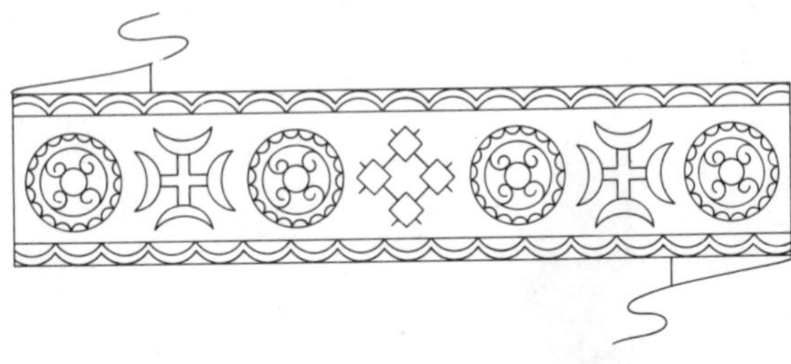

"I have two fine bows here," Holds Him Fast said as he pointed to a beautiful pair of perfectly made bows, "and these will belong to the person who will find my mare and colt. They wandered from the camp yesterday and I have been unable to find them."

At the offer of this reward, the boys lost no time in scrambling for their horses. The group split in natural confusion, and went in separate directions. Tame Elk and Coyote's Way rode with Spotted Calf and Hawk.

They rode for three hours, when as if by magic they saw the mare and her colt. Ropes in hand, the boys galloped after the prize. The mare looked up at the approaching riders and then continued to graze, unconcerned. Their loops were thrown almost in unison. But to Hawk's disappointment, his only fell on the mare's neck and slid off. The other three found their mark. The mare was led away by Spotted Calf with her colt following a short distance behind. Tame Elk and Coyote's Way decided to share one of the bows Holds Him Fast would give them. Hawk waited for his friend to mention sharing the other prize with him, but Spotted Calf said nothing. His disappointment at Spotted Calf's silence sat in Hawk's chest like a stone.

"Let us now go look at that cave!" Coyote's

Way said as they headed back toward the camp. "It is a good time."

The boys kicked their ponies into a run. The excitement of the cave made Hawk forget his bad feeling for the time being. They were soon strung out in their run for the caves. Hawk's horse was in the lead with Spotted Calf's bringing up the rear. Hawk saw the large cave and rode straight for its opening. When he reached the opening, Hawk's horse shied and bucked, backing nervously and fighting for its head. Coyote's Way was the next to reach the cave, and his horse also balked at its mouth. Coyote's Way stung his nervous pony with his quirt, and it danced sideways into the cave. Hawk, who was without a quirt, kicked his horse viciously, calling fire on his mount's head for this new disappointment.

The others had just reached the cave's entrance when Hawk saw Coyote's Way's pony fall. The horse scrambled to regain its footing and ran back for the opening. Tame Elk reached for the frightened pony and caught its reins, jerking it up short. Hawk dismounted, handing his reins to Tame Elk, and ran into the cave. Coyote's Way was lying motionless on the floor of the cave. Hawk started to run to him when he heard a vicious hiss that stopped him in his tracks. A huge wolverine stood just to Hawk's right, between Hawk and where Coyote's Way was lying unconscious on the floor of the cave. The wolverine hissed again and made a challenging movement toward Hawk. Hawk slowly backed up a few steps and stood there. The wolverine stood its ground, hissing and snapping its teeth.

"What can we do?" Spotted Calf yelled almost in his ear. "We have got to do something quickly!"

"Let us get help!" Hawk answered, his voice shaking. "We have nothing with which to kill this animal."

"You know we cannot do that," Spotted Calf said. "The wolverine will kill Coyote's Way if we leave, and if we do not do something right away."

Hawk stood there paralyzed. He was looking around wildly and trying to decide what to do, when Spotted Calf dashed past him into the cave. He leaped over Coyote's Way and ran to the back of the cave. The wolverine answered this new challenge and moved back toward Spotted Calf. Spotted Calf teased it, and drew it further into the cave.

"For the sake of wholeness, Hawk, get Coyote's Way!" Spotted Calf screamed. "Hurry! Do not just stand there!"

Hawk seemed to come out of a dream. He ran to his friend and grabbed his shoulders. The wolverine stopped its advance toward Spotted Calf and answered what it believed to be its second challenge. It moved quickly toward Hawk. Its ugly head and body wobbled, jelly-like, as it slithered toward him. Spotted Calf yelled and hit the wolverine with a rock. The beast turned again and rushed back to battle with Spotted Calf. Hawk dragged his friend into the sunlight, and ran back to help Spotted Calf. Spotted Calf had climbed to a ledge at the back of the cave, and was now poking with a stick at the enraged wolverine from a safe distance.

"Go get some bowmen," Spotted Calf grinned from his perch, "and hurry. I am

hungry."

Spotted Calf was a hero. Robes were given to him and also to Hawk that same evening.

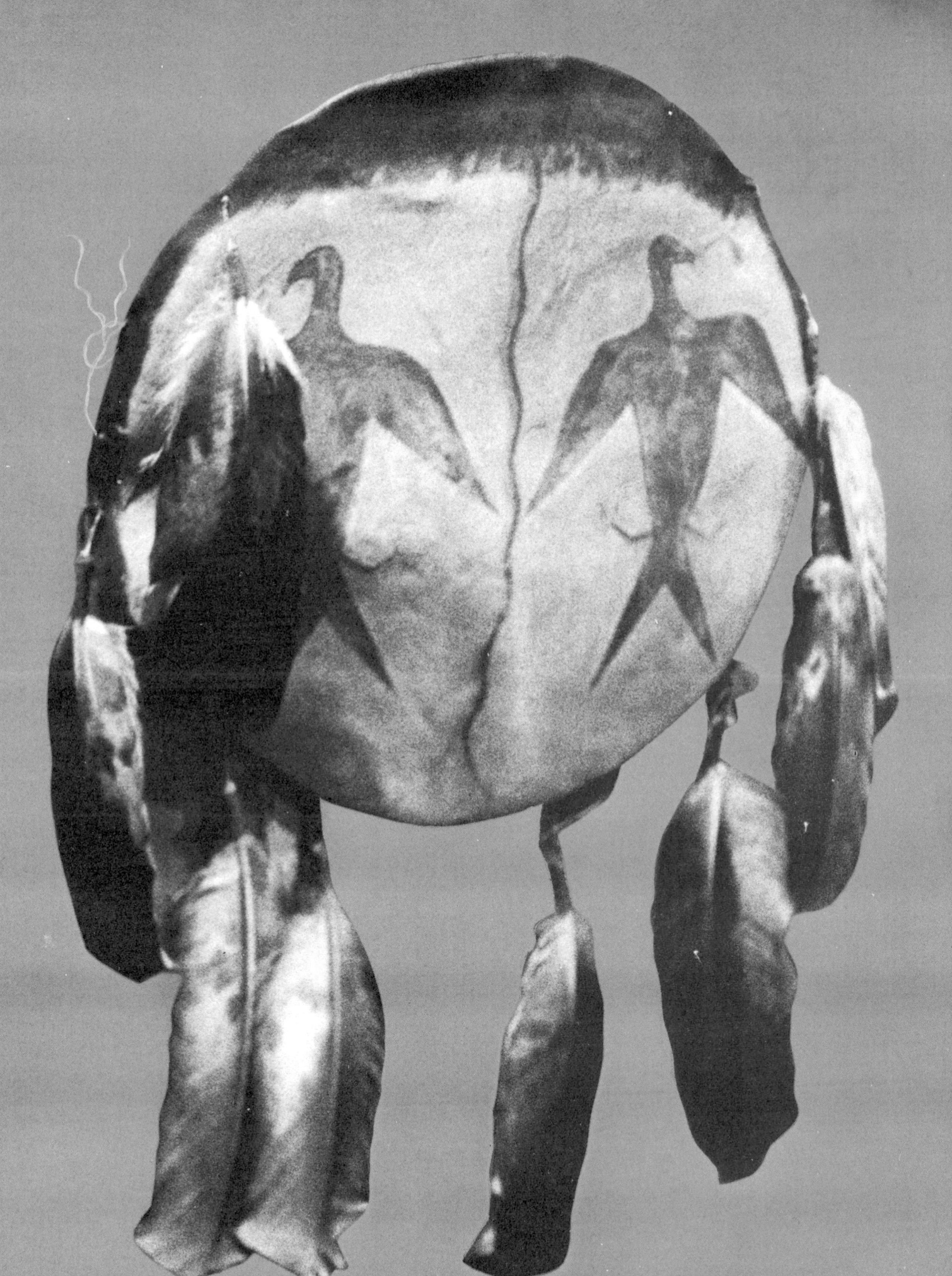

Spotted Calf made his way to Hawk through the crowd with his horse, and stopped. His horse backed and shied nervously when Hawk went up and gripped his arm.

Spotted Calf had grown and filled out even more than Hawk since he had left the camp a year ago, and now he seemed to radiate a new power.

"What have we here?" he asked, looking at Day Woman. "Are you sleeping with my brother?"

Day Woman blushed and looked at her feet. Spotted Calf jumped from his horse and stood between them, hugging them both, laughing. They remained this way as they walked to Hawk's lodge. Spotted Calf's horse tried to follow, finally stopping when it stepped on one of its dragging reins, and then began to graze on some grass it found nearby.

The camp at Sand Creek bustled with activity. It seemed almost like the coming together for the Sun Dance. Women excitedly visited old friends, happy to see each other again, and settled in to talk. Children and dogs mingled, fought, laughed, cried, and played together. Girls giggled and boys shuffled their feet, both amazed at the transformation of each other's bodies and minds in just one short year.

There were many new things to see. The miracles of the whiteman's magic were visible everywhere. Hawk's people, who had seen very little of these marvels, exclaimed with disbelief, surprise, and envy.

There was the stinging water, too. The first taste of the stinging water brought whoops of delight from some, and sour expressions to the faces of others. Still others sat by just watching, waiting to see what happened. Some of the men were already drunk. They staggered and danced, delighted in themselves and their spectators. This was not a Renewal time. There would be no Sun Dance, and the air was thick with the strangeness of it.

There was excitement because of the many visitors, too. Throw Away Boy People, Little Black Eagles, and the People of the South, the Comanches, were there. Their stories were as different as their personalities, as they gave their accounts of the changing world and the whitemen they had met. Some of the men spat out their experiences in tones of hatred and

bitter sorrow. Others laughed because of good trades they had made, while still others refused to talk at all. Evidence of the disintegration of the Brotherhood of the Shields and the Sun Dance Way was everywhere.

Hawk and Spotted Calf sat together at watch on a hill near the camp. It was early evening, and growing dark quickly. Clouds massed themselves in the west and were lit by the flash of distant heat lightning. Little gusts of wind blew awkwardly at the boys' small fire, tipping the flames in different directions, and sighing in the pines over their heads.

Hawk felt the smoothness of the heavy weapon that lay across his lap. Spotted Calf had instructed Hawk in the use of the thunder iron the day before. The iron belonged to Sun Goes Slow, one of the men who had ridden into the camp with Holds His Braids.

"This thunder iron used to belong to a filthy Little Black Eagle," Spotted Calf said, touching the weapon that lay in Hawk's lap. "He rolled into the dust like a common dog when we shot him." Spotted Calf laughed, and began again. "I can still remember the surprised look on his face. Sun Goes Slow carries his hair now."

"A filthy Little Black Eagle?" Hawk replied in disbelief. "I do not understand! Sun Goes Slow's own mother and father are People of the Little Black Eagle. The Sign of this is right there." Hawk pointed to Spotted Calf's shield and to the Black Eagle that was painted there. "That is the sign of the Spiritual Father of the Little Black Bird. You are a Little Black Eagle yourself, Spotted Calf. How is it that you say 'filthy Little Black Eagle?' "

"It is not the same!" Spotted Calf answered contemptuously. "The world is not what the

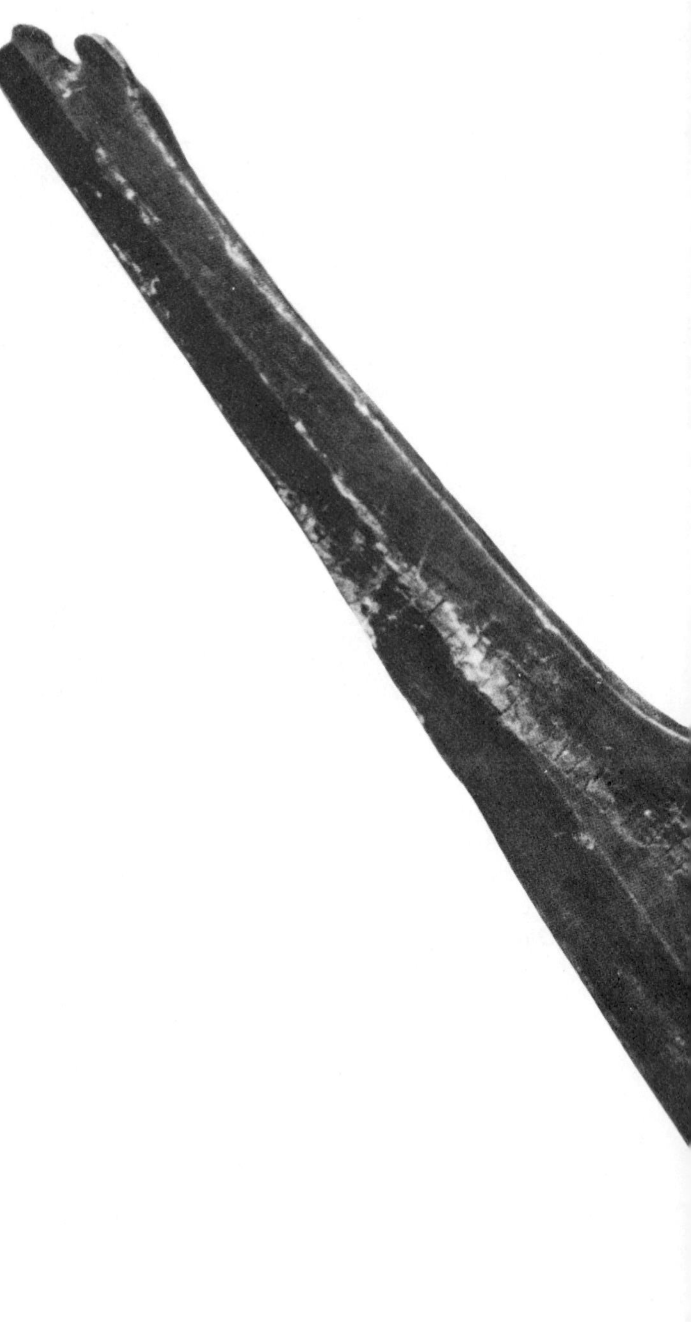

Peace Chiefs say. There was no doubt a time when the Brotherhood of the Shields was strong, but those days are dead. While I lived in the old camp I believed as you do. But one year away has taught me much. The outside world is different, little brother. There are powerful things of the whiteman to be seen everywhere. It is a hard world, one full of danger, and only those strong and brave enough will live in it. The rewards are great. Greater than your mind can imagine!"

"What rewards?" asked Hawk. "Death?"

"You are a child," Spotted Calf said putting his arm around Hawk. "Maybe you will be a Peace Chief. You have no understanding of these things. You believe in the Medicine and teach it. I believe in this." Spotted Calf raised the iron above his head. "This is my reality. The war god of the whiteman is strong and is generous with rewards. I have chosen this new Way."

Before, when the camps had come together, the Sun Dancers had stood in a line within the Medicine lodge. The drum had been its heartbeat, and the singers' voices had been strong. The People had stood there in the Renewal of the Brotherhood and watched the sunrise. The Power had been strong and because of this the People had been strong. But this time, the sunrise that came the next morning at Sand Creek was not the same. The morning exploded with the frightening crash of thunder irons, as hundreds of Pony Soldiers charged into the camp at a full gallop.

Hawk was awakened by screams and by the roar of horses' hooves and exploding weapons. He grabbed his bow and quiver and ran outside. He saw his mother clutch at her stomach and roll over in a sudden pool of blood. She spilled her cooking pot as she fell, and the steam rose from it into the air.

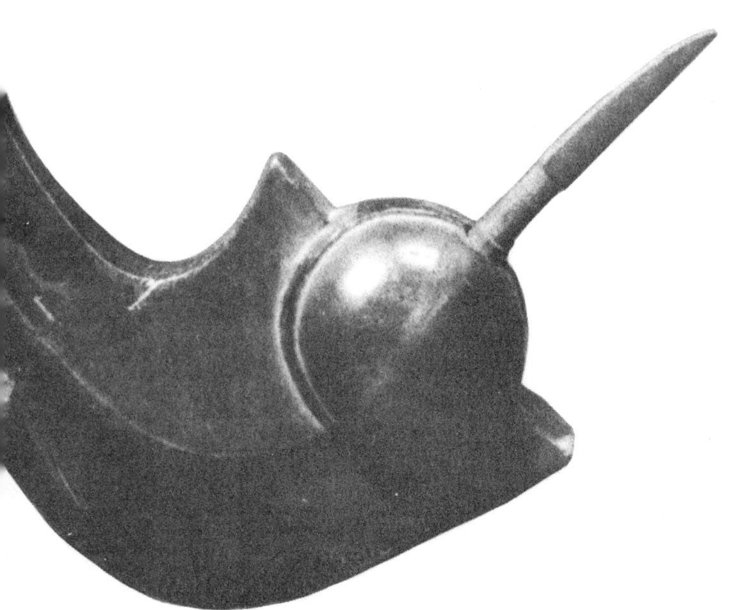

Hawk stared in disbelief at the charging whitemen. A part of his mind told him he should either run or fight, but he was unable even to move. The wave of attacking men was nearly upon him, but all he could see in his astonishment was that the white soldiers were all dressed absolutely alike, and that they looked completely identical. Their bright blue figures were everywhere, and men, women, and children were falling before their long knives and thunder irons like cut grass. Warriors ran from their lodges for their ponies, and were killed even before they could reach them. Hawk saw Spotted Calf leap to his horse and charge alone to meet the enemy. He fell from his horse dead within a few feet of Hawk. Hawk saw Singing Flower standing by her lodge screaming, rooted to the spot with terror. Her mother and father were already dead. He ran to her, scooping her up in his arms. Then he ran blindly on, without direction.

The attack on the camp was over quickly. As Hawk ran, he heard only the sporadic sounds of exploding irons mingled with the shrieks of the wounded women and children. These sounds continued until sundown, and then even they ceased. Then all was quiet, except for the strange and unintelligible voices of the Pony Soldiers, and the neighing of their horses.

Hawk stayed hidden for two days with Singing Flower by the river. On the evening of the second day, they left their hiding place and headed out onto the prairie. They traveled all night. When it was nearly daylight, Hawk killed a rabbit and they ate it raw. Then they tried to sleep. Hawk had not slept since the morning of the attack, and now he found he was so tired he could not sleep.

Unable to rest, he thought again about the attack. He thanked the Power he had fallen asleep fully dressed the night before, because Singing

Flower had still been undressed when they had been surprised. Now, he had taken off his shirt and given it to her. Also, neither Hawk nor Singing Flower had escaped with their moccasins. Hawk had torn the sleeves from his shirt and wrapped them around Singing Flower's feet, using the fringes from the sleeves to tie them.

Still unable to sleep, Hawk decided he would explore the wash they were hidden in for water and food. As he walked down it the wash became deeper, and he hurried along hoping it would lead him to a creek. Hawk made a turn with the wash and froze dead in his tracks. Ahead of him were Day Woman and Prairie Rose. Both girls screamed at Hawk's sudden appearance, and then began to cry in relief.

"Stay right where you are," said Hawk, and ran back for Singing Flower. He returned with Singing Flower and she ran to the other two girls, crying. Hawk then left them and explored the wash further, finding a small stream hidden within banks it had cut for itself. He made a small shelter for them there and then returned for the girls. He noticed that Prairie Rose walked stiffly and wondered if she had been wounded.

"It seems hard for you to walk," Hawk said to Prairie Rose. "Were you hurt?"

Prairie Rose removed her dress. Her body was bruised from neck to knees, and even after three days the places where she had been bitten about her breasts and stomach were still clearly visible.

"Fifteen or twenty of the Pony Soldiers took their turns with me," Prairie Rose said as she put her dress back on. "I was lucky. Many were treated worse than I."

They stayed hidden there for five days. Hawk hunted for them, and the girls worked hard outfitting their camp. When they left they traveled north, moving only at night. Their progress was slow and with its share of everyday misfortunes.

"You have not spoken to me yet about your escape," Hawk said to Day Woman one evening while they ate. "It is better for you to talk about it."

She sat for a very long time before answering him, and then suddenly she blurted out her reply. "I have killed two men!" she said and began to cry.

"Good!" Hawk exclaimed, "Why should you cry about a thing like that?"

"No," Day Woman said through her tears. "No, it was different. I am still confused. I know it seems right that I killed them. But, *Maheo!* I do not know. It was a mixed-up thing. It was not the same with me as with Prairie Rose."

She wiped her tears away and walked a short distance. Then she sat down, drawing her knees up under her chin.

"The two men who took me away with them were different. They caught me down by the river. From the minute they found me they acted strangely. They looked this way and that, and then sneaked with me to a place that was thick with bushes. I was so frightened I could hardly walk. They poked me with their irons and motioned me inside the cover of some bushes. I expected them to kill me and to take my hair, but instead they sat down and motioned me with their irons to sit. They kept looking at each other oddly, and then at me. My hands were shaking so badly I could not stop them.

"Then one of them put his hands upon mine and pressed them. I think I cried out, I do not remember. Then they just sat there looking at me and talking in their own tongue. I looked around for a place to run, but could not find one. It was like a dream. I wanted to kill them both and run.

"They both laid down their irons and motioned for me to undress. I got up on my knees and took off my dress. They both were looking at me hard, but gently. Yes, I know what you are thinking, but they were! It was all very confusing. They spoke to each other again and then one left, walked a short distance from us, and sat down with his back to us. Then each in turn made love to me. Touching me gently, caressing me, and kissing my mouth. Both of them were shaking. Their hands trembled before they made love to me.

"After they were finished I put my dress back on and sat there. From the camp I could hear the cries of women and children as they were dying. I grabbed one of the whitemen's irons the way Spotted Calf had taught me, and killed one of them. His eyes grew wide when I made the iron speak.

"The other grabbed his iron, pointed it at me and said something. I saw him begging me with his eyes. Yes, it is true! I actually saw him beg me with his eyes. He pointed to me and then to himself, shaking his head. He was saying something to me as he did this. Then he laid down his iron. I got up to leave. He did nothing. I could have gotten away easily. But the hate welled up inside me, and I killed him. He reached out to me before he fell in his death."

Prairie Rose went to her side and comforted her.

"Strange!" Hawk finally said. "How very strange."

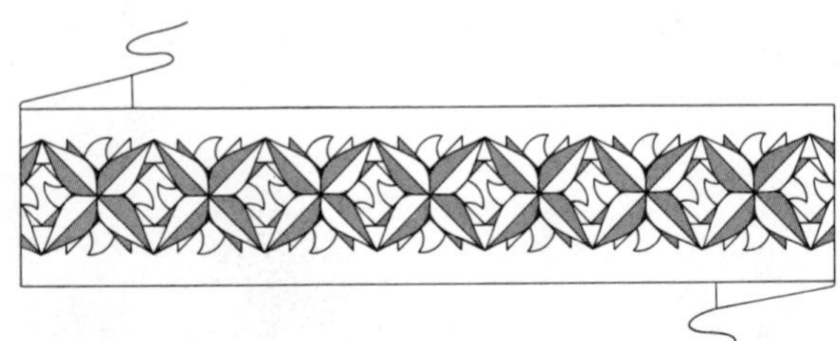

Blue Weasel sat in his lodge trying to make sense out of the message that had been brought to him. Yellow Robe sat across from him in numb silence.

"Dead?" Blue Weasel mumbled. "All my brothers of the Painted Arrow dead? It is hard for me to believe."

"The whitemen killed them in reprisal," Yellow Robe answered his friend.

"Reprisal!" thundered Blue Weasel. "Their people kill us at will, and then the Pony Soldiers kill us in reprisal."

"True," Yellow Robe answered, "but many of the People of the Shields have taken this path of war also."

"What shall we do?" Blue Weasel asked in a quieter voice. "It does us no good to sit with them in councils of peace. They never honor the peace. Should our village join with Crazy Horse? His name fits him. Crazy New Way.

"The whiteman is a madman. In some of our villages he even moves among the People quietly, either ignoring what is going on elsewhere in the world or in ignorance of it, I do not know."

"Let us hear Crazy New Way speak tomorrow, and then make up our minds as to what to do," Yellow Robe answered.

The next day, Blue Weasel and Yellow Robe stepped from their lodges to meet Crazy New Way. His main camp had been made only a short distance from the camp of Blue Weasel.

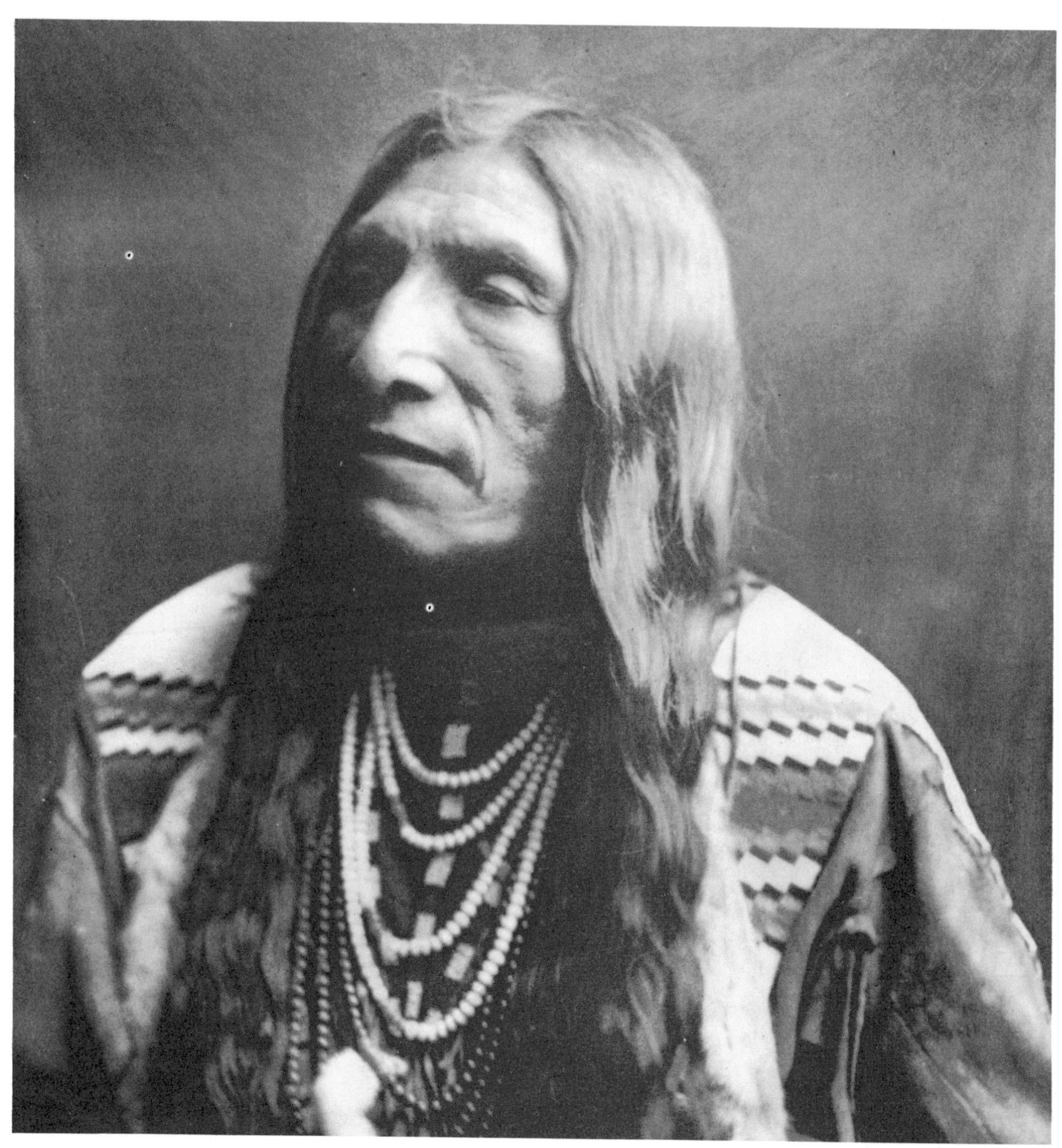

Now, he rode into camp in a reckless run, with thirty or forty warriors riding hard after him. After they had dismounted and exchanged greetings, a council circle was formed and the Pipe was passed. Crazy New Way spoke.

"People, I have been given the name Crazy New Way, and I am Crazy Horse. The old Way is dead or is dying among all the People. There is a new Power, the Power of the whiteman. This new Power has one simple rule. It is to be strong. It brings with it a new Way of touching. It is the taking of scalps. The rewards of this new Power can be seen everywhere. The whitemen are only men just as we are. It is his God who is so powerful. If we meet the whitemen on the battlefields, we can kill them.

"Look," he said throwing his iron into the middle of the circle. "This is a reward. It can bring more food to the lodges of the People than our bows and arrows. And it can kill our enemies at a greater distance. If you do not fight then you will die. The whiteman will find you. It may take him a year or more if you try to hide, but he will find you. And then you will certainly die! But the things he has we also can have. It is a thing easily understood. We must kill as he does, and his Gifts will be ours."

"Kill, Kill, Kill!" Yellow Robe was the speaker. "We have been taught by the Men of the Shields all of our lives not to kill, that it is a greater man who simply touches his enemy and shames him. Any animal can kill. It is only man, the great Medicine Animal, who has the Power of Decision. He can either shame or he can kill. The animal who has no mind knows only one law, and that is to kill. You call yourself Crazy Horse. The Crazy New Way. I say to you that it is truly crazy. You say there is a new Power. There is only one Power. It is the Mirror of the Universe, and it is the Sun Dance. The Sun Dance will not die!

"The Men of the Shields have taught us that man is here to learn and to grow. The coming of the whiteman is no different for us than dissension, cruelty, or loneliness. It is a learning for us. I know that you will take many of my people with you when you leave here. They will leave for many reasons. Some will leave for gain, others because of their bitterness and hatred toward the whitemen, and others for glory. But I choose to stand by the Medicine Shields. I choose to be a Sun Dancer. I choose Peace. I have spoken."

"You are a fool!" shouted Crazy New Way. "The Way of the Great Shields has been dying for years. Can you remember within your lifetime when the Brother People, the Painted Arrows and the People of the Little Black Eagle have not been at war? Your People of the Little Black Eagle have been warring with the People of the Painted Arrow for so many years that even you have forgotten."

"It is true I am of the People of the Little Black Eagle, the Crow. But I have still grieved at the death of my brothers of the Painted Arrow, the Cheyenne. Yes, there have been wars. But not the kind you and the whitemen have been fighting. Our old wars were for touching the enemy and shaming him, not for taking his life. We cut off his braids, not his whole hair and scalp! And every four years we met within the Renewal Lodge and were brothers. The woman who gave me birth was a Painted Arrow woman, and the man who loved her was of the Little Black Eagle. They met at one of these Renewals."

"I know you," Crazy Horse laughed. "You are a soft Peace Chief! You hide behind your Shields because you have always been afraid to fight. Do you remember your Teaching of the

Dogs? The Dogs who run out into the night to bark at the fearful things of the night? The ones who will lay their lives down for the People? The Dogs who will fight the biggest bears to save their masters? It is these Dogs that I have come for! Not the ones who tremble in their lodges. There is an animal bear who is coming here to kill us all in our villages. This bear is the whiteman, and I am here for Crazy Dogs who will fight him! I have spoken."

Crazy Horse strode from the council and mounted his horse.

"Only Dogs!" yelled Crazy Horse, holding his thunder iron over his head and piercing the air with the cry of a dog. He kicked his horse into a run and left the camp. The party of men who had come with him copied their leader's yell, fired their irons into the air, and galloped after him.

Later the flap of Yellow Robe's lodge opened and a young man stuck his head inside. "There is a young man here who is looking for you, Yellow Robe. He has two women with him and a little girl. He says he is of the Painted Arrow People and that you are his father."

"It is Hawk!" Yellow Robe exclaimed excitedly. "He is indeed my son! Tell him to bring his sisters and himself to my lodge."

The head disappeared and soon Hawk, Day Woman, Prairie Rose, and Singing Flower were well fed and asleep in the lodge of Yellow Robe.

Hawk slept until mid-afternoon the next day. The skin of the lodge had been rolled up on its poles, and he could see Day Woman and Prairie Rose sitting under an arbor outside. They were busy repairing some moccasins they had been given. Prairie Rose said something, and they both laughed. It was the first laughter Hawk had heard in months, and he lay there listening to the music of it.

"What is so funny?" Hawk said as he rolled over. The two young women laughed again and busied themselves once more with their moccasins.

Hawk got up and found a large turtle shell lying on its edge against the lodge. He poured water into it from a buffalo skin that hung in the shade and washed his face.

"You two people are showing mystery," Hawk said, as he sat with them. "Our journey to this camp took a full twelve changes of the moon. How is it you still have mysteries from me? Have we something to eat?"

Singing Flower, who was playing with some children, looked up, saw Hawk and came running.

"You are going to have some children," she giggled excitedly and sat down upon Hawk's lap, "and they will both be boys."

"Both?" Hawk said in surprise. "What are you talking about, little one?"

"We are both with child," Day Woman smiled, "and we know that they will be your children."

Well, it seems that I will have children, my father, signed Hawk to Yellow Robe.

That is good, Yellow Robe signed in answer. *This will keep you with your father. It will not be long before you are speaking our tongue. You are loved and will be happy in the lodge of your father.*

Good, signed Hawk. *I will hunt for the lodge and will be a good son.*

And I will teach you the making of the Shields, smiled Yellow Robe as he signed.

It was late fall and the evenings had already begun to turn cold. Hawk hunted every day and his wives dried the meat he brought back with him. Prairie Rose was asked by the camp women to join with them in their quilling.

Then Winter Man came with a ferocious determination. The snow was deep, but the Medicine Spirit was generous and the camp had fresh meat almost every day. Hawk learned the language of the Little Black Eagle quickly and became popular with the men of the camp. He was invited to many lodges, and also to join with the men in their hunting.

Four years had passed, when one day a young man in the village asked to accompany him on his Vision Quest and to build him his Shield. Hawk was beside himself with joy.

"Bull Looks Around has asked me to build his Shield," Hawk told Yellow Robe the following day. "Will you help me in the making of it?"

"You have learned well, my son," Yellow Robe told Hawk. "Begin with him tomorrow. And if you have any questions, then come to me."

Bull Looks Around led his horse to the lodge of the Painted Arrow the next day. It was still dark when he reached the lodge. Hawk was already standing there waiting for him.

The older man climbed silently on his horse. Bull Looks Around got on his own horse and followed him at a walk. The sun was beginning to lighten the sky when the men stopped. Bull Looks Around slid from his pony and waited for instructions.

"Come with me," said the man and led him to the top of the hill. The camp lay almost at the foot of the hill below where they now stood. "I will leave you now, but I will stay where we left the horses," the man said and laid down a large soft buffalo robe on the ground. Then he took another one he had carried rolled up and laid it upon the first robe. Bull Looks Around knew the custom and removed all of his clothes. The man took them and began his walk down the hill.

Bull Looks Around ran to the edge of the hill and looked down. The camp was waking up and he could see the individual people quite clearly, but at that distance he could not quite tell exactly who they were. He then explored his surroundings carefully. There was not much to see. The hills rolled away from where he sat in every direction except one, where there was the prairie. He saw an eagle glide in a lazy circle above him, and he lay on his back on the robe a long time watching it. The eagle then disappeared and there was only the sky left to see. He turned his attention next to himself. He examined himself carefully, which aroused him sexually and his thoughts turned to Little Star Woman. As he lay there he began to daydream about her.

"She is the most beautiful girl in all the camp," he dreamed, "and one day she will be my woman."

In his dream, she was walking down to the river to get her grandmother some water. He examined her from the top of her head to the bottom of her feet as she walked toward him. Her dark eyes saw him and smiled. Her lips were beautiful and full and were saying his name. Of course she didn't see Bull Looks Around, and she walked on, completely unaware that he was watching her so closely. As she walked, he saw the curve of her small, perfectly shaped breasts under her dress. His eyes followed the rhythm of her body as she walked, down to her belly. His eyes saw under her dress. The scented black hair hid perfectly the soft gift of her womanhood. She stopped at the river and took off her dress. Suddenly he was there running his hands over her skin, feeling its satin smoothness. His hand found and cupped her breasts. She lay back in the grass as soft as the buffalo robe he lay upon, and his hand sought her warm moist gift. They kissed. Bull Looks Around's hand heightened the pleasure of the dream to its finish.

Bored again, he got up and walked to the edge of the hill to see if he could really see Little Star Woman. He strained his eyes hard but could not see her. He then threw rocks over the edge of the hill for almost an hour, but finally tired of that and returned to the robe to sit. He thought of his mother, father, brothers, and cousins. He thought of everybody he knew, and still he found time heavy upon his hands. His mind then turned to the camp again, and he went to the edge of the hill and looked down upon it. He saw people coming and going, saw women busy at campfires, men going and coming from the hunt. He watched the children closely at their play, and became excited with the discovery that he could pick out individuals he knew by their behavior and by the way they walked.

By nightfall he was very lonesome. He walked to the other edge of the hill and looked for the horses. The trees were very thick, but he could tell that the horses were still there. Night came and he huddled in the second robe. By now his thirst and hunger were unbearable, and he wondered if he could last through the night.

"I wonder what they would do if I were to come down now," he thought, "maybe just to get a drink of water and then go back up." He hesitated for a while and then suddenly he made up his mind again.

"No. I will remain here."

The darkness closed in on him and he made a fire. Someone had been up there before him and left the wood all piled up, waiting for him. "It must have been the Painted Arrow who did it," he thought.

The sounds of the night began around him, and his fire was little comfort. He thought he heard something behind him and turned quickly to see what it was. He saw nothing. Fear welled up inside him. He wrapped his robes more tightly around himself and tried to be calm.

"There is nothing," he thought. "It is only my own fear."

His loneliness grew and he wished he was back within the warmth and security of his mother's lodge. He even wished after a while that his brother, Walking Turtle, was with him, even though he did not like him. His mind then began to think about all the things he disliked about Walking Turtle. The dislike he felt for the boy helped ease his fear.

"But what if Walking Turtle was the only man in the world," he thought. "Well, even that would be better than this!" As he thought of how he could become better friends with the boy, suddenly he heard another sound!

"Who is there?" he called out loud. The sound of his voice was strange to him up here. "Is there someone there?" he called again. But there was no answer.

He began to remember then what his father had told him the night before he had left. "The Spirits of this world are Seven Arrows. They only reflect what you feel. If you feel fear, they reflect fear. If you feel joy, then Seven Arrows reflects joy. Talk to him. Talk to him out loud about your fears and he will talk to you."

Bull Looks Around began to talk and soon it was morning.

The man called Hawk was there at the sunrise. He rolled up the two blankets. "I am

taking these from you now, little brother. Pray here for a while and then come back down," he said, and left.

Bull Looks Around thanked the Medicine Power for keeping him safe through the night and started down. When he was almost to the bottom, Little Star Woman met him. She was carrying a newly-made quilled shirt and pants. She handed them to him and he dressed. They walked the remainder of the way together. His mother, father, and cousins were there to meet him. They had a big feast. There were hoop games and arrow throwing. Bull Looks Around was the center of attention and everyone was happy.

The following evening, the man called Hawk came to his lodge. He told Bull Looks Around a story about a Mouse called Jumping Mouse, and they talked about it for a very long time.

The following day Hawk returned again.

"You have begun your Vision Quest, little brother," Hawk said. "The things you experienced when you were on the hill were the things that you are. When a man seeks to discover who he is, he ultimately discovers also who his brothers are. And he learns about the Universe that is around him. Who are you, little brother?"

"I do not know," answered Bull Looks Around. "I did not learn very much about myself that day and night."

"Did you feel fear?" asked the man.

"Yes, I did," answered Bull Looks Around.

"Fear is part of you, little brother, as it is a part of all men. Did you talk to Seven Arrows concerning your fears?"

"Yes, but all it did was make me feel a little better. I had no answers from Seven Arrows. I never heard him speak."

"Seven Arrows speaks, little brother, but first

you must learn to listen to him. When you began to talk you felt better because you trusted. Trust is what made you feel better.

"Was there anything else?" asked Hawk.

"No, I do not think so. I thought of Little Star Woman," Bull Looks Around answered.

"Did you experience loneliness?" asked the man.

"Yes, I did. I was very lonely," said the boy.

"Loneliness is a Teacher of Giving, little brother," Hawk began. "When you thought of Little Star Woman you dreamed of what she could give you, and what you could give to her. Companionship is a Giving. Man, of all the animals, is the only one that feels loneliness. The Buffalo gives away portions of his total being, but still remains one with himself. It is this way with the Eagle, and also with all other beings in that they all know of each other, and speak with each other in all places. But the Power gave each man his own Medicine Wheel. And the Medicine has given man this Mirror to enable him to Sun Dance with his brothers and sisters.

"There are women in many of the camps of the People, married and unmarried, who are lonely. Men must learn to give to these women. Give with sexual things, companionship, and understanding. And there are lonely men, my little brother. These men push people away from themselves in their loneliness and are afraid, causing them even more loneliness. Understanding is what these men crave. Give them understanding and they will respond to your companionship."

The following day Hawk returned again. It was early morning when Bull Looks Around felt Hawk shake him awake.

"Come, little brother, and follow me," the man said.

Bull Looks Around dressed and followed Hawk. They walked until they came to the river. Hawk sat down and motioned for the boy to do likewise.

"Today I want you to walk around. Walk wherever the Spirit leads you. Whether it is into the hills, or onto the prairie, or along the river. Go where the Spirit leads you. Do not think about it, just walk. Listen to your heart and your mind, and listen to the world. Take your time. You have all day. Go until the Medicine paints its colors in the west. Then come back to the camp. Pick up things along the way that you wish to keep. They will be your Gifts. Let these things talk to you."

Hawk got up and motioned the boy to follow him. "This Wheel I have made for you, upon the ground in front of you, is the Great Medicine Wheel. A man begins on this Wheel from whichever Way in which he first perceives. With some this will be from the North, in wisdom. White is the color of the North, and of wisdom. With others it may be from the South, within innocence of heart. Green is the color of innocence, and of the South. Still others may touch the Medicine Wheel first from the West, from looking-within. This color of the West, of introspection, is black. And yet others may find the Wheel from the East, through illumination. The color for the East is yellow. Each man's Way of Perceiving is his Medicine Gift. Every man has one of these Beginning Gifts. But men must not let themselves be tied for all their lives to only one Way of Perceiving. Men must learn to Perceive in all Four Ways in order to become Full. Think about your Way of seeing things. Learn what it is today, and you will be ready to complete your Vision Quest," Hawk said, and left the boy.

"It has been seven days, good father," Bull

Looks Around said when he returned to the lodge of Hawk, "and I have thought about your last Teaching. I am ready to continue my Vision Quest."

"Good," said Hawk. "We will leave this very evening. Have you asked four men to meditate at a distance with you?"

"I have asked three," the boy answered. "I was hoping my Teacher could be the fourth."

Thank you, little brother," Hawk said. "I am honored. I will be your fourth helper."

The boy smiled within his new joy and ran toward his own lodge.

Just then Yellow Robe walked up to Hawk. "I have news," he said. "Little Coyote, who was in the camp at Sand Creek, survived the massacre. He is living with our Medicine Song Bird Brothers of the Shield to the south of us. Word has come to us that some others escaped also."

Yellow Robe sat down with Hawk for the meal Day Woman had begun to serve. Day Woman and Prairie Rose listened to the news and talked with Hawk about who else might have survived the Sand Creek attack.

"I have been in the lodge of Strikes a Blow all night. His daughter has been very ill," Yellow Robe said later between bites of food. "Grandmother Deaf Woman, the Medicine Woman, doctored her all night with her herbs. White Wolf and I were there with our prayers. Just before dawn she turned for the better and now is resting well. The girl's mother is one of the kindest women I have ever known, and her grief touched me deeply. Her daughter was given her name by my wife before she died. The little girl's name is Mountain Mist. She will probably be up and playing before this day is over."

"The boy, Bull Looks Around, will begin his Vision Quest today," said Hawk. "I am going to

take him to Eagle Butte."

Yellow Robe laughed. "I remember well my Vision Quest. I was scared to death and so excited that if the Power had coughed I probably would be still running!"

Hawk laughed with Yellow Robe and added, "My Vision Quest was a wonderful time for me, too. There were no Men of the Shields in my camp when I made my visit. And I never had the chance to talk to one of them about it for almost three years afterward. I talked with many of the men in my own camp about the visit."

Hawk laughed out loud, a good laugh. He began again. "But their answers were all different and confusing to me. It has taken much time for me to untangle the lessons I learned from these men from the completely different set of things I learned on my Vision Quest. It has taken me almost up to this very moment to do this thing."

"Yes," Yellow Robe answered, his face suddenly sobering. "This has been one of the problems that has existed with the Way of the Shields. I met a young man a few years ago who had the symbol of the horse in his name. As you know, the horse is the symbol of the new Way. He called himself Crazy New Way. He too had made his Vision Quest, but I am afraid the men who guided him were as confused as he turned out to be.

"Now, the People are leaving the Medicine Way in larger and larger numbers. The Teachers are becoming a novelty. In some camps they are even perceived as something to fear. I have visited several camps with gentle Lightning Mouse where the children have been afraid of him. The People in these camps treated him as someone to be near, but not too near. He was as confused as I was about what to do about the problem. Black Robe teachers and others had

visited these villages, and had brought fear into the lives of the People. The young man, Crazy New Way, said their Medicine was one of death. I believe this completely."

"I spent much time with a Man of the Shield who visited our camp not long ago. There was not one day that I was not with him while he was among us. He spoke four of the tongues of the People. He would sit with anyone who would listen to him, but most of the time I was his only listener. The Dog Soldiers of the camp argued with him constantly."

"Aaai ya hey!" exclaimed Yellow Robe. "This has always been true. Do you know why the Center Pole in the Great Lodge is Forked?"

"No," answered Hawk. "No, I do not."

"There is a Twinness about man," began Yellow Robe. "A Twinness of his nature. And there have always existed the Twin Parts of the People. It is always the Other Man who does

not understand, or the Other Man who is the one at fault. This Other Man is represented by the Forked Tree, the Center Pole of the Sun Dance. It is Forked, but Both Parts of this are One Thing. Leaves are left upon the Forked Tree as a Sign to the People that these things of Twinness mirror Twinness again within the People. The Two Forks look exactly the same. And each Fork branches into many leaves that are exactly the same. But the question is always, which Reflection is which? Which one am I? Or am I both? It is a great Teaching, and that is why it is symbolized in the building of the Sun Dance Lodge. It has healed the wounds between many divided Peoples, and has brought these many different kinds together in brotherhood within the Renewal Lodge."

"This Twin Part of myself is quite evident," Hawk offered. "I have found myself moved many times to do things that have become entangled in the lives of others and have been misunderstood by them. I have very seldom in my life set out to hurt someone else intentionally, but I have sometimes brought pain to people anyway."

"Yes," Yellow Robe agreed. "This is part of the Teaching. One Half of you loves, and the Other Half of you at times hates. This is the Forked Medicine Pole of Man. The clever thing the Medicine has taught us here is this. One Half of you must understand the Other Half or you will tear yourself apart. It is the same with the Other Half of any People who live together. One must understand the Other, or they will destroy each other. But remember! Both Halves must try to understand. Even within yourself it is hard to know which of the Forks is which. 'Now why did I do that?' One Half of you

asks the Other Half. You do things quite often which you do not mean to say or do, sometimes to yourself and sometimes to others. But you would not kill yourself for these mistakes, would you? I am quite certain that you would not. Yet there are those who have done this, who have killed either themselves or others. These are men who have not learned. An entire People can be like this. These People and men are not Full, they are not Whole."

"Tell me more," Hawk said. "I am interested."

"When Lightning Mouse and I visited the camp I was telling you about, we found a problem among them in their Understanding. It was a lesson to be learned in the Sign of the Forked Medicine Pole," Yellow Robe said.

He then called for his Pipe. Prairie Rose filled the Pipe and brought it to him. Yellow Robe lit the Pipe and took a long puff. He then handed the Pipe to Hawk. He began to speak again.

"These People had been taught by the Black Robes that good and evil existed as separate things. We talked with them about this philosophy and discovered their confusion. They had these two things set apart. But they are not separate. These things are found in the same Forked Tree. If One Half tries to split itself from the Other Half, the Tree will become crippled or die. These People we discovered were trying to split this Tree with their law. But you cannot split these things with law. Rather than taking this barren Way, we must tie together the paradoxes of our Twin Nature with the things of One Universe.

"Before our Sun Dances can begin, many Forked Poles smaller than the great Center Pole must first be formed into a circle. This circle becomes the outside of the Medicine Lodge. The Forked Poles for the circle are given by the People, and they represent the People. But remember these are Forked also. This is the sign of their Twinness. There are twelve of these placed to form the circle of the Great Lodge. They represent the Twelve Great Peoples of the world. Only the two at the opening that faces East represent the People of the Shields. The others represent the other Peoples in this world. One of these People is the whiteman.

"These smaller Forked Poles also represent all the things of this world. Let us pretend for a moment that they alternate as we go around the Lodge. The first one will be called good and the next bad. But the question will still be the same as before. Which is which? They are perfect Twins and look exactly the same. They are all Twins.

No, my son, there is no such thing as good and bad. This is only a tool used by the whitemen to create fear among themselves. It is only the man who searches for good who will also discover things that he will perceive as bad. If this man then tries to dictate his own perception of what is good to others, he will ultimately become a bad man himself. And now here is the next paradox, which is the Other Twin. The man who dictates his own perception of what is bad to others is also bad. One is mirrored into the other. Because in truth they are one of the same Forked Pole, and are always perceiving the mirrored image of themselves.

"The answer to this conflict is the Give-Away. Whenever one gives from his heart, he also receives. Every man has his separate Way. And every man is a separate Way. But we all Dance within the Renewal Lodge in Renewal of the Brotherhood and in Giving. We, all of us, are the great Center Pole. We must bind together all the things of the Universe by the

Giving of the Pipe. The Dancers within the Lodge, the Pledgers, Dance in representation of the People. The Dancers Give-Away. The Medicine Power is within all People, and all of the things of the Universe. The Power has been generous in his Giving and has taught us Understanding so that we might also Give. But the Medicine is also the Coyote, the trickster. We must Give to the People, and Give all the things of the People, in order that we may receive.

"Now this boy, Bull Looks Around, is beginning his Vision Quest. He wishes to understand who he is within the circle of the great Medicine Wheel. As he seeks to discover who he is, he will also discover who his brothers are, and what his position is within the Harmony of this world. When a man seeks *Maheo,* he ultimately seeks both his own identity and also that of his brothers and sisters. Bull Looks Around will learn on that mountain, and from your Teaching, that we are all One. He will come to understand that all of the People are one great Medicine Wheel.

"He will also learn of his personal Medicine. One of the Medicines will visit him. It may be the Wolf, the Guide. The Guide is a great Medicine. And through this, he will learn much about himself. If he finds that the Wolf is his Medicine, he will also learn that a Wolf can be both vicious and lonely, and many other things as well."

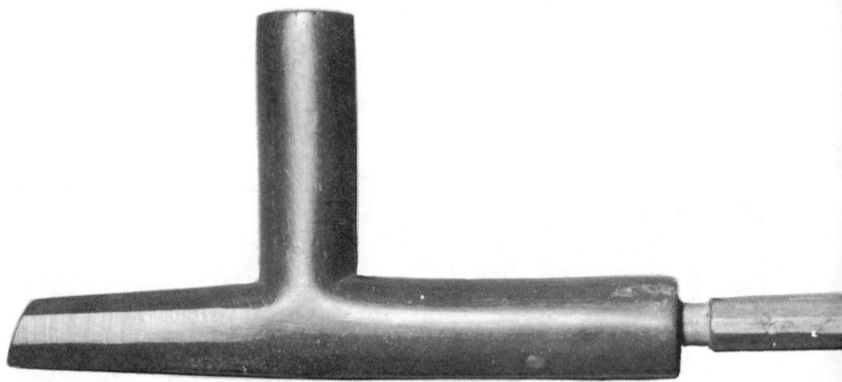

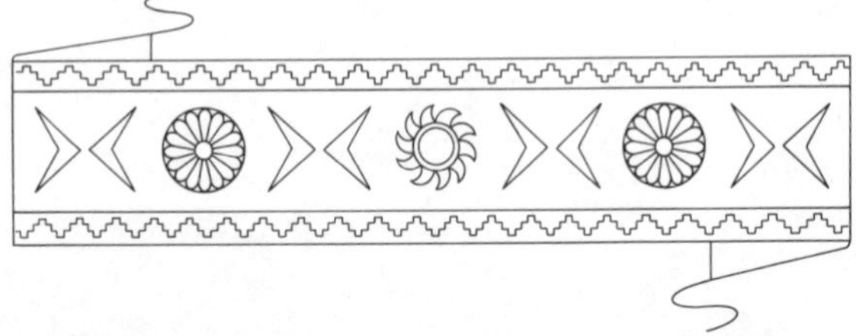

Hawk was washing his face in a small stream when he looked up and saw Bull Looks Around coming back from the mountain. This was his final day, his third, and Hawk knew he would have much to tell him.

Hawk called the three other men who had accompanied them to the mountain. All four met the boy. Bull Looks Around grabbed each man's arm hard, one by one. Hawk noticed that the boy was changed. There was a shining deep within his eyes. Bull Looks Around opened a robe he had taken with him to the mountain but which he had left behind him when he had gone up for his Quest. Four of the things the boy held dearest to him lay on the unrolled robe. He handed the articles one by one to each man until only one remained. It was a bow, one of the finest bows Hawk had seen in his entire life. Bull Looks Around handed it to him and smiled.

That evening, according to custom, a Give-Away and dance were given by the four men Bull Looks Around had chosen for his helpers and by the boy's family. Day Woman and Prairie Rose had worked hard in the three weeks Hawk had been with the boy. They had prepared robes and moccasins for the Give-Away, finding enough time in between to work on the beautifully quilled new dresses they wore at the dance.

Early the next day, Yellow Robe and Hawk began construction of a Shield for Bull Looks

Around. The boy was called to the Lone Dwelling Lodge of the Shield-Maker. He entered and took his place at the North side of the Lodge. Hawk and Yellow Robe sat to the back of the Lodge. White Wolf was sitting to the South. Four young girls entered the Lodge and sat in front of the men. One sat to the South, one to the North, one to the West, and Little Star Woman sat to the East. She filled the Pipe and passed it to the boy. He lit the Pipe from the small fire that was in the middle of the Lodge, smoked it, and passed it on. Each man smoked and passed it on to the next until it came back to Little Star Woman, who held it.

"This is the Way to sit with your brothers," said Yellow Robe. "Smoke with Peace in your heart."

Little Star Woman then took the Pipe outside and returned with a bowl of water and also one

of Buffalo meat.

She handed the bowls to two of the other girls. The bowl of water was given to the girl on her left and the bowl of meat to the girl on her right. The meat and water were then offered by the girls to each of the men, who either ate or drank, depending upon which bowl was handed to them. The men then passed the bowls back to the girls, who in turn handed them on to their sisters until they had all been returned to Little Star Woman.

"The Water," said Yellow Robe to Bull Looks Around, "is the Medicine and it is Life. It is a Gift of the Great Spirit. The girls you see seated here are your sisters. One of them you may even marry some day. These girls sit here in representation of their clans and their societies. The Buffalo is the Power's greatest Gift. His meat fills our stomachs. His skin keeps us warm in our lodges, and we wrap his robe around us when we are cold. The Buffalo is used for many things among the People. The Buffalo is the North where you now sit. Be a Gift to your People, little brother."

Little Star Woman then brought in the Shield. She handed it to the girl on her left, who handed it to White Wolf. White Wolf tied a strip of buckskin diagonally across the Shield. He sang a song and painted the strip green.

"White Wolf," began Yellow Robe again, "is representative of the South. This Shield-Maker has shown you that you must always try to find your Medicine and your understanding of the Power, and of your brothers, through Innocence and Trust."

White Wolf then handed the Shield back to the girl who sat in front of him. She passed it on to her sister, who then gave it to Hawk. Hawk sang a song and painted the bottom of the Shield blue, and tied a red bird's tail in the

middle of the band.

"The Medicine Bird of Fire," Yellow Robe spoke again, "has been tied to your seeker band. You must seek the Spirit through Innocence. When you make your Medicine, little brother, always make a small fire and sprinkle cedar before your prayers. Do these things in trust of the Medicine and it is his promise that your prayers will be answered. Blue has been painted upon your Shield. It was your Gift from the People. It is the sign of their prayers."

Hawk then handed the Shield directly to Yellow Robe. He carefully painted the image of a black bear on the upper half of the Shield. He then painted four stars around the bear. He then handed the Shield to one of the girls, who in turn passed it to Little Star Woman. She in turn took the Shield outside and placed it upon a three-legged tripod. The girls got up and followed Little Star Woman out. Yellow Robe sang another song and all the men filed out, the boy taking the lead. Once outside, Yellow Robe held his arms up in blessing.

"My People!" Yellow Robe announced. "This boy has made his Vision Quest. He has been given a new name. It is Night Bear. Come, children. Come and touch the Shield of Night Bear and receive its Gifts."

The warriors gathered around Night Bear, hugging, jostling, and teasing him. Night Bear had his Shield.

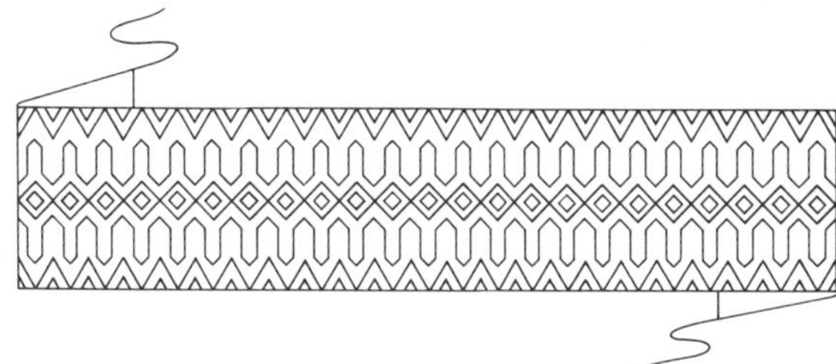

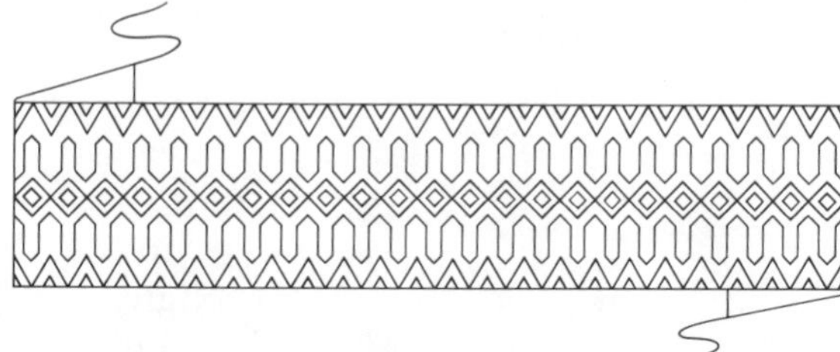

It had been one full week since Night Bear and his best friend, Red Fox, had set out with the trading party for the long ride to the next camp. They had kept pretty much to the prairie as they followed the River down its length to where it joined the Yellowstone. It had been an uneventful journey so far. At its best, their excitement had consisted of nothing more than scaring up a covey of prairie chickens, or surprising a stray wolf or coyote, and the two boys were bored. Night Bear was only half listening to the conversation of the two warriors who rode near him. They had been discussing something about a man named White Shirt and some kind of misfortune that had befallen his family, when suddenly a thunder iron spoke its deadly sound from somewhere to their front. One of the men who had been talking slumped forward and fell silently from his horse, dead.

The whole air then crackled with exploding thunder irons from almost every direction, turning the quiet afternoon into a nightmare of dying men and wounded horses. Another warrior near Night Bear raised his own thunder iron to his shoulder to fire. Night Bear's horse screamed and leaped forward, throwing up its head. Blood from the mouth of the other warrior's horse splashed into Night Bear's eyes, blinding him momentarily. His horse fought for its head, trying to run. Night Bear wiped the blood from his eyes in time to see his mount knock down the warrior whose horse had just

been killed beneath him. Night Bear slid to the ground to help the man, holding his rearing pony with one hand and reaching for the man with his other free hand. But Night Bear could tell that the man was already dead. His head was terribly twisted and it was obvious that he had broken his neck.

Night Bear scooped up the fallen warrior's iron from the ground, leaped onto the back of his horse and let him run. Their pack horses loaded with trade furs were running wildly over the prairie in all directions. Every man in his small party had been leading one of them, but many had already died and the others had released them in order to fight. Night Bear grabbed the reins of one of the fleeing animals just as he saw his attackers for the first time. They rode out from their cover screaming their war cries. The men were painted and were carrying Shields. But the Shields they carried were the new Shields, the Shields of war.

By some miracle, Night Bear's friend, Red Fox, had not been killed and was running on foot across the prairie just ahead of him. Night Bear pulled his horse to a stop by his friend. Red Fox ran through the dust to the pack horse and began to slash at the leather that held the furs to the back of the animal. Night Bear turned to see one of the attackers riding hard straight for them. He almost dropped the thunder iron in his hands as he instinctively reached for his bow, but then realizing that he held the iron he raised the weapon just as the other man fired. Night Bear saw Red Fox stagger from the impact of the bullet, as his own iron roared. The enemy rider jerked his head up, pulling his horse to a stop. The horse then began to walk toward Night Bear. The man sat straight and

calmly on his mount as he approached. Then he pitched forward slowly, slid from his horse, rolled onto the ground, and lay still on his face. The eagle feathers on his Shield fluttered quietly in the wind. A figure of a mouse was drawn on the upper half of the Shield, and around the figure was the Clan Sign of the Four Stars.

Night Bear turned his attention back to Red Fox. His friend was now sitting on the pack-horse, holding his arm and looking down at the dead man. Night Bear looked around quickly and saw that they were alone. They were in a small valley, out of sight of the main part of the battle. Night Bear jumped to the ground and grabbed the dead man's iron. The man's horse stood calmly as Night Bear tied the weapon to the harness on its saddle robe, and took up its reins in his hand. Then Red Fox and Night Bear ran their horses to their limits before letting them walk.

"Those people were Painted Arrow People," Red Fox finally said, as they rode down and across a small stream, "and the one you killed was your brother."

"Yes," answered Night Bear quickly. "I know. I saw the Stars on his Shield."

Night Bear pulled his pony to a stop in the shade by the stream and dismounted. He tied both his horses and walked over to Red Fox's horse, helping him down. He sat his friend down by a large cottonwood tree and began to cut away the shirt from his bloody arm.

"My arm is stiff," Red Fox said, "but it does not hurt too much."

Night Bear finished cutting away the shirt and looked at the wound.

"The thunder arrow point has gone through

your arm," Night Bear said at length. "But it did not touch your bone. *Zahuah!* You were very lucky!"

"Lucky?" answered Red Fox. "How can you say I am lucky? You suffered no wound, and now you even have two thunder irons."

"You may have one," Night Bear answered quickly. "And I would be much happier right now if it had been I who had suffered the wound. Instead, I have killed one of my brothers. There will have to be a Renewal. I know full well that my Medicine Father, Hawk, will be grieved. And my family, too."

"Renewal? Grieved?" Red Fox snapped back angrily. "Are you crazy? Those Painted Arrow People are dung! They are murderers! I have never loved them and I will see that they pay dearly for this killing!"

"Finally the two men mounted and headed back for their camp. After many days they reached it. Each went straight to his own lodge. Night Bear's mother saw him coming and ran out to him, tears streaming from her eyes. She was one of the most beautiful women of the camp, and as she ran toward Night Bear she had never looked more radiant."

"What is this?" Night Bear asked, hugging her. "The most beautiful woman in the camp is ruining her face with these tears."

"Crying Bull returned with the news three days before you," she said, wiping her tears. "He was wounded badly. He told us that as far as he knew no one but himself had survived." She broke into sobbing again, wiped her eyes and continued. "There was hatred and sorrow in our camp, and the People were screaming for revenge. A war party left the camp only a short time ago to punish the People who did the

killing. Crying Bull said that they were the People of the Throw Away Boy. The men have gone south to attack their camp. Your father went with them."

"The Throw Away Boy People?" Night Bear asked in surprise. "Those People were not Throw Away Boy People! They were Painted Arrow People!" Night Bear leaped to the back of his horse and kicked him into a run. He jerked his animal to a stop at the lodge of Yellow Robe and darted inside. Yellow Robe stood up in surprise, knocking over a bowl of meat that had just been handed him by Prairie Rose.

"Crying Bull was wrong!" Night Bear almost yelled at Yellow Robe. "He must have been made crazy with his wounds! Those People who attacked us were Painted Arrow People!"

"Are you sure?" Yellow Robe asked, shock reflecting in his eyes."Are you sure?" he repeated.

"Yes!" answered Night Bear. "Red Fox is at his lodge and can speak for the truth of what I say."

"*Mahka-Zaughan*!" Yellow Robe exclaimed, his voice shaking. "Our warriors are on their way to kill the wrong People!"

Yellow Robe ran from the lodge, calling for Hawk. Three other men came running with Hawk. They had seen Night Bear riding for Yellow Robe's lodge. Realizing something was wrong, they had come as quickly as possible to learn of the trouble. Yellow Robe quickly explained the situation. Hawk and the others ran for their horses, and they galloped out of camp.

It was four full weeks before Hawk and a handful of men returned. Hawk slid from his pony and slumped against a tree in the shade.

His face was etched with lack of sleep, and with sorrow.

Yellow Robe had been at White Wolf's lodge when the small party returned, and now he and White Wolf walked hurriedly to where Hawk sat to ask what had happened.

"We drove our horses as hard as we could to catch up. Borrowed Spirit struck out ahead of us, pushing his horse until he killed it. It was our last desperate try to catch them. But we failed. We were one night and one day behind them." Hawk stopped talking long enough to take a drink from a buffalo skin bag that hung near him, and went on. "They surprised a small village and had killed over half the people in it before we arrived. We found our warriors scattered around what remained of the camp. Many of the men had taken scalps and had them hanging at their waists. It was the camp of Charging Eagle, the same man who visited with us only three moons ago. Seventeen of the thirty men who left this camp are dead. We told as many as we could find about the mistake, but it was too late for us to tell Suns in the Sky, Night Bear's father. He had begun his attack at almost the moment we arrived, and he was killed."

"What will become of us?" Yellow Robe said, turning to White Wolf, his voice shaking with emotion. "Are we all to die?"

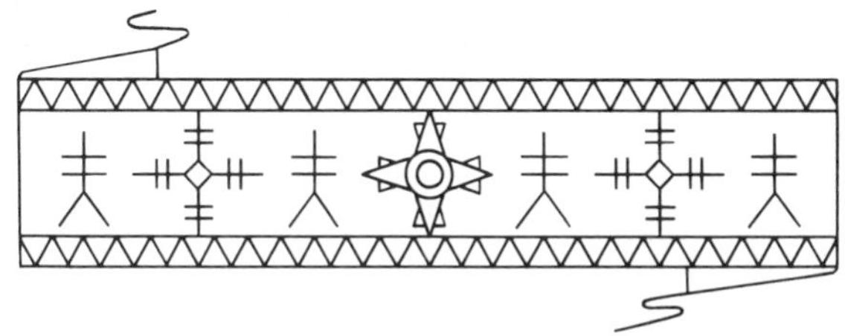

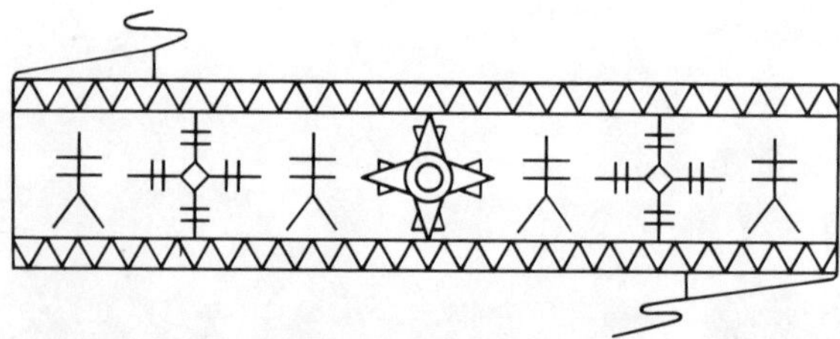

During the coldest part of the winter the camp of Yellow Robe was forced to move. Game had become scarce as the cold spell hung on, and when the weather finally broke a council was called. It was decided that it would be a good time to move to better country a little farther down the valley.

Night Bear and his mother were among the last people in the line that moved slowly down the valley. They were to meet at a place that was familiar to everyone, about twenty-five miles from the old camp. Night Bear rode a young mare he had broken to ride only the summer before, and he was having trouble keeping her from throwing him. He called to his mother to wait, and began untying one of the pack animals to make a change of horses. As he was finishing, the wind came up suddenly and began to blow the loose fallen snow into a blizzard. Night Bear worked quickly until he had made the change. He rode up beside his mother and tied their horses together, halter to halter, leaving only enough room for safety in case one of the animals might slip or fall.

Soon new snow began to fall, adding itself to the blizzard. Night Bear had to squint through its fury to see his mother, who was a scant six feet from him. "It would be death for her if she were to stop," thought Night Bear, as he paused for a moment to think.

"We will go on this way, Sweet Water," Night Bear called to his mother, using the most

jovial voice he could find. "If we remain in a straight line, and cross two hills that are to the front of us, we will be there. Once we reach the valley we are heading for, we will turn left down its stream. Keep looking for a tree, a big one. It is at a place where another valley enters the one we are going to. Then all we have to do is follow the next valley left and we will be at a place where two streams meet. It will be simple from there on."

Sweet Water knew only too well that his cheerful voice was for her benefit, and that the next few hours of traveling would be difficult and dangerous. She hid her own fear and called out that she would do as she was instructed. They climbed two of the hills, almost losing one of their animals in the ravine that cut between them. Then they crossed a third hill and followed the valley they came upon on the other side. The going was very hard. Night Bear had no idea of the length of the valley and hoped that it would not be too many miles. After some time they came to a tree. Night Bear studied the tree closely. He decided it was the one they were looking for, and turned to the left into another valley. They continued down this new valley throughout the rest of the day. At nightfall the storm finally stopped as suddenly as it had begun.

Night Bear halted and immediately gathered wood for a fire. Sweet Water took two robes from her pack animal and made them into a shelter. They ate dry meat and warmed themselves by the fire. The moon came out and turned the countryside into a daytime of deep blue. After resting for a while they struck out again. The wind had blown the snow shallow on the high ground, and they moved along the

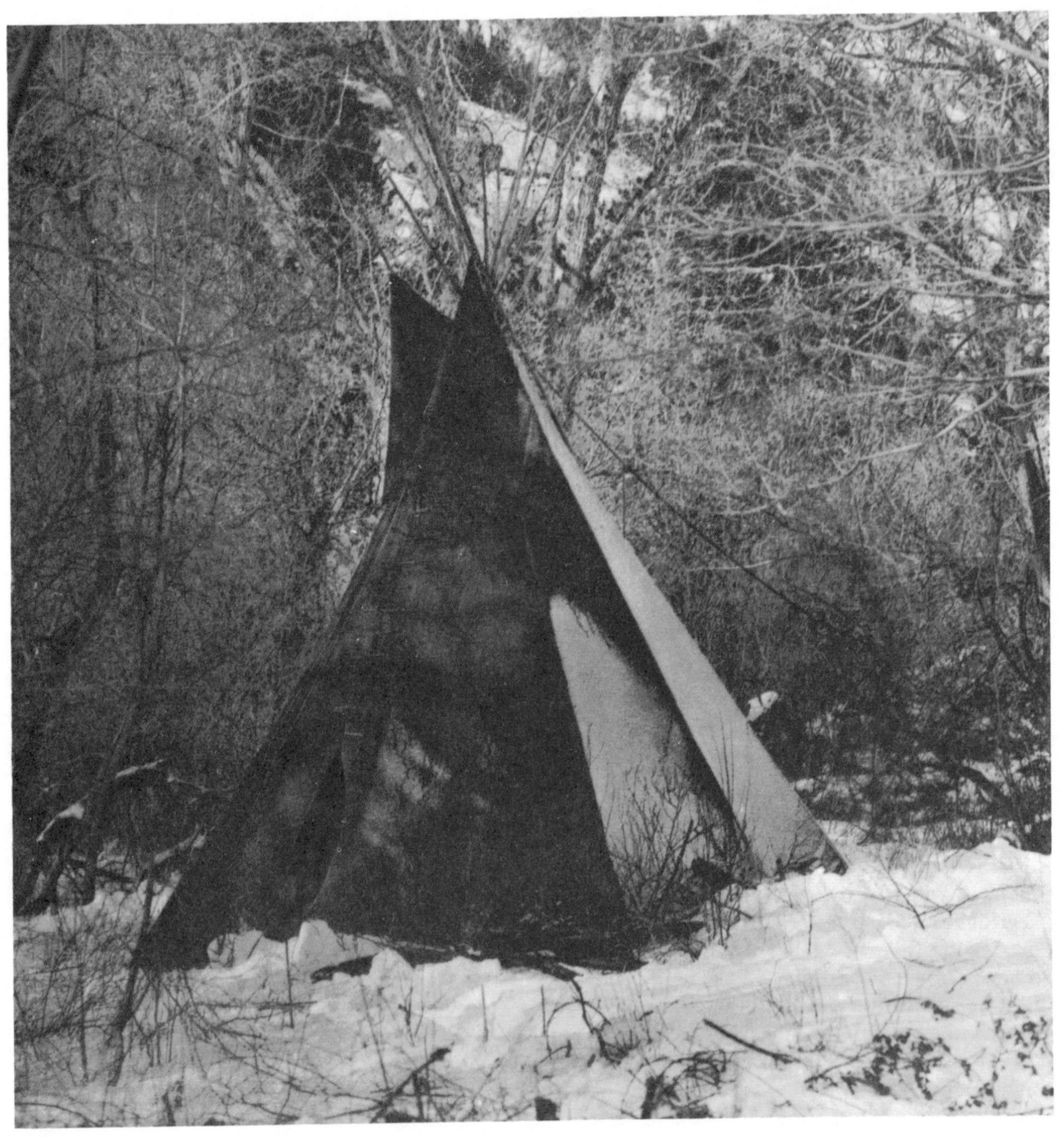

ridge above the river valley quickly and smoothly.

As they rode, they talked. They teased each other, and Night Bear enjoyed Sweet Water's musical laugh. She too enjoyed his, because it pushed away her fear.

They rode for hours until it was almost daybreak. Night Bear then pulled his horse to a stop and dismounted to study the features of the valleys and hills. A mountain taller than all the rest was to the south of them, and Night Bear looked at it hard. He thought he recognized its shape, but he was not sure. Then as he studied the valley they had come along, he slowly realized it was not the one they had been looking for. There was nothing familiar about it. They turned around, and then again, and again, until finally they camped, hopelessly lost.

Night Bear cut lodge poles and helped Sweet Water set up the lodge. After they had lined and banked the lodge with snow, they kindled a warm fire and rested. Night Bear had chosen a place where game was plentiful and they settled themselves to wait for spring.

After the initial shock of being lost and alone had worn off, Night Bear and Sweet Water began to talk. As the days and weeks went by they began to speak more and more of their innermost feelings.

"Have you ever wondered about all this?" Night Bear asked, moving his hand in a sweeping motion.

"You mean the world?" Sweet Water answered.

"Yes, but I mean everything," Night Bear said, leaning back on his hands. "I mean everything in it, and everything that happens in it. I speak of the animals, and of the many different Peoples, and of the things they do. Of the way in which things happen, and of the things people think and say."

"It is too much to hold in one's mind, I will have to admit that," Sweet Water said as she comforted herself by lying on her elbow, so that she could face Night Bear.

"There is always somebody who has something to say about something, no matter what it is," Night Bear said, getting up on his elbow too. His muscles stood out on his chest and arms as he moved himself into place. He was good-looking, a mirror of his mother. Sweet Water watched him and saw the sincerity in his eyes as he spoke again. "I told Yellow Robe that I was going to make love to you."

Sweet Water moved nervously, but covered it up by reaching for a pair of moccasins she had been working on.

"And all he did when I told him was talk and talk and talk. I talked to Hawk about it later," Night Bear went on.

"'How is it, Hawk,' I asked him, 'that I should not make love to Sweet Water, my mother?'

"'Do you love her?' he asked me.

"I answered, 'Yes, more than anyone else. Is my wanting to love her wrong?' I asked.

"'No, it is not,' he answered. 'It is natural. She is your first love.'"

Sweet Water lay down on her back. Night Bear studied her body as she lay there. Her face was framed in her black braids. Her face was more mature and overshadowed that of any other woman Night Bear had ever seen. Sweet Water's beauty was richer and more full. His eyes found her large breasts, and his mind returned to the dream he had once had on the hill during his Vision Quest. But instead of just Little Star Woman and a dream, he now faced a reality. A reality so much greater that he became giddy with it in his whole being. His eyes moved down Sweet Water's body. Her dress had pulled itself above her knees, and showed the greater part of her shapely legs.

"I do not know," Sweet Water answered. Her voice was smooth and steady. "I too have thought of this. You mean so much to me. I love you more than my whole life and this adds to it. But there is a thing about this that must always be looked at."

"What is that?" asked Night Bear.

"Children," answered Sweet Water. "Children of such a love are born wrong."

"Have you ever seen one of these children?" asked Night Bear.

"No, I have not. And I have never known anyone who has. My aunt was discussing this very thing one time with my mother. She said that it would be impossible for a son to give his mother birth."

"Then it is like everything else," Night Bear said. "It seems an easy thing to hear when a son kills someone, even his mother, but it is hard on people's ears when they hear of a son loving his mother."

Night Bear moved to Sweet Water's side and sat on his legs. Sweet Water felt his hand upon her leg, close to being under her dress, and her stomach tightened. Her mind was a mixture of fear and another emotion that was not sexual desire.

"I must follow this through and have it over with," she thought as she lay there. "I will not order him away," she said to herself, "because he has been honest and has trusted me. But still," she went on in her mind, "I wonder if I should do this."

"Take off your dress," Night Bear said softly.

Sweet Water hesitated a moment, then sat up on her knees and began to remove her dress. She placed the dress in a neat pile at her side.

"Lie back down, I want to look at you," Night Bear said. A warmness spread over Night Bear's body when she removed the dress. He kissed her breasts gently and removed his own clothes.

Sweet Water's mind tumbled in confusion when she suddenly felt a sensual drive explode in her body, greater than she had ever felt in her life. A warmth so beautiful she moved her body with the joy of it.

"I love you," Sweet Water said, as Night Bear began his descent. "This is good and it is right. I would do this over and over again for you, no matter what the consequences."

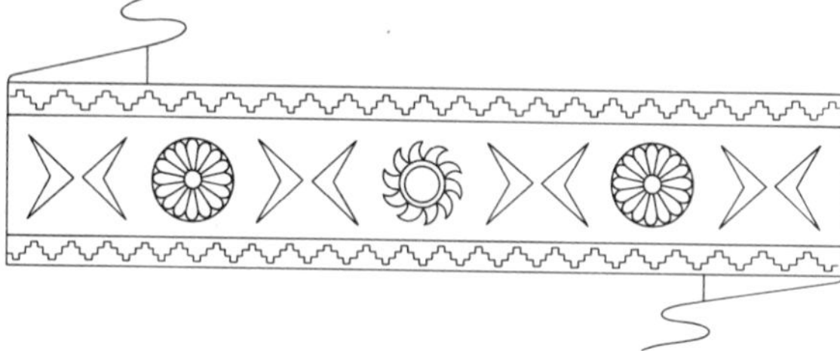

"Before the Power Gave us our Medicine, Men Kept their Hearts and the things of their Hearts to Themselves."

It was White Wolf who was doing the speaking. Night Bear, his mother, and some of his cousins and aunts were taking a sweat bath. They were in total darkness. The water White Wolf placed on the rocks in the lodge hissed, and the old man's voice went on.

They Sat in Darkness as we Do Now, Unable to See Each Other. And in those Days, there was Killing and Shame. Man Carried a Rock in his Hand that was Heavy with his Law. The Rock Kept Down the Skin Upon his Lodge and he could See Out Only in One Direction. Then Sweet Medicine Came to the People. He Brought the Sacred Arrows, which were a Touching. They were Truth. And the First Shields were Built. People Began to Write their Names for Everyone to See. And he Put each Man's Medicine Upon that Man's Shield. The Truth of Each Man's Inner Being was Put Upon his Shield. And the People Began to Seek their Medicines. As they Sought their own Names, they also Found their Brothers and Sisters.

"Sweet Water has told me she slept with her son the whole winter. And they found truth in what they did. It was a Gift to them and they have learned from it. They have called us here together for us to hear of their Gift so that we might enjoy the sound of its truth.

"One woman of our camp said that Sweet

Water had done an unreal thing. But I saw that it was real. Man accepts war and its killing. He accepts suffering, lies, deceit, and greed. But I, White Wolf, tell you that these are the things that are unreal. Sweet Water entered within this Gift in love and found love. Night Bear wishes to return his great Gift to the Medicine and has asked me to teach him in the ways of the Medicine Painting. And he is ready to visit all the People. And he will teach the Way of the Shield to all who will listen. Little Star will walk with him."

Red Fox moved his horse into the stream of warriors. They were following the ridges above the river looking for the men who had attacked their brothers.

Ten Bulls was riding near Red Fox. He was looking at the thunder iron Red Fox carried, and at length he asked him about it.

"Is that the thunder iron you won as a coup when you and Night Bear killed the Painted Arrow?" he asked.

"Yes, it is the same one," answered Red Fox. "But I have no arrow points for it."

"You will have some soon," the other young man grinned.

"You mean," asked Red Fox, "if we find those stinking Painted Arrow People?" And he laughed out loud.

Coyote Inside His Robe motioned for the party to stop. Everyone dismounted and muzzled his pony.

"The camp I told you about is just over there," the leader said to Ten Bulls. "We shall divide our party in half. You will take yours to the west and I will take mine east."

"You have already seen the camp of the Painted Arrows?" Red Fox signed to Ten Bulls.

Ten Bulls smiled and motioned Red Fox to hurry. They walked about two miles, leading their horses, and then halted. Each man waited for Coyote Inside His Robe to begin the attack. Red Fox was unable to see the camp and wondered how far he would have to walk, when

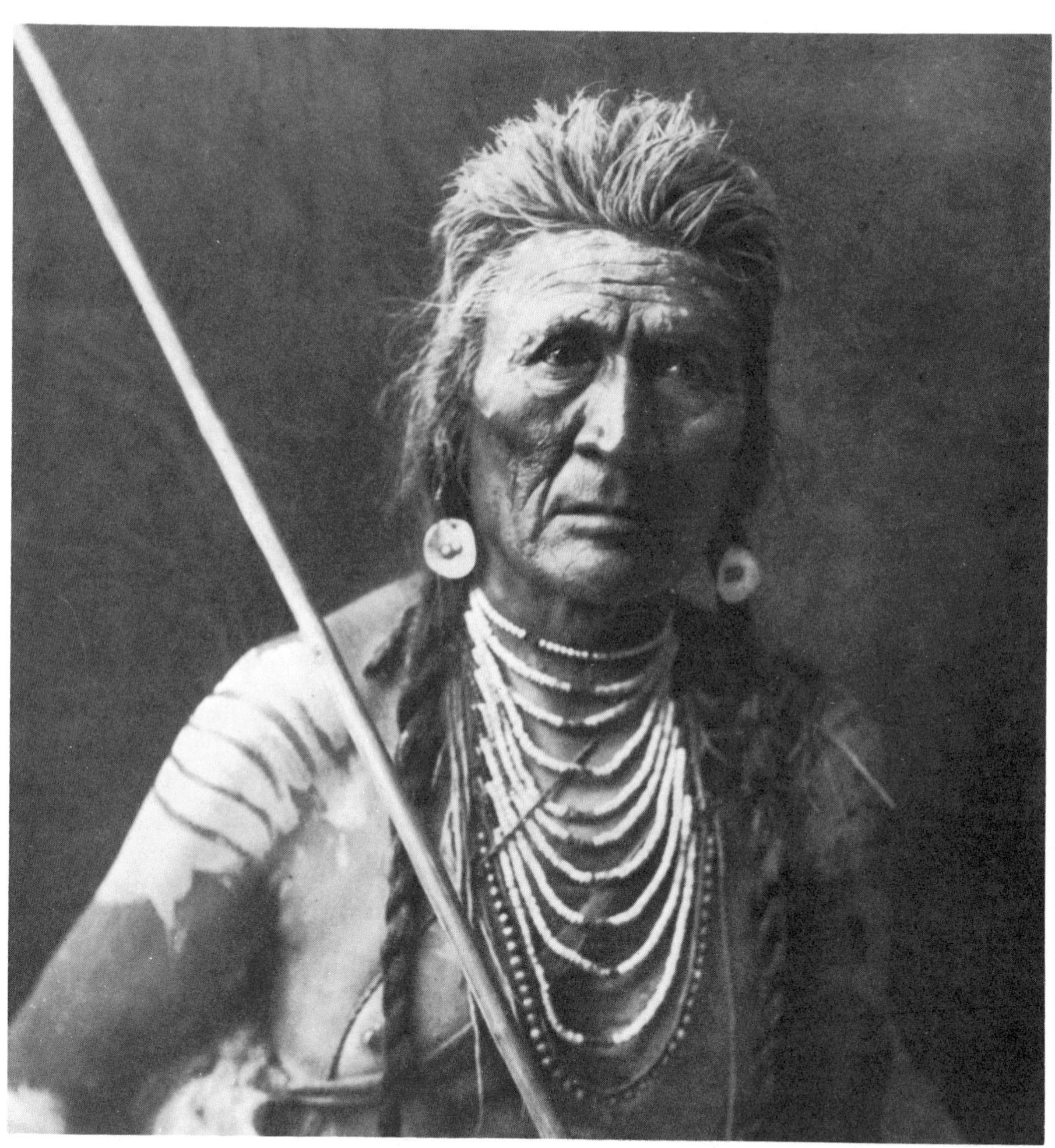

suddenly Ten Bulls sprang to the back of his pony. Ten Bulls kicked his horse into a dead run, leading the rest into a clearing which held a circle of lodges.

Men ran from their lodges to reach their ponies and weapons, but they were too late. Red Fox saw in a flash that it was not a camp of the Painted Arrows they were attacking. These were the Black Feet, the Walks in the Introspective Way People. Red Fox held back in confusion as he watched his brothers killing and then cutting the hair from the dead men.

"Now you have many arrow points for your thunder iron," Ten Bulls said as he rode up to where Red Fox still sat on his horse. He laughed and held up a scalp in his hand. "Do you see how easy it is to be rich? Look at the Gifts we have taken! Horses, robes of many colors, beads, and much more. And part of this is yours."

"But these People were not our enemies!" Red Fox told Ten Bulls, looking at him incredulously. "You have killed innocent people."

"Did you hear that?" Ten Bulls yelled to the other men. "Little Red Fox has just told me these people here were innocent."

All of the young men laughed and hooted. *"Eeeesheeeh, eeeesheeeh,"* they teased Red Fox.

"Have you no stomach for a man's work?" Coyote Inside His Robe asked. *"Eeeesheeeh,* you think these people were innocent?" He laughed again. "The people of this innocent camp have killed your beloved Painted Arrows for these things which we have now taken from them."

Red Fox returned to the camp with the others, carrying his share of the prizes they had captured. As they entered the camp, Yellow Robe ran from his lodge.

"Where did you get these things?" Yellow Robe asked. The warriors only laughed and rode by the old man. "You have killed for these things!" Yellow Robe said, as he reached out to grab Ten Bulls. Ten Bulls turned and slapped Yellow Robe to the ground.

"Do not touch me as if I were a common camp child," he warned Yellow Robe. "We ran into those same Painted Arrows who attacked us before," he grinned, "and took back only what belonged to us."

The People began to gather around the group of warriors, asking excitedly about the fight and looking at the great prizes they carried. Yellow Robe got slowly to his feet and walked up to Ten Bulls.

"I am sorry that I accused you," he said. "Were there very many of the enemy?"

"Not enough for us, were there, little Red Fox?" Ten Bulls laughed. "Not nearly enough!"

Red Fox walked to his lodge. The People that passed him smiled and some stopped to congratulate him. But he was sick. Inside his heart he wished he had never gone with Ten Bulls at all. Night Bear came from his lodge, grinning from ear to ear.

"I hear you shamed those Painted Arrows completely," Night Bear said, as he hugged his friend.

Red Fox avoided answering until he was in Night Bear's lodge. Sweet Water was mending her dress when he entered, and she rose to greet him. The young man sat down across from his friend and bowed his head.

"What is the matter?" Sweet Water asked. "Are you ill?"

"Yes, I am," Red Fox answered softly. "Those were not Painted Arrow People and we did not shame them. We killed them."

"Killed?" Night Bear asked in astonishment. "Who did you kill?"

"Actually my hand killed no one," answered

Red Fox, his head still hanging. "But I was with them, and I wanted to kill! It is all the same."

"No, it is not," Sweet Water broke in. "You said your hand killed no one and your grief tells of your real heart."

Red Fox told them all that had happened.

"You have witnessed death and do not find it to your liking," Night Bear began. "And as for the revenge you felt, you can see what that brings. Give away what you have taken. Give it back to Ten Bulls. Tell the old ones what has happened."

A council was called. Red Fox told everyone present what had happened. Ten Bulls stood up and began to speak.

"These old men here," he pointed to Yellow Robe and White Wolf, "treat us as if we had done a wrong. But the warriors who sit here know that the Walks in the Introspective Way People have killed and killed again. They have killed our People as well as many others. It was a brave thing my brothers did. We never fell into a fight with women. It was men that we killed in battle."

Green Hat suddenly got to his feet. He was wearing one of the captured multicolored robes and a pair of blue cloth pants.

"How is it you speak this way?" he snapped. "When before have warriors been asked to defend their actions in a council? We have defended this camp bravely and have raided our enemies many times before."

White Wolf's quiet reedy voice answered. "There have been raids, yes. But never like this one. Our young men have gallantly stolen horses, and many times they have shamed their enemy. But this time what was done was murder. Have our warriors become like savage animals?"

"The old man is right," Swallow Wings added. Other sounds of approval traveled around the group of men.

Coyote In His Robe laughed out loud and pointed at Swallow Wings. "You laughing dog! You were among the raiders last year who struck the camp of Charging Eagle. What we have done was nothing compared to your butchering then."

Swallow Wings got to his feet and knocked his antagonist to the ground. Painted Rock leaped up and pinned the arms of Swallow Wings.

"Stop this!" Yellow Robe said, getting to his feet. "This is no way for brothers to act. Sit down, Swallow Wings, and you hold your tongue, Coyote In His Robe. Say what you have to say, but do not strike each other like painted snakes. The poison ones at least warn their victims."

Coyote In His Robe sat up wiping the blood from his mouth. His eyes were burning. "No man has the right to tell me how to live!" he spat at Yellow Robe. "No man! If I choose to run naked with the beasts, it is my right! But I have not killed any Brothers of the Shield. I have killed only wild animals."

"No man is a wild animal, little brother," White Wolf answered. "That is why Sweet Medicine gave us the Power to See. And that is the reason for our council tonight. It is to try to stop you, our sons, from walking in a Way that will destroy you."

"This is madness!" Hides His Way spoke up. "You people are dreamers. I for one have had enough of these old men's dreams. This world we live in is hard, and only the strong will live. The animals of the prairies and mountains are proof enough of this."

"If this were true," Yellow Robe answered, "then all men would have perished long before

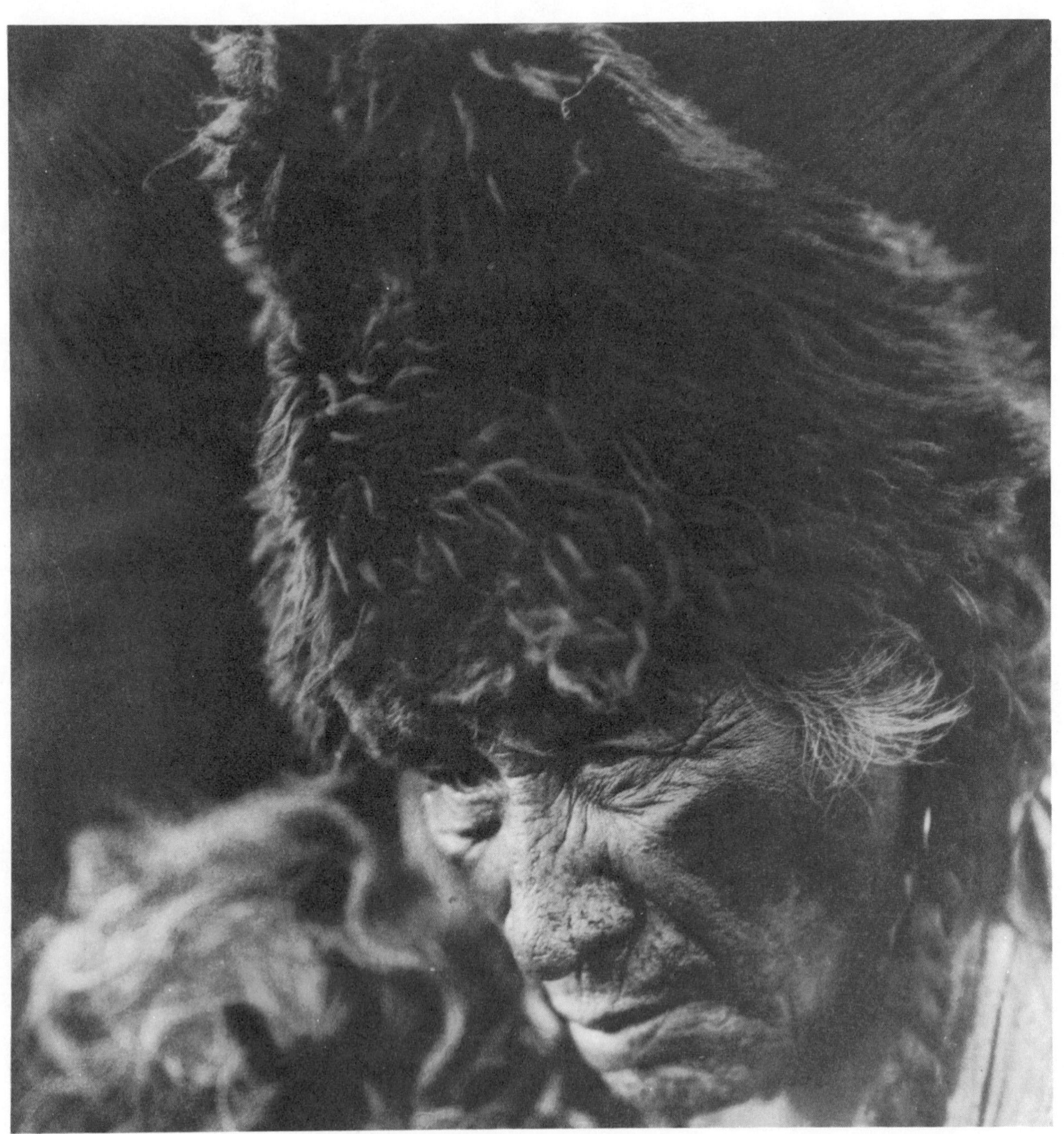

now. Man is weaker than even the mouse. Only the Gift of the North has saved man from disappearing from this world. It is a great Gift, my son! The Gift of mind has saved us from destruction. It is this Gift which makes us different from all the other animals of the world. It is this Gift which gives us the choice of either killing or touching our enemies in battle."

"What you say is true," Sees In The Morning spoke out. "But if our braves do not stop these new enemies before they reach our village, then we will all be attacked and killed by them. Even our women and our helpless young ones will be killed. Our warriors have no choice but to defend us by seeking out and putting an end to these enemies. It is the sacrifice they must make to protect our camp circle and our Way of life."

White Wolf's eyebrows went up in surprise. "What are you talking about, Sees In The Morning? We do not have to seek out the enemy in other places. The enemy is always right here among us. If we seek always the enemy, then after a while even everyone here would have to be killed. The Medicine Way is not to be protected. It needs no protection. For if it did, no matter what enemy was among us, then it would not be a Living Spirit. The only things needing the protection of men are the things of men, not the things of the Spirit."

Sees In The Morning spoke again. "Be reasonable, old one," he began. "If another People became our masters, then our Way of life would be ended. They would force us to walk in their Way, just as we have heard the whiteman's Pony Soldiers are already doing now with many of the Peoples of the Plains."

"What you say is true, but only in part," White Wolf answered. "The everyday things of

our lives would be different. But if our Spirit is a true Spirit, then it can know of no boundaries or masters.

"It is not the whitemen who are changing our world. It is our own brothers who are doing this. Our own brothers, like some of you young men here in council before me, have given in to these new Ways of the whiteman, and have become victims to it. And what you propose would only add to this terrible thing. We must not go out to seek the enemy in war. We can save our camp only by holding strong to the Way of the Sun Dance, and by remembering the Teachings of the Shields. There is a place for every man within the Great Lodge, because it is a whole Medicine Wheel.

"I have never agreed with the sacrifice men, the Dog Soldiers, and their piercing of their skin within the Lodge. They believe that if they take suffering upon themselves in this Way, they will then keep suffering from the People. It is a noble thought, but one I have never agreed with. But I have Danced within the Lodge with these men all of my life. They Danced their Way and I mine, and still we were always together in brotherhood.

"But there is no such thing as the protection of Spirit and mind. The Medicine will protect these things itself. It is a Gift to man and will remain a Gift. The People were put upon this world to learn of themselves and of their brothers and sisters. We are these People. We are the Fallen Star. Our laws of men change with our understandings of them. Only the laws of the Spirit remain always the same.

"You are right, Sees In The Morning. Our entire Way of life will change. The coming of the whiteman will make this change, because they are now among us and they will remain among us. We are all one camp with them, and must be one camp by the great River. I have witnessed this shrinking of the Way of the Shields among our People. And I have no doubt it will become worse. But it will never die, because it is of the Spirit. It is a Truth, and Truth cannot die."

The following winter was worse than anyone living could remember. Starvation crept through the camp, tearing at the young and the old. But the dissension that visited the People was even more cruel to them. Many of the young men were accused of treachery and of bringing disharmony to the camp. The chiefs tried desperately to hold the People together, but soon realized that this was futile. Because of the deep snow and poor hunting, the camp circle had to be broken. All of the People left the mountains to seek shelter in the lowlands where it was still possible to hunt. A few of the People became lost and made their way to the forts of the whitemen, where some were taken in and survived. Most were fortunate enough to find other camps of the People, instead of either going to the forts or dying on the prairie. Night Bear and Hawk had been among these, staying with a camp of the Shoshone's, the Buffalo Grass People. But during the long winter, Day Woman, Prairie Rose and their children had all died, taken by sickness. Sweet Water had lingered on until spring, but finally she too had died of the same illness.

When spring finally came, Night Bear and Hawk made their way back to the camps of the Painted Arrow. The camp they found was a large one, and it was bustling with activity when they arrived. It was mid-afternoon and it was unmercifully hot. The young men who

rode out and surrounded them would have killed them both immediately, but when they saw their Shields they lowered their striking arms.

"Why do we not take the hair of these women?" one of the young men called to another. *"Aaieh!* It is clear under this sun that they are the enemy." He kicked his horse and was about to drive his lance through Hawk when he was struck by another man near him.

"You fool!" the man said angrily. "These are Peace Men of the Shield! They are Teachers and may even be of our own People. Their dress means nothing."

Welcome to the camp of Little Wolf and Morning Star, the man signed. *I am called Blue Hair.*

"And I am called Hawk," Hawk answered in his own tongue. "This is my brother, Night Bear."

"You speak our tongue?" the young man who was about to kill them asked in surprise. "Are you of the Morning Star People?"

"I am of the Brotherhood of the Shield," Hawk answered.

"You are truly an ignorant fool," said Blue Hair to the young man. "These men often speak many tongues. And they have forgotten to which Peoples their mothers and fathers belonged." He turned his attention back to Night Bear and Hawk. "Come, good fathers. I will take you to the camp. You will be welcome among our People."

"Look!" one of the children of the camp called to his friends, pointing to Hawk and Night Bear as they walked into the village. "Two of our fathers visit us," he said excitedly.

"That is my son," Blue Hair said proudly. "I have taught him the Ways of the Medicine Lodge."

They walked into the shade near Blue Hair's

lodge. The children followed the men and were talking excitedly together. "Is he not a Black Crow?" one of the children asked as he stared at Hawk.

"No," answered another. "They are Morning Star People. They dress any way they want to." And he giggled.

Hawk noticed that a party of men was approaching. Two of the men in the group walked proudly and purposefully toward him. He knew it must be the two men Blue Hair had spoken about, Morning Star and Little Wolf. Both of them were young.

The two men sat down across from Night Bear and Hawk.

Welcome, the younger of the two signed. *It is my understanding that one of you speaks our tongue.*

It is I, Hawk signed.

My name is Morning Star, the younger man began his signs again. *And my brother here is called Little Wolf. We have been chosen as leaders from among our People.*

Night Bear signed his answer. *I am called Night Bear and my brother's name is Yellow Hawk Tail. I do not understand what you mean by leader. How is it you are a leader?*

Little Wolf chose to answer the question. *We have a new Way in our camp. There is so much war these days that it has become necessary for us to have war leaders.*

Then you are war leaders? signed Hawk.

No, Morning Star signed. *But we sit in council with the chiefs of war. We have been chosen always to speak for peace. It has brought a balance among us in our decisions.*

How very strange, Night Bear signed. *It is a strange new custom, but one I find favor with.*

How is it you now find yourselves among us?

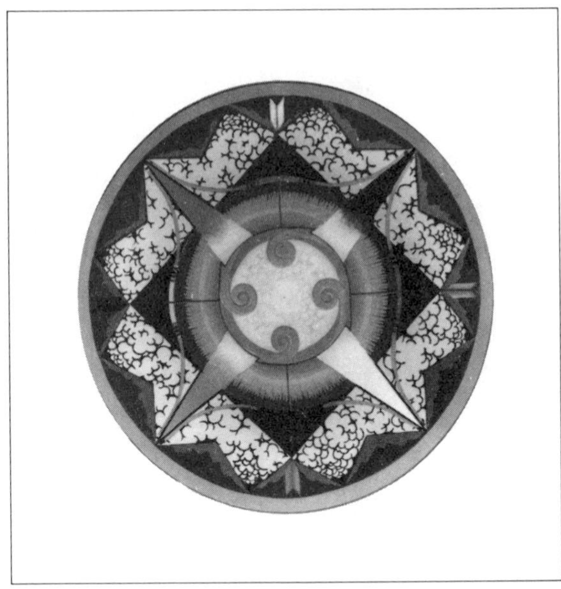

Little Wolf signed.

Hawk took his turn in answering. *My brother, Night Bear, lost his wife, who was called Little Star Woman, and his mother this past winter to the sickness. I too lost both my wives and my children to this same illness. It made our hearts sad to remain among the People we had been living with. There were too many memories.*

I am glad you have chosen our camp, signed Morning Star. He then removed a Pipe from the pouch he carried, filled the Pipe and held it in both his hands for Night Bear. *I bring you this Pipe.*

Night Bear accepted the Pipe. *What is it you wish my brother and me to do, for we accept your Pipe?* signed Night Bear.

Our People requested that we ask you and your brother to be our Sun Dance Chiefs. We will begin the ceremonies whenever you tell us. Our warriors need the Power to make war, Little Wolf signed.

War! signed Night Bear. *How does one do this in the Sun Dance? This is a time for receiving the Power of Brotherhood and Healing for the People.*

Can one not find protection from death within the Sun Dance Lodge? signed Morning Star.

Yes, Hawk signed the answer. *There is great Power within the Lodge. One can find the protection for his life always within the Medicine. But it is not used to make war. Tell your People that the Sun Dance is for the Giving and the Receiving of love. Tell them that we are Men of the Shield. We are men of peace, not war! We will accept your Pipe and be your chiefs for this Sun Dance, but it must be a Dance of Peace."*

That evening Little Wolf returned and sat with Hawk and Night Bear again.

"*Many of the young men in the camp were angry with what you told us,*" Little Wolf began.

"But many spoke out for you, telling the others that you were right in what you said. Still others have refused to enter the Lodge because they believe you to be enemies. Morning Star and I will dance with you, and I am sure there will be many more. What is it you wish for us to do?"

"Put two lodges together," Hawk began, *"making them into One Lodge. Place this in the middle of the camp, and your Sun Dance will have begun."*

The next evening Hawk and Night Bear went into the Lodge that had been put up for them in the middle of the camp. Only a handful of young men were there. Hawk was disappointed, but his heart was also pleased that any were there at all.

"Welcome, my brothers," Hawk began. "Night Bear, my brother, will sign you a Story, and I will tell you of the Story. It is a Story about the Other Man, and it has been given the name Buffalo Wives. The Story is actually Two Stories, because it is about the Twins. It is about the great Medicine Pole that you will Dance to in a few days. It is Two Stories, because it is a Forked Story like the Medicine Lodge Pole, but in reality the Two Stories are One. Listen closely and decide which of these Ways you are. You may be One or the Other, or you may be part of Both. The Medicine of this Story is important for you to take with you into the Sun Dance."

Night Bear began to sign, *Once the Tribe was Scattered Out, Living in small Camps in Different Places.*

Hawk spoke, "These People were not in Harmony with the Power. They were not within the great Wheel. Their camps were not put within a Circle."

Night Bear signed, *In One of the Camps was a very Handsome Youngman. His Father Loved him dearly, and used to Put Up a Lodge for him in which he would Live by himself.*

Hawk spoke, "This youngman, my little brothers, was a lonely man. It was the fault of his Teachers that he was alone. Because these People were scattered about, they also were alone. And this boy's father made him alone."

Night Bear signed, *Several of the Girls had Wanted to Marry him, but he Refused them. Then one Day a Girl who had Yellow Hair Visited his Village. He Liked her and Took her to his Lodge and Married her. After a Time, another Beautiful Girl Visited the Camp. Her Hair was Black and he Married her, too.*

Hawk spoke. "Two things came to the boy's mind and heart. They were illumination and introspection. The Medicine had sent this man a

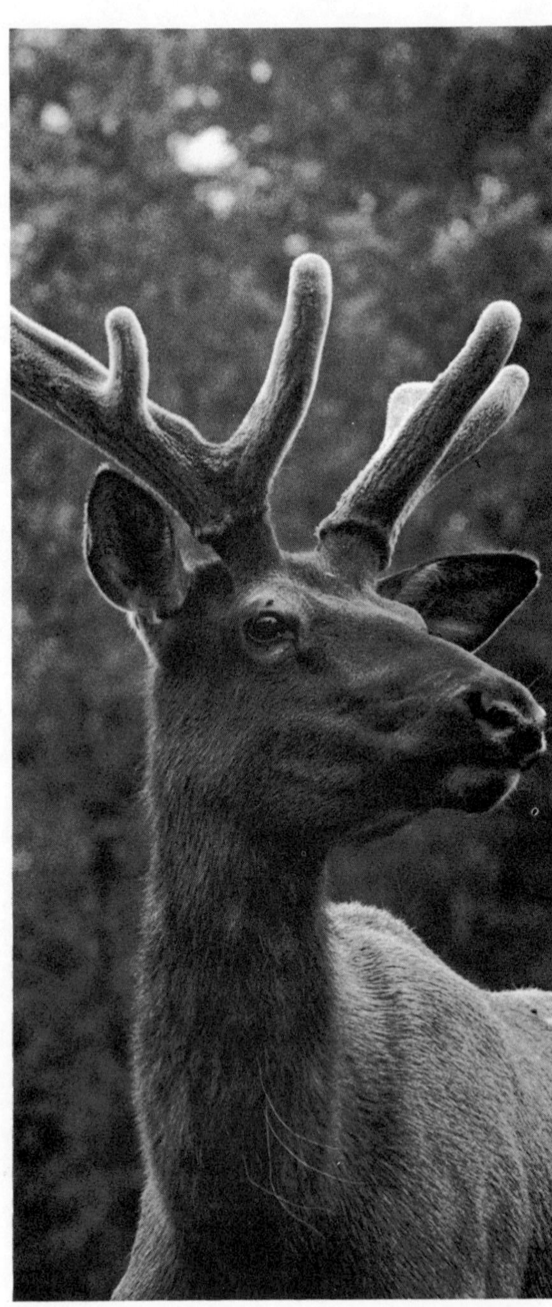

Gift, the answers to his loneliness. Men find the answers to the questions illumination has brought them by pursuing introspection, or looking within."

Night Bear signed, *The First Girl, the One with the Yellow Hair, was an Elk, and the Second was a Buffalo Cow. But the Youngman did not Know this. The Youngman Lived with his Two Wives. After a Time Each had a Boy Child.*

Hawk spoke, "When men live with illumination and introspection, these give birth to concepts, to Ways of understanding, or seeing something."

Night Bear signed, *These Boys Grew Up until they were Big enough to Run about and Play Together.*

Hawk spoke, "In order for a man to become full, he must seek. The man in this story has been given the Gift of the East and the Gift of

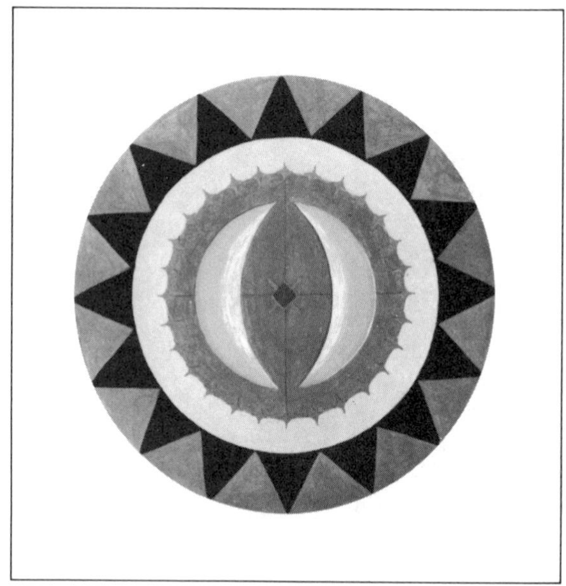

the West. He has intercourse with these things and is given his third Gift of the South. It is innocence. But he must have the other Direction. He must have the North."

Night Bear signed, *One Day the Two Girls began to Argue about something, and soon they were Fighting.*

Hawk spoke. "This man did not call his People into a Circle and give to them his Gifts. He was still alone and never shared. He never discussed his Gifts with anyone, and soon he began to dispute these things inside himself."

Night Bear signed, *The Two Women began to Dispute, each One Taking the Part of her own Child. One Day they Quarreled and the Elk Girl Went Away from the Camp, Taking her Boy with her.*

Hawk spoke. "Illumination will dim with argument and will leave when it is argued with in this way."

Night Bear signed. *The Buffalo Woman, too, Decided that she would also Leave and so She Left with her Boy. This Happened while the Youngman was Out in the Hills Looking for his Dogs.*

Hawk spoke, "Many men are looking for their dogs, for things to serve them, when they should be looking for greater things."

Night Bear signed, *When the Youngman Returned to his Camp he was Angry and said to his Father, "Why did you Let my Loves Go Away? Why did you not Try to Stop them?" The Youngman Put Together some Moccasins, and said, "I am Going After One of them to See if I can Get her to Come Back."*

Hawk spoke, "The youngman got together the few things his father and mother could give him and set out in pursuit of what he had lost."

Night Bear signed, *He Left the Camp and Climbed a Hill. He Stood there a while and Made up his Mind which One of his Wives he would Follow. He Made up his Mind to Follow the Buffalo Woman with the Black Hair.*

Hawk spoke, "This, my little brothers, was when you went upon your Vision Quest alone in the hills. This youngman did as you did, but he made up his mind to follow the looks-within. It is easier for men to follow the Black-Haired Woman than it is to follow after the lightning of the beautiful Yellow-Haired Wife."

Night Bear signed, *He Followed the Trail of the Woman a long Way, and at Length the Tracks of the Child and the Woman Disappeared. And he Saw only the Tracks of a Buffalo Cow and her Calf.*

Hawk spoke, "But when he began to pursue his wife he only found the Spirit Way, her tracks. There was no doubt in this youngman's mind now that he had been given a Gift, and that he must pursue this Gift in order that he might grow."

Night Bear signed, *He Followed these Tracks Late into the Evening. At Length he Saw before him, Far Off, a Lone Lodge and he Went to it. It was his Wife's Lodge. The Little Boy was Playing Outside and Saw his Father Coming. "Mother, my Father is Coming," said the Little Boy to His Mother. "Go and Meet your Father and Tell him to Go back Home. Let him Come no Further than where he is when you Meet him. Tell him I am Going to my Home Far Away," the Little Boy's Mother Told him.*

Hawk spoke, "This man pursued his Gift until he was tired. But he immediately felt separated from what had been given to him. For some men these spiritual and philosophical things are hard to follow. And when they get to them again, the birth these men have given the

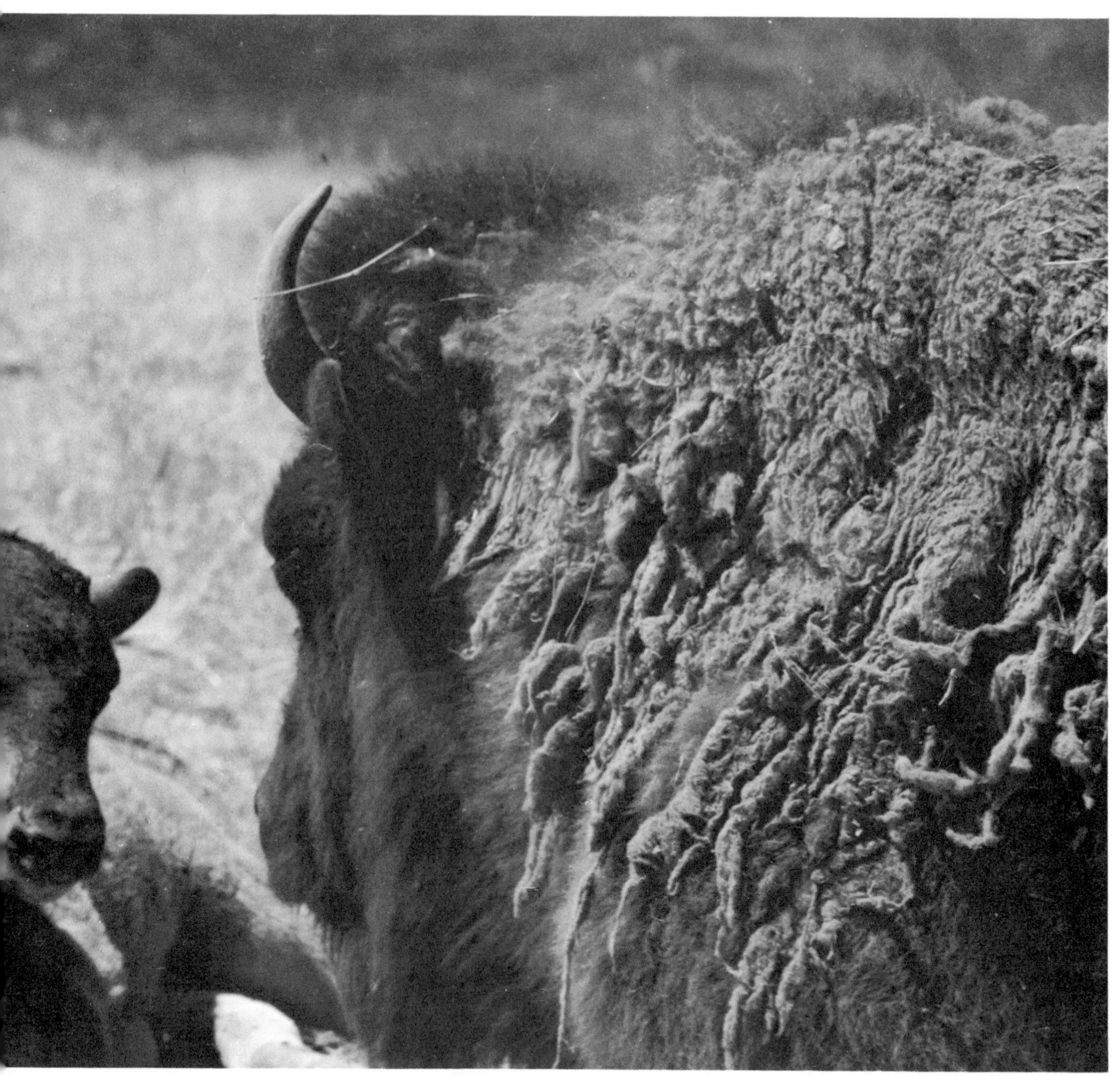

Woman through their intercourse seems always to deliver a message to turn back. This man, my little brothers, has to fight the negative reflection within himself."

Night Bear signed, *The Boy Went as he had been Told to do, and when he Met his Father he Told him to Turn About and to Go Home. He then Told his Father what his Mother had Told him. But the Youngman Refused to Turn Back. "No," he said, "I love You, my Son. I am Determined to Follow you," and he Went into the Lodge. Everything was Nicely Arranged. At Night when he Went to Bed he Lay down to the Left of the Opening in the Lodge, by his Little Boy.*

Hawk spoke, "When this man entered the lodge of introspection he found everything nicely arranged. Because, my little brothers, he wanted it nicely arranged. He was calling for the place his arrows were to hit. But he lay down with the boy, on the side of innocence, to the South of the opening of the lodge."

Night Bear signed, *His Wife Lay to the Right of the Lodge, but he Slept with his Son. When he Awoke in the Morning he was Lying on the Open Prairie and there was No One there.*

Hawk spoke, "He should have slept to the North in wisdom with his wife. He should have had intercourse with her again, but he did not. What he did, my little brothers, was neither right nor wrong. It was good, but he still had to learn another Way. When he awoke, he sat there in the middle of life, wondering."

Night Bear signed, *He could See the Trail where the Lodge Poles had Dragged Along, and he Followed them Crying. Then the Lodge Poles Disappeared and there again were the Tracks of the Buffalo Cow and her Calf.*

Hawk spoke, "You should be thinking yourselves of what is meant by the lodge and by the tracks of the lodge poles. This is for you to discover. Because these are every man's own things."

Night Bear signed, *He Followed these his Second Day, and by Night he again Saw the Lodge. It was by a little Stream. The Boy again Saw him Coming and Ran to Tell his Mother. She Sent the Youngman's Son to him with the same Message. That Night he Lay Down by his Son again and Held him Close so that he could not Get Away. But in the Morning when he Awoke, he was Once more Lying upon the Prairie all Alone.*

Hawk spoke, "As you have probably guessed, this man is making his Sun Dance. But we are speaking of more than that, little brothers. Because these things are also all part of life and men. The sign of the river, you all know, is life, and the things of the Medicine. You will thirst your second day in the Lodge, and you will know more fully this sign then."

Night Bear signed, *The next Day he Followed the Trail, Mourning and Crying, and that Night he saw the Lodge again. His Son Told him the same thing and Added that things were Going to Appear even more Harsh for him. The Youngman Told his Son he Loved him and that he would not Go Back. That Night he Tied his little Boy to him.*

Hawk spoke, "Now I must tell you here, little brothers, these Gifts never really leave us. They are always there, although sometimes it may seem to us as though they had gone."

Night Bear signed, *That Night in the Lodge the Boy Told him that he would soon be Meeting his Grandfather and Grandmother and they might Overpower him.*

Hawk spoke, "These signs of the Grandmother and Grandfather are the tradition of these things, and believe me, little brothers, they have overpowered the spirit of many men. This man tried to tie the little boy to him. This means he tried to tie down or fix this thing to its place. But we can never fix these things for long. These things of the Medicine and the Spirit must flow like water or they will die."

Night Bear signed, *That Night before the Youngman Went to Sleep his Beautiful Wife Lay Down Beside him, but he was Busy Holding on to the Rope he had Tied to his Son.*

Hawk spoke, "This man's fear kept him blind to his other Gift. She lay down right beside him, but he was too busy fixing his son to one place to see her."

Night Bear signed, *The Boy had Told his Father that where they were Going it would be very Dry, and there would be no Water. "If you Follow us," said the Boy, "Where I Step Off to One Side you will Find Water in my Track."*

Hawk spoke, "Your Third day in the Sun Dance will be very dry. And like this man you will find drink in the Way of the Spirit. But remember that we are telling the story of the Other Man. This Other Man sees things in this manner. Not all men see these things in this Way. The boy is always telling him to return home. He feels that he is not wanted and he sees fearful things that might befall him."

Night Bear signed, *The Boy Continued his Father's Instructions. "When you Get there," said the boy, "Sit to One Side. My Relations will Charge on you."*

Hawk spoke, "One has to face fear or forever run from it. This is the sign here."

Night Bear signed, *The Man Remembered what his Son had Said to him. The Cow and her Calf Went a long Way, and as they Went it Became very Dry and the Man Became very Thirsty. The Man Found the Water in the Tracks his Son had Left, and he Found Food that had been Left for him.*

Hawk spoke, "We will not only find water to drink in the Way of the Spirit, my sons. We will also find food for our bodies and our minds there."

Night Bear signed, *Now, this is the Way this Other Man Saw it. The Buffalo Saw his Daughter Coming. The Buffalo Said among themselves, "What shall we Do?" They Determined that unless he Went Away they would Overpower him. And they Sent his Son to Tell him this.*

Hawk spoke, "This is the sign of the Mirroring. It is what happens when one meets Seven Arrows. Seven Arrows will only Reflect what you feel and think. As you can see, my little brothers, this man sees the Gifts as something to fear."

Night Bear signed, *When the Other Man Came into Sight of the Buffalo, he Sat Down on a Hill, Mourning and Crying. After a little while the Boy Came to him on the Hill and Spoke to him in his Time of Fear. "Maybe you had better Leave this Hill. My Grandfather and Grandmother may Overpower you."*

Hawk spoke, "This man experienced fear when he went on his Vision Quest. He saw the Gifts as something to fear, and his mind told him to leave."

Night Bear signed, *The Man Became Determined even though he Felt Fear and Saw the Buffalo as something that might Overpower him. "No, my Son," he said, "I Love you and I am Determined to Follow you."*

Hawk spoke, "This man is a remarkable man. He trembles with fear and he perceives everything as dangerous, but still he continues."

Night Bear signed, *The Chief of the Bulls Sent his Son up the Hill to Overpower him, and as he did, he Stopped and Pawed the Earth, Making a great Dust. When he Came near the Man, he Put down his Head and Charged him, but the Man did not Move. Before the Young Bull Reached the Man he Stopped. He Looked at the Man and said,*

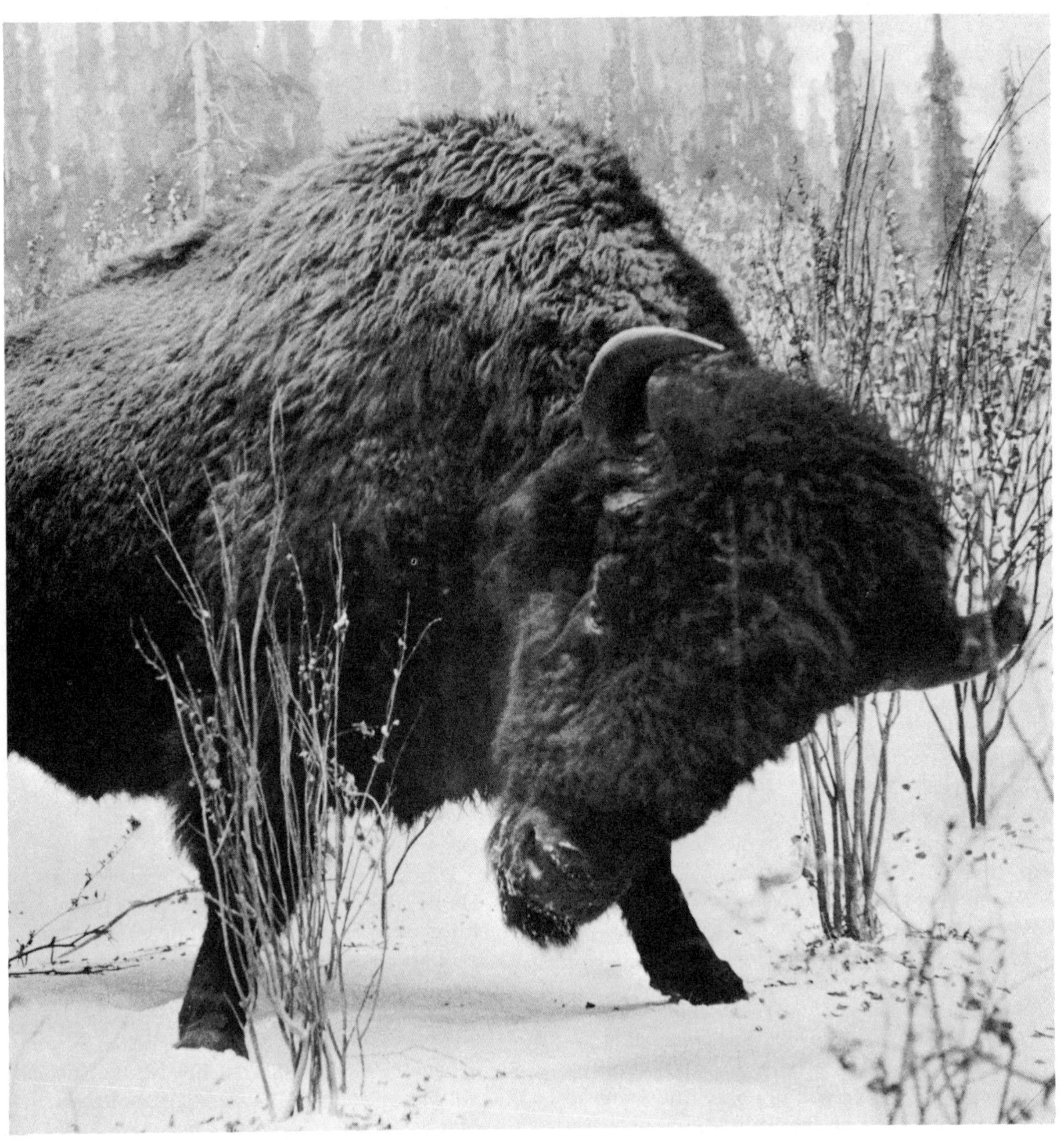

"My Brother-In-Law has a Strong Heart." The greatest of the Bulls then Charged the Man. But still he did not Move and the great Bull was Impressed with the Man's Courage.

Hawk spoke, "I am quite sure you all see the lesson learned here. It is very simple. It is that all of you must have strong hearts."

Night Bear signed, *The Buffalo Counseled Together to Test the Man, and they Sent the Man's Son to Tell him.*

Hawk stood up and stretched. "I think," he said, "this would be a fine time for all of us to rest from the story for a while."

Everyone agreed and the meeting broke up. The young people scattered, some to the brush and others to talk to friends.

Hawk was taking a drink from a buffalo skin bag when a tall young man approached him.

"I find it hard to follow what you have been saying, good father," the boy began. "Who is the Other Man? What is the meaning of this Story?"

"This is not something anyone understands fully the first time they hear it, my son," Hawk answered the boy and handed him a drink. "I find more in this Teaching every time I hear it. It is a flower that can be opened in many ways. Each time you hear it, the understanding it brings you depends upon where you are standing upon the great Medicine Wheel. Every man will see this Story from within his own perceiving. He may perceive it closely, broadly, introspectively, or with wisdom. Some will see it through the eyes of Eagles, some will see it as Wolves, and some as Mice. A true adult, my son, will unfold the petals of these stories one by one, and he will see a great deal. It is foolish for anyone to think that they can comprehend it

all the first time they hear it. The Spirit will grow in men, and so will the meaning of the Stories."

"There are parts of your Story that I do not seem to feel in a clear way," said the young man.

"These feelings will become clearer for you later. I will give you an example. Even a very little girl or boy has sexual feelings." Hawk began to walk as he spoke. "But they do not know what they are. They have to mature before they can understand these things. Some men and women who are forty and fifty winters old still may not possess the understanding of it. It has nothing to do with the maturity of age. Some may understand it while they are still very young. Experience has much to do with it, but it is more than just experience. It is a Gift of special wisdom. It is the same with these Stories."

"But what must one do to gain this wisdom?" the boy asked, now even more perplexed.

"I am sure you have heard the Story of Jumping Mouse," Hawk said, turning to the boy. "It is like this. This Story uncovers each petal of a great flower. Think of it this way. There are many things that perplex men, things whose riddles men cannot solve. The Medicine has given us these Stories so that we can unfold the mysteries of these things that perplex us.

"Think of a flower that has two stems. On one stem of the flower is a sun flower and on the other stem is also a sun flower. Let me show you a picture of one of the Forty-Four Shields of the Peace Chiefs. And then we will talk more.'

Hawk began to draw the face of the Shield in the dirt. "You see, I have drawn a Circle. The

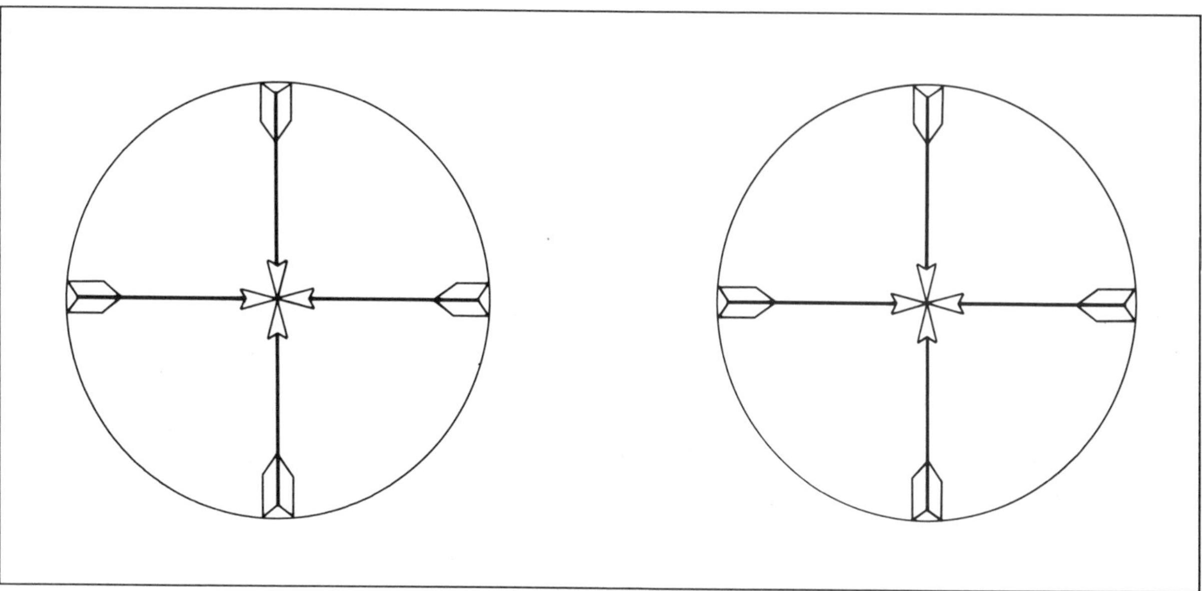

Circle of the Shield is the great Medicine Wheel. The flower in the middle of the Shield tells that these things are one. But to make an understanding for the People, the Medicine gave us the stories of the Forked Pole. This Sign of the Two Flowers on the One Stem represents the Two Stories. The Story Night Bear has been telling you unfolds, petal by petal, one of these two blooms, so that you may see and understand its riddle. The Other Story you will hear soon will represent the Other Flower, and it too will open for you petal by petal. But after you have heard both Stories, you will see that they are really One. We have no talking leaves like the whiteman, so we have to memorize these Stories. Then as we tell them they unfold for the People. It is the Way given to us by the Medicine, *Miaheyyun*. Let me show you more."

Hawk drew two more Shields in the dirt. "You have heard of the Four Medicine Arrows that were brought to us by Sweet Medicine?" Hawk asked. "This is their sign.

"Every story is meant to be unfolded from each of the Four Great Ways. From the directions of Wisdom, Innocence, Sees Far, and Looks-Within. These are the North Arrow, South Arrow, East Arrow, and the West Arrow. The Medicine points the Way for man to learn about himself, his brothers, the world, and the Universe. These Two Medicine Wheels I have drawn upon the ground with the Arrows are the same as the Two Flowers on the other Shield I drew for you before. They are Two Stories about One Teaching. This Teaching is of Man.

"Come with me," said Hawk, and he walked to the edge of the camp with the boy. "Now look at the camp," Hawk instructed the boy. But Hawk had thrust his face almost within an

inch of the boy's, and every time the boy moved his head to see around him, Hawk moved his own head to block him. This sudden and unexplained action unnerved the boy, who stopped trying to see the camp and looked down at his feet.

"Now lie down in that grass on your stomach," Hawk said, pointing to the ground. The boy looked at Hawk oddly and lay down. "Now look again at the camp," he ordered. When the boy had done so, Hawk said, "Now get up and follow me," and he led the young man back to the center of the camp. "Look at the camp now," Hawk said, but as the boy began to turn around Hawk slapped him hard. The young man's face turned livid with rage.

"You are making a fool of me," the young man said through clenched teeth.

Hawk swiftly drew his knife and held it to the boy's throat.

"Turn around and look at the camp again," Hawk said, his face empty of expression. The boy turned slowly, looking everywhere for help.

"I was making no fool of you, little brother," Hawk said as the boy finished turning. "I love you deeply. I needed you angry, and I needed you afraid to make you understand. Here, you can have the knife."

Hawk sat down on the ground, and the boy sat down limply beside him.

"I do not understand," the boy said after recovering his balance. "What were you doing?"

"How did you feel when I kept you from seeing around my face?" asked Hawk.

"Foolish!" answered the boy.

"But you could see little more than my face

and you were surprised. You were perceiving a common camp within one of the many emotions of men, but you could not see the camp because of my face and your feelings," said Hawk.

"And what did you see when I made you lie in the grass?" Hawk asked.

"I could still see little of the camp, because of the tall grass and because your feet were in my way," answered the boy.

"Again you were perceiving with another type of feeling and perspective. The perspective of a Mouse. And when you were slapped?" asked Hawk.

"I could not see the camp again because of my anger and my fear," the boy answered.

"These are the problems that face men all the time, in everything they do. These are the difficulties they must overcome in trying to see both themselves and others," said Hawk.

"And the Stories that are told to us by you and the other Teachers are meant to show us these things?" the boy asked.

"Exactly," Hawk answered. "The man in this first Story is perceiving the Sun Dance, the Universe Dance, and the things of the Medicine Wheel, in ways that are common to many men.

"But now I see that our young Pledgers, your brothers, have returned. Let us join them and continue the Story."

"Are there any questions?" Hawk asked when he had joined the circle of men again. Hawk waited but there were no questions.

Night Bear began signing once again. *The Buffalo Counseled Together to Test the Man Further and then they Sent his Son to Tell him of their Decision. The Boy Went to his Father. "Father," he said, "If you cannot Pick me and*

your Wife and your Other Relations out from Among them they will Overpower you. I Intend to Try and Save your Life. When you are Looking through the Buffalo to Find me, I shall be on the Left of the Other Calves and I shall Keep Moving my Ears. I will Put a big Pine Burr on my Mother's Hump, a Burr in the Middle of my Grandmother's Back, One on my Grandfather's Head, and One on my Uncle's Rump."

Hawk spoke, "All of us must find our Gifts among the great Gifts, but this man is going about this in a strange way. He is putting markers on his Gifts."

Night Bear signed, *The Chief of all the Buffalo Told his People to Stand in Straight Rows. The Young Bulls in One Row, the Old Bulls in Another, the Cows in Another, and the Calves in Another. And he Sent for the Man to Come Down to Pick Out his Relations.*

Hawk spoke, "These Gifts are placed into straight rows by the man. They are fixed into positions. He does not let them come together in a natural Circle and separate themselves out in a natural Way."

Some of the young men began to laugh. "*Wheey, Wheey,*" one of them said. "This one is surely a strange one."

"True," Hawk said. "But you would be surprised how many men try to fix the Gifts of this Universe into nice little bundles."

Night Bear signed, *The Man did as his Son Told him and he Found All of his Relatives. The Other Buffalo were Astonished. And the Buffalo Said, "Eezaugh! Eezaugh! This Man has Accomplished a great thing."*

"He really thinks he has done something, does he not?" It was the boy Hawk had talked with.

"Yes," said Hawk. "I fear that he does."

Night Bear signed, *Now quite Suddenly on the Prairie the Man Saw many Possible Bundles. In these Possible Bundles were the Possessions of the Buffalo, and they were all Ornamented with great Signs in Quill Work.*

Hawk spoke. "These Possible Bundles, my brothers, have within them the Possibilities of all the many talents the Power has given to you. But as you see, this man puts all the Buffalo into convenient places or rows for himself. It then becomes simple for him to put limits on all the Possible Powers of each Gift. He does this because he fears the Gifts, and is afraid to seek the full beauty of their many parts."

Night Bear signed, *The Boy then said to his Father, "They will Ask you to Look Among these for my Mother's Possible Bundle. I will Mark her Bundle with a Forked Stick so that you will Find it." And when the Buffalo Told the Man to Look for his Wife's Bundle he Found it by the Forked Stick that was Placed there. This Astonished the Buffalo People and they Let him Stay with them. Then the Buffalo Put Up a Lodge for the Man and they Asked themselves, "What shall we Give him to Eat?" "Let a Buffalo be Taken and Let him Taste it and See if he Likes it," One of them said.*

Hawk spoke. "See, my Brothers, what this Man has come to? We must all take our Buffalo so that we may eat and let the meat of the great Gift give us strength, but this man's Way is really a strange one."

Night Bear signed, *They Took One of the Buffalo for the Man and he Ate it. The Old Bull Asked his Daughter if her Husband Liked it. She Said he Liked it. It was Good.*

The young men in the Lodge roared with laughter.

"Yes," Hawk said after the laughter died down. "But you must remember that part of your laughter is at yourselves. Because many of us have tried to do what this man is doing in very many different ways. There are many Gifts in this world that frighten us, but it is because we do not understand them. It is not because they are bad. Let us bring this understanding down to a real thing. My brother received a Gift from his mother that many of the people found frightening. It was out of the ordinary, and so it frightened them. My brother could also have seen the Gift as bad, but if he had, then many other Gifts would also have become bad for him. And pretty soon he too would have begun to see these things in the same light as this man. But let us let the Story illustrate this point. Watch for it in the Story and remember that it has its subtle turns, this Medicine Wheel, but that it is common to all men."

Night Bear signed, *While All of this had been Happening, War Parties of Buffalo had been Continually Separating themselves from the Herd and Looking for the Camps of the People and Fighting Them.*

Hawk spoke, "This man sees some of the Gifts as fighting the People."

Night Bear signed, *The People had no Bows and Arrows to Use Against these Buffaloes.*

Hawk spoke, "The meaning here is that the People were not armed to fight these things, and therefore they were victim to them."

Night Bear signed, *The People would not Eat any of the Buffalo because they Feared them All. The People Believed that the Buffalo Ate People. One Day the Man could Stand it no longer and Went to See what the Buffalo were Fighting.*

Hawk spoke. "This man is taking action. His

fear and his own experience make it possible for him to see, as we all must, little brothers. Within these things is a strange paradox. Because it is true that fear blinds man, but it is equally true that fear is the source that drives men to seek and to become illuminated. Upon the beginnings of this man's day, his illumination, he goes to see what the Buffalo are fighting. But what do the Buffalo fight? These Buffalo, or Gifts, are fighting within each of us, and so must be perceived from within. But let us continue with this Story, the Marriage of the Buffalo Wives, and see what this Teaching Way will tell us."

Night Bear signed, *He was very Afraid, but he Went Straight to the Fight. He Saw that the Buffalo had Killed some of the People. It Made the Man Sad to See this Happening. One Night the Man Dreamed. His Wife of the Yellow Hair Visited him and Told him of things that would Pierce things a Long Way Off. He Went out into the Hills and Thought about this Way for Three Days and Three Nights.*

Hawk spoke, "This man now goes on his Vision Quest."

Night Bear signed, *He took Sinew from the Buffalo that had been Eaten, and he Took a Tree and Made a Bow.*

Hawk spoke, "The man took the building things of the Gifts and made himself a bow. The Sign to us here is that of building from a Gift. Sinew is used in your clothes, moccasins, and almost everything else we have in the camps, even to holding the robes together that make our lodges."

Night Bear signed, *After he had Made these things he Took them Immediately into the Hills with him and Began to Look for Arrows. He then Learned how to Use these New things.*

Hawk spoke, "This man has found a new Way for the People. It is a Way for them to touch the Buffalo instead of the Buffalo killing them."

Night Bear signed, *The Man Went Out One Day and Saw some Buffalo that were Fighting with the People. He Went Toward them in a Circle and then Went Among them. He Saw the People Building all kinds of things so that they could not See the Buffalo, and they Fought Behind these things.*

Hawk spoke, "Little brothers, this is a Sign to all of us. When things are lined up and put each one in its place, these things happen. The problem with the laws of men is this. These laws defend against whatever is attacking us, but they also hold out new things. They do not let us grow. The law that protects us in these things ultimately kills us. They will starve us to death."

Night Bear signed, *The Man Rushed at the Buffalo and Began to Shoot his Arrows at them. The Buffalo that Ran Away when the Man Began to Shoot his Arrows at them had Killed some of the People. These Buffalo had Hid the People About their Necks. This is why the People Call this Meat the Human Fat.*

Hawk spoke, "This man brought the Ways of Seeing to the People. This understanding drove away the Buffalo that were killing people. This Human Fat that is about the Buffalo's neck represents the superstitions of the People. But, little brothers, the Human Fat is found about the neck of all Buffalo. It is part of all the Gifts. The fat upon the neck can be eaten as all the rest of the Buffalo can be eaten. But this can only be done when it is eaten in love. The arrows of love can never destroy, they can only Teach."

Night Bear signed, *The Man Told the People to Eat the Buffalo he had Touched with his Arrows. The People Found that it was Food and that it was Good. He Made Many Bows and Arrows for the People. And from that time forth they Scattered over the Prairie to Live like People. The People Tasted all the Fruits of the Prairie, the Roots and the Berries and the Plums. And the Lodges were Brought Together in a Circle. And when the Lodges were Brought into a Circle, there Standing in the Middle of the Circle was the Elk Woman. They Took her to the Lodge of the Man. The Buffalo Wife Ran out to Greet her and they Hugged each Other.*

"Tomorrow will be the telling of the next Story," Hawk said, getting to his feet. "If any of you have questions, I will be at the lodge of Blue Hair." The next morning many of the young men who had been in the Lodge the night before came and talked with Night Bear and Hawk.

"Have you ever seen a whiteman?" Blue Hair asked Hawk later that morning. "There will be one visiting our camp today."

"Visiting here?" Hawk said in surprise. "I thought the People were at war with them!" Hawk was so perplexed that he was embarrassed.

Blue Hair saw the confusion in Hawk's face and began to explain. "I know what you are thinking. If you and Night Bear had not been Men of the Shield, you would have been killed when you first rode into our camp. And so would nearly any other man, whiteman or not. But this one who comes is different."

"Different?" Hawk spoke his thoughts out loud.

"It is hard for you to understand, I know, but have patience with me and I will try to explain to you the madness of it," said Blue Hair.

"Many of the People have been in contact with whitemen for a very long time. Some for their whole lives. Yet still others of the People, like yourself, have never seen a whiteman."

Hawk was moved to tell of his one experience with the whitemen, but his feeling was a fleeting one, and he sat in silence while Blue Hair went on.

"The whitemen are a strange People. Some of them seem not to care for anything but trade. Others of them, like their Pony Soldiers, are interested only in killing. Still others come to visit our camps endlessly, and talk about their god. The man who will visit us here today is one of those who trades. The other man who follows him is the talker of his god."

"There will be two who visit?" Hawk asked, his eyebrows showing his new surprise.

"Not always two," Blue Hair explained. "Most of the time it is only the one who trades. There has been an agreement this time to let the other one come and talk."

Later, Hawk and Night Bear sat in the shade of an arbor and watched the crowd of people collect around the trader and the other man as they entered the camp. Both men were monstrously ugly. Their faces appeared nearly identical, with only the coloring of the hair upon their faces different. The warriors pressed around the trader, each of them eager to trade first. The trader never became hurried or rushed. He took his time examining each of the pelts the different men brought to him.

The talking man left the crowd of traders and began to walk through the camp. He walked stiffly and jerkily. He stopped here and there speaking to children, men, women, and in fact to almost everyone he passed. He either lifted his hat, bowed, or waved to everyone. It appeared to Hawk as if the people were a herd of buffalo, and the talking man was a sage hen walking through the herd, squawking at some, ruffling his feathers at others. The thought was

so completely right for the scene that Hawk burst out in loud laughter that shook his whole body. Every time he looked up and saw the talking man's skinny legs strutting through the camp, he fell back into uncontrollable laughter again.

"Zahuah," Hawk said through his tears and laughter. "He is the funniest creature I have ever seen in my life. He opens greetings with everyone, but stops for no one. If one of our young buffalo in the camp were to lower his head and playfully charge the man," Hawk began to laugh again, "he would probably lose all his feathers right there on the spot."

"Feathers?" Blue Hair asked.

"It is nothing," said Hawk. "It is just that I suddenly thought the man looked like a prairie hen."

Blue Hair saw the resemblance and joined in Hawk's laughter.

Later, Hawk was working on some of his riding equipment and was talking quietly with Night Bear when the talking man walked up behind him. He had completely forgotten about the prairie hen man, and the thought that he might be somewhere nearby had not even entered Hawk's mind. Then Night Bear suddenly looked up, staring behind Hawk with a strange and frightened look on his face. Hawk turned his head slowly to see what it was that Night Bear saw. He had the feeling that either a monster or a man with a war ax must be standing behind him. When he saw that it was the prairie hen standing almost on top of him, he was frozen to the spot. The surprise of seeing the man so close, and the trick his mind had played on him, caused Hawk to sit there expressionless.

Night Bear rose to his feet and greeted the man. The prairie hen seated himself, and Night Bear offered him some dry meat. Hawk watched the man bite a piece from the meat and begin to chew it. He saw that the man was frightened to death. Hawk marveled that he could sit there as calmly as he did, his fear was so apparent. Once before, Hawk had seen eyes that reflected the same expression as those he now looked into. They had the same haunted look Singing Flower had still shown in her eyes hours after she had stopped her screaming.

Hawk was embarrassed. He looked down at his hands.

"Speak the People's tongue?" the man asked in Cheyenne. Then just as quickly he added in Crow, "Speak the People's tongue?"

"He speaks both tongues!" Night Bear said in a surprise that was overly visible.

"Me alla time speak plenty good," the man said and grinned. The fright never left his eyes.

"That is good," answered Night Bear. "Where did you learn the tongue?"

"Me learn tongue plenty fast by pony fort," the man said. "I bring you plenty talk about Medicine Way. The People heap plenty bad their Way."

Hawk began to become curious and questioned the man further. "What do you mean when you say the People are bad, and that their Way is bad?"

"The Big Medicine that hugs the People is bad. The People do not know Geessis," the man told Hawk.

"Geeshish?" repeated Hawk.

"No," the man corrected him. "Geessis."

"What is this Geessis?" asked Night Bear.

"Geessis is heap plenty good power. Kills people who bad are."

"It is true then," thought Hawk. "Their Power is one of death."

The man went on. "Geessis give people heap plenty riches. If people believe Geessis plenty fast he riches gives. Geessis is new Way."

"Strange, isn't it?" Night Bear said, turning to Hawk. "It makes my braids loosen themselves just to think of it. I do not see how these people can find their rest at night with a Power like that."

"Plenty sleep now with Geessis," the man broke in. "Geessis together sleep with relations dead."

"Remarkable!" Hawk finally said. "Have you noticed the fear in his eyes? I saw this same fear in Singing Flower's eyes when the Pony Soldiers were killing the People. This Geessis must be a cunning and terrible Way."

Hawk then turned to the man. "Tell me, brother," Hawk said, carefully pronouncing his words. "Does this Geessis get angry with you much of the time? Do you fear him?"

"Yes! Yes!" the man smiled. "Gifts are given who people fear great their Father. Geessis died for anger, fear and the Father. Yes, I fear him."

"These People are insane!" Night Bear blurted out. "I can see now why it is so hard to understand them. You seem to have better luck with the man than I do. Ask him where the whiteman gets all these wonderful things like the talking leaves and the iron horse we have heard of."

"Tell me," asked Hawk, speaking slowly, "where do the whitemen, your brothers, get their wonderful Gifts, the iron horses and their talking leaves? Where do all these wonderful things come from?"

"From the Medicine Father," answered the man. "If people Geessis path follow they rewarded rich Gifts. Medicine Father talking leaves Gift people giving. You too follow path Geessis and many plenty prizes giving. Iron horse took sharing with."

Later that evening many of the young men who had been with the first group of Pledgers did not return for the meeting with Hawk and Night Bear. The warriors who had traded with the whiteman earlier in the day were staggering drunk with the stinging water. Hawk looked around at the tiny group of young men. Disappointment rose in his stomach, choking him into anger.

"Is this all who will listen?" he asked, controlling his urge to yell or cry.

"There are no more," answered the boy Hawk had talked with. "The others accuse you of having women's meetings."

"I will be back shortly," Hawk said as he rose to leave. "I will talk with these young men and be right back."

The anger inside Hawk grew with each step as he drew nearer to where the men were drinking.

"Who was it of you who said that we have meetings of women?" Hawk demanded as he stopped at the group. A man of about forty or more years staggered to his feet and walked up to Hawk.

"I say that you have meetings of women," the man said. Hawk noticed the man's dull eyes, which he had learned were typical of men who had been drinking.

"And one day, Medicine Man, I myself will be the one who will cut the top leaves from the great Forked Pole. There will be no more leaves on the pole, no innocence, no mirroring. These things have never been the Way of the Dog Soldiers. And today I, Limping Horse," the man slurred his name and spun around wildly, "I will cut the great Pole. There will be no more leaves. The Pole will belong only to the Dog Soldiers!"

Hawk stood there unbelieving. "How can he speak this way?" Hawk thought to himself in confusion.

"Cut them off!" the man said over and over as he danced around the other men.

Hawk realized that it was useless to stand and argue with these men when they were in this state of mind, so he turned to walk back to the Lodge. Someone grabbed his arm. Hawk stopped and turned to see who it was. It was a boy called Raven's Wing. Hawk had met him briefly the day he and Night Bear had been surrounded and brought into the camp. The boy was now so drunk that he clung to Hawk for support. His face was a scant two inches away when he spoke.

"I tell you this, Crow lover," he began. "We Dog Soldiers will win."

"Win what?" growled Hawk. "A Geessis Gift?" He pulled the hands from his shirt and let the boy stagger away looking for another support. He heard the other men giggle and hoot as he walked away. Someone threw a rock that bounced a few feet past him to his left. Hawk never turned around.

Hawk returned to the Lodge and sat down.

"It is heartbreaking, is it not?" Morning Star asked quietly. "They will all be sick tomorrow. Sick in their hearts and sick in their minds."

"I know," Hawk said. "But it seems so hopeless. It is something I cannot fight. I do not know where to begin." Hawk raised his head and looked at the young faces of those who sat around him, and then over to the milling, staggering group of men who were only a short distance away. "Those brothers over there," Hawk said to the young men around him, "will Sun Dance with you. If for no other reason, it

will be because of their desire to find protection for their lives. They will Dance. I have a request I wish to ask of each one of you here. I want no one to tell me his answer. But I wish for the ones among you whose hearts are willing, to Pledge their Second Day to these your brothers."

Then Night Bear began the second Story, signing, *This is about the Other Man. The Whole Camp was Moving. They came to a big River and Began to Cross Over to the Other Side. The People Began to Cross and Soon nearly Every One of them was on the Other Side. The Last Family to Cross Saw an Old Woman Sitting by the Water. And the Woman of the Family said, "My, my, here is an Old Woman, an Old Woman who has been Left on this Side of the River. Get on the Traveling Poles my Dogs are Pulling, and I will Take you Across."*

"No," answered the Old Woman. "I will Wait here for a little while." She Remained Sitting there and would not Cross.

The Woman Went On, Leaving her. When the Woman Reached the Camp most of the Lodges were already Set Up in a Circle. As usual, there were Stragglers Following Behind, mostly Young Men and Boys on Foot. At length some of these Reached the River and Seeing the Old Woman said, "Well, well, they have Moved Off and Left the Old Woman on this Side of the River."

They Sat down and Began to Take off their Moccasins and Leggings before Wading the River. One of them Said to the Others, "Let us Carry the Old Woman Across the River." They Talked and Joked about it for a while, and Finally one of them said, "I will Carry her Over." He Spoke to the Old Woman with her Cane of Braids that Lay before her on the Ground. "Old Woman, I will

Carry you Over."

"No!" she answered.

As this Crowd of Young Men Sat there Talking, Another Crowd of Young Men and Boys Came Up. The First Lot, as they Walked into the River, Called Back to the Others, "Bring your Grandmother Over the River."

The Second Lot Began to Say to One Another, "Get the Old Woman and Carry her Across."

One by One they Went to her and Offered to Carry her Across the River to where the Camp was. She Refused them All. Among them was a Handsome Youngman who was very Quiet. He Carried a Contrary Bow. The Other Youngmen Spoke to him and Said, "Go Over and Ask her if she will Let you Carry her Over." And he said, "Grandmother, Let me Carry you Over."

She answered, "Yes, yes, my Grandson, Carry me Over."

Hawk spoke, "Now we hear the other side of the Medicine Pole. This is the Other Man. The People came to the Medicine of Life, but typically the old woman, tradition, refuses to cross with the young men. Tradition is something the young must learn, but tradition is a stubborn, cantankerous old woman and she is afraid to get her feet wet. The young men know they must get the old woman across the river with them, but she refuses. The tradition of the People refuses to cross. The young respect tradition, but they are frustrated by it also. But one among them will carry her across. It is the boy with the Contrary Bow. He is a boy different from all the rest. He is the contrary side of men."

Night Bear signed, *The Youngman Gave his Moccasins to Another Youngman to Carry for him and said to the Old Woman, "Put your Arms*

Around my Neck." He Turned and Squatted on the Ground so that she could Get on his Back. When he Reached the Other Bank, he said, "Now Get Off here." The Old Woman did not Answer, nor did she Get Off either, and he could not Get her Off.

The young men in the lodge roared with laughter.

Night Bear went on signing, *She would not Get Off and she would not Say a Word. The Youngman Went to his Close Friend and said to his Friend, "Please Try to Get this Old Woman Off my Back." His Friend Tried Hard but could do Nothing. He could not even Get her Arms Loose. Then the Youngman said, "Put on my Moccasins for me." And his Friend Did so.*

Hawk spoke, "All of you here have the Old Woman on your back. Remember these Teachings are for you. You too, must ask for your moccasins, for the things of the People."

Night Bear signed, *They all Started Toward the Camp Together, and as they Went On the Youngman who was Carrying the Old Woman felt Ashamed. And he said to himself, "The People will all Look at me when I Come into the Camp." When he Reached the Camp, he was Told to Go to the Center of the Camp and that the People would Try to Get her Off his Back. All of the Other Youngmen Left and Went their Ways to their Lodges.*

Hawk spoke, "This will happen to any young man who is a Contrary. He will feel shame and his friends will abandon him. Tradition, little brothers, will normally hound a People. It follows them wherever they will go. But this young man did not understand tradition. Little brothers, I say too much. It is for you to study this Story, and to grow with the Spirit of its Teaching."

Night Bear signed, *The Youngman who was Carrying the Woman Went to the Center of the Circle and Sat Down there. The Other Youngmen Went about the Camp Telling the People that the Contrary had an Old Woman Stuck Fast to his Back and something ought to be Done to Get her Off. An Old Man Went around the Camp Crying that in some Way the Old Woman should be Gotten Off the Contrary's Back. Then All the People Came Together at the Center of the Camp and they Tried to Pull her Off but they could not Do it. At last they Gave Up their Attempts, but One Man Spoke Up and said, "Vihio is in the Camp. He may have some Plan for Getting her Off this Youngman's Back. "They Found Vihio and Brought him there. "Build a large Fire in the Center of the Camp," said Vihio. "And have the Contrary Sit with his Back to the Fire."*

Hawk spoke, "You have all heard many of the tales of Vihio. Vihio, which also means 'white,' is symbolic of the North, or Wisdom. But we all know that Vihio is also the Contrary. He is a clown. He is a knowledgeable fool."

Night Bear signed, *All the Youngmen Ran to Bring Wood for they Liked Contrary. And when Contrary Sat with his Back to the Fire, the Old Woman Squirmed this Way and that, then Finally she Fell Off his Back and Coiled herself as Women Do and Sat there.*

Hawk spoke, "Firewood is the thing brought by the hands of the People. The fire is the Spirit of their Brotherhood."

Night Bear signed, *The People Looked at her for they had never Seen her Sitting this Way in the Middle of them. "Leave her and Let her Starve to Death," they said. They all Moved Away and Left her Sitting there By Herself. Contrary Went to the Lodge of his Parents. Night Came and the Youngmen Went through the Camp Yelping and Singing as Youngmen do. But toward the Middle of the Night these Sounds grew Quiet, and soon Everyone was Asleep. Contrary was Tired and Wanted to Rest and to Sleep, but yet he Felt that he must Go Out. He could not Resist the Feeling and he Got Up and Stepped from the Lodge. When he Looked toward the Center of the Camp he Saw a Beautiful Great Lodge, a Dwelling Lodge, and it was Glowing with Light.*

Hawk spoke, "Follow the Spirit of these things, little brothers."

Night Bear signed, *He Saw a Large and Beautifully Painted Lodge with a Light in it. He Looked at it, Astonished. And as he Looked at it her Heard a Baby Crying, and a Woman Singing to the Baby. He Wondered who Camped there and he said to himself, "I Believe I should Look Into that Lodge."*

Hawk spoke, "Because of this young man, now tradition is changed. There are beautiful things of tradition, my sons, but it is the young mother, not the old woman, whom one should love."

Night Bear signed, *He did not Go into the Lodge the First Time, but Went Back to his own Lodge and Lay Back Down. As he Went into his Lodge he said Out Loud, "Someone is Camped in the Middle of the Circle. There is a big Lodge there with a Light in it." The next Morning when he Looked Out of the Door, there was no longer a Lodge in the Middle of the Circle, but the Old Woman was Sitting in the Same Place where she had been Before. That Day the People kept Talking about what they should Do with the Old Woman. They were Wondering about it and toward Evening they Held Council Over it. It was Decided that they would Move Away and Leave her there to Starve to Death. Late that Night while most of the People were Asleep but still Others were Up and About, an Old Man Stepped Out of his Lodge and Saw the Big Glowing Lodge Clearly Standing in the Center of the Camp. The*

Old Man Called to the People, "Look at this Lodge in the Center of the Camp!" But No One Bothered to Look and the Old Man, who Needed his Rest, Went Back Inside to Sleep.

That Night the Contrary said, "I Think I will Go Out and Look into that Lodge." He Arose from his Bed and Went Out. He could Hear the Baby Crying and he Heard Clearly Someone Singing to the Baby. The Voice said, "Hush, Little One, your Father is Coming. He will Be here soon." The Youngman Entered the Lodge and Saw a very Beautiful Girl Sitting at the South of the Lodge. She had Beautiful Long Black Hair and she Held the Child in her Arms. The Lodge was finely Furnished with Backrests and Buffalo Robes Hanging on the Backrests. As the Youngman Entered the Lodge the Beautiful Young Girl Looked at him, and Followed him with her Eyes. The Youngman said to her, "Hand me my Son," and she Put the Baby in his Arms. He was very Happy to See the Child. As he Held him, the Girl Gave her Husband Pemmican to Eat, Berries of the Prairies, and Buffalo Meat. They Both Made Ready to Go to Sleep. The Robes on the Beds were Quilled with the Medicine Signs. The Youngman was Glad for the Gift. He Slept with the Girl and Put the Baby Next to him.

Hawk spoke, "As you can see, the Other Man in this Story is quite different from the Other Man in the first Story. He is not protected by his father, nor does he see things as always bad. He trusts, and as you can see, he sleeps with the woman. He has intercourse with her immediately. Notice also my sons, that this man is not even aware that he has had previous intercourse with the girl. He has to learn of his own child. Notice the difference in the two Stories, but notice more the difference as it is

reflected in yourselves."

Night Bear signed, *The Youngman Awoke in the Morning and Found himself Lying Alone in the Sweet Grass Within the Middle of the Camp Circle. When the People Awoke that Morning, the Old Woman was Gone.*

Contrary Went Home to his Lodge. He Wondered which Way his Wife had Moved, and so Before Anyone was Awake, he Went Out in Search of Signs. He Saw the Tracks of the Lodge Poles and Followed them. He Followed the Tracks the Whole Day. By Evening he Began to be very Tired. He Stopped Upon a Hill and Looked Beyond and Saw a little Creek. He Saw Pines that Grew Along the Creek and Below them was a Lodge. When he Came Close to the Lodge he Stopped and Sat Down to Rest. He then Moved Toward the Lodge. The Girl Came Out and Moved the Wings of the Smoke Hole of the Lodge. She Spoke to Her Child, who now was Large Enough to Sit Up, and said, "Little One, your Father is here." Contrary Went In and Sat Down at the Left Side of the Lodge. He Took the Child in his Arms, and his Wife Gave him something to Eat. It was the Neck Fat of the Buffalo. That Night they Sat Together and Talked.

Hawk spoke, "Do you see how this man watches his son grow? How this man loves his baby? He takes the food of mind, heart, and body from his wife. And, my sons, notice that with the food is the Neck Fat of the Buffalo. These things, my sons, will make us grow. That is if we also talk with our wives, our Gifts, as this young man did."

Night Bear signed, *The Next Morning the Youngman again Awoke Alone on the Prairie. The Lodge was Gone and he did not Know which Way it had Gone. All he could See were the Tracks of a Buffalo Cow and her Calf. He Followed the Tracks,*

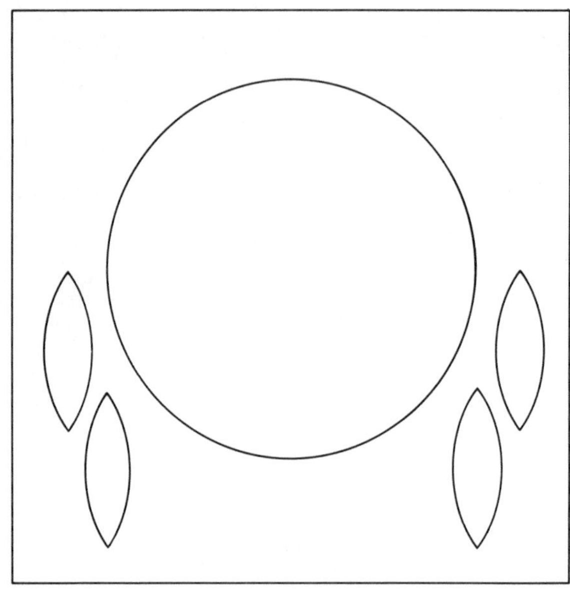

and after a while the Tracks Turned into the Tracks of the Lodge Poles and he Followed them.

Hawk spoke, "This man sees the Tracks of the Spirit, but he also sees the same thing in the Lodge Pole Tracks of the People. He sees the Spirit of these things in the People."

Night Bear signed, *The Youngman Stopped and Rested Four Times. He Sat the First Time Facing the South. He Rested the Second Time Facing the West. The Third Time he Rested he Faced the North. And the Fourth Time he Rested he Faced the East. In the Evening he Saw a Lodge a long Way Off. As he Drew Near, the Girl Came Out as Before and Fixed the Wings. When he came Close to the Lodge he Saw the Boy Toddling Around and Playing. The Mother Spoke to the Child, "Your Father is Coming, my Little One." The Child Laughed and Ran to his Father, Holding Out his Hands. The Father Took him Up in his Arms and Carried him into the Lodge. His Wife Gave her Husband something to Eat. They Talked again and they Slept.*

Hawk then called a halt to the meeting as he had before. He and Night Bear decided they would go for a short walk, but as they started out the young man that Hawk had talked with the day before joined them.

"My name is Singing Rock," the boy said as he ran to catch up with them. "Could you show me another of the Shields of the Forty-Four Peace Chiefs, good father?"

Hawk smiled and signed to Night Bear the words the boy had spoken.

"Let me draw him the Shield of Two Moon," Night Bear said, "and you can explain it to him in his own tongue as I draw."

Night Bear began to draw the Shield.

"The Shield you see drawn upon the ground

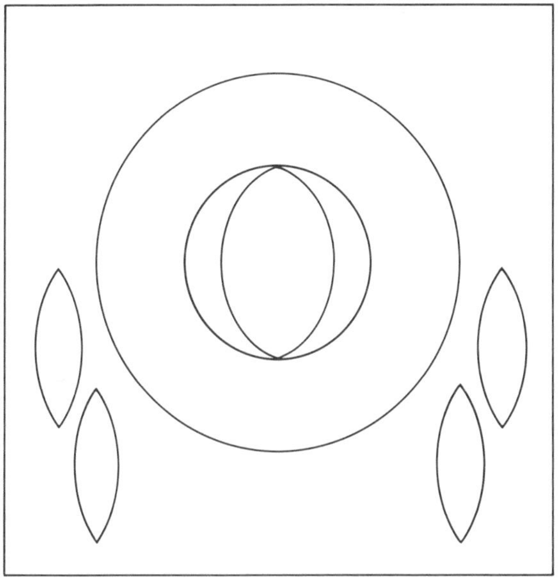

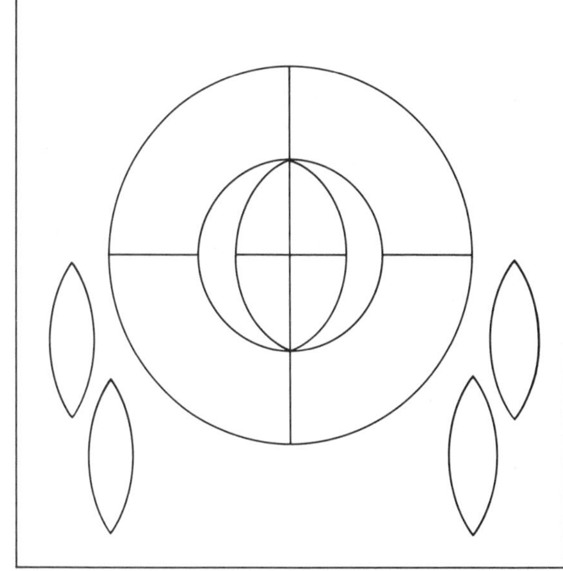

is the Medicine Wheel," explained Hawk. "It represents the things of the Universe. The feathers you see on the Shield are two Red Hawk Feathers and two Black Hawk Feathers. The People must put these upon the Shield. They are the Sees in the Day Hawk and the Sees in the Night Hawk. The feathers are wrapped at their stems with White Mink and Black Otter. These are Signs of the healing of the Medicine Water. They are also the Signs of Wisdom and of Looking-Within. But these small animals are also playful, as you know. They play in the Medicine Water. Men are also playful, and must be as children in the Medicine Water."

Night Bear then added two Half Moons to the face of the Shield.

"Man sees half of the Medicine Wheel when he is in darkness. But he must then seek the other half in the same darkness. Because in the darkness, my son, are found both fear and joy. The two Half Moons are another Sign of these Twins, as in the Forked Medicine Pole. Both represent the Twinness of Man," Hawk explained.

Night Bear drew again.

"This Shield is painted Blue, Red, Green, and Yellow," continued Hawk. "The Blue is the Cedar of the Sacred Mountains. It is prayer. The Green is for Innocence of Heart. The Red is the Sign of the Campfires of the People. It is the Spirit. And the Yellow is for the Eagle of the East. Man must See Far. He must perceive these things broadly. You will see the Eagle on top of the Forked Medicine Pole in the Sun Dance Lodge. This is a Sign of these things. Remember this, little brother. The Eagle Sees Far, but this Eagle cannot live forever within the sky. His thirst and his hunger will bring him to

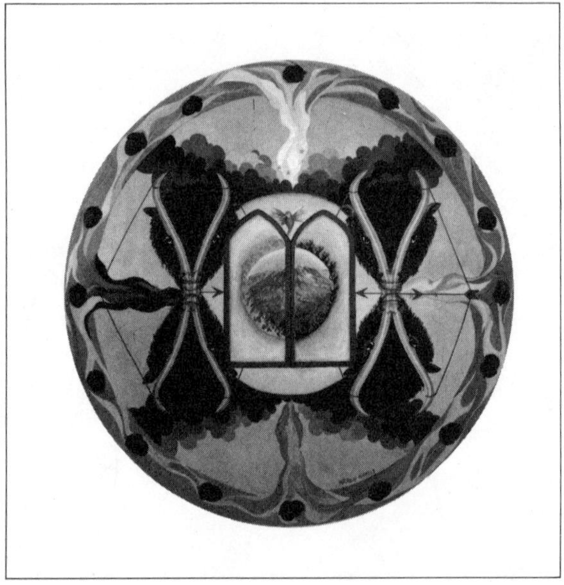

the earth to find nourishment. But, little brother, this Eagle could also choose, as many men have chosen, to starve to death instead of seeking nourishment. The arrows of the People cannot touch the Eagle, because he hides high within the sky robe. But the Power brings the Eagle down to the Great Lodge for the Give-Away. That is why the Eagle is represented in the Sun Dance Lodge upon the Forked Tree. This Sign of the Eagle Plume is the sign of man's Truth. It is also like the Buffalo, the Sign of the Give-Away."

Night Bear drew again, finishing the Shield.

"You are one of the Half Moons and your brother is the Other Half. Together you are One. This last Sign of the Shield is the Mirror of the great Medicine Lake and of Seven Arrows. You Mirror each other, my son, you and your Brother. And you both together are a Mirror of the Great Spirit. This Sign of the Circle is seen as the Sun Sign, the time when men can see far and clearly. It is the great Medicine Wheel. It is the Universe," concluded Hawk.

"*Wheey! Wheeey! Eezaugh!* This Shield is a mighty Sign for the People," Singing Rock exclaimed. "I shall seek the Name of Two Moon," he said as he walked along with the two men. Then he stopped suddenly and added excitedly, "The Name is Two Moon, not Two Moons! Because they really are One Moon, is that not true?"

"Yes," answered Hawk. "Yes, my son, they are One."

Later, after everyone had returned to the Lodge and settled themselves, Night Bear again began his signing.

The Next Morning the Youngman was Alone again on the Prairie. He Found the Trail and

Followed it. He realized that they were Going in the Direction of the Sunrise. Before him he could See Far Off some Blue Ridges.

Hawk spoke, "You must seek the East, little brothers. And like this Other Man you will then see the Signs of the Sacred Mountains."

Night Bear signed, *When he Reached the Ridges he Stopped and Sat Down. Then he Went On again. Ahead of him he Saw Another Distant Ridge, and he Went Toward that Ridge. It was Getting Along toward Evening when he Reached the Second Ridge. He Climbed to the Top, and Suddenly Below and Behind him where he had already Been he Saw the Creek. Along the Creek was the Lodge. The Man Went Down to the Camp. The Little Boy Saw him Approaching, and he said Excitedly, "Mother, my Father is Approaching!" The Little Boy Ran and Met his Father and Took his Hand. His Wife was Bringing in Wood for a warm Fire. His Wife Cooked him something Over the Fire and Gave him Something to Eat. After he Finished Eating, he Told his Wife that he was very Tired. "I Want to Talk to you for a while Before you Rest, my Husband," she said. "I Came for you, you are the One I Came for." And they Went to Sleep Together.*

Hawk spoke, "Many of us will shoot over the marks we aim our arrows toward, my sons, like the Other Man. But do not become alarmed when this happens. Look down and you will see the Woman's Lodge. She will bring for you too the things from this world that make the fire. And you will be warm from this fire. You will also enjoy the food this fire cooks for you, and it will take care of your hunger. All of you are hungry, my sons, and you will also be given water to quench your thirst. You will neither eat nor will you drink in the Sun Dance Lodge for three days and three nights. You will learn of the Spirit of these things in the Great Lodge. The Sun Dance is four days long, but you will only Dance three of these together. Your fourth and final day will be spent alone. It is the alone time. And you will fast that last day."

Night Bear signed, *The Youngman was very Tired and he Slept Soundly and Long. The Next Morning he Slept so Hard that he did not Wake Up in Time and again the Camp was Gone. He Followed the Trail all Day long and Rested Four Times. As Before, he Faced Each of the Four Directions with Each Rest. That Evening After his Fourth Rest, he again Saw the Lodge. When the Youngman came Closer to the Lodge, he Saw his Young Son Playing Outside. The Boy Ran to Meet him and Hugged his Father. Then they Walked Together Back to the Lodge. His Wife Cooked something for him to Eat. After he had Finished Eating, his Wife Explained how it was that she had First Come for him.*

"My Father Gave me to you," she said, "and Sent me for you. Before this I have been Sent to Others in the Same Way. Whatever it is that Happens, you must not Give Up. You must be Strong. In the Morning if you Look in that Direction," she Pointed, "you will See a Beautiful Blue Ridge a Long Way Off. It was from there that I was Sent for you."

The Little Boy was Glad to Have his Father With him again. He Played and Ran Around the Lodge. He Ran again to his Father and Threw his Arms Around his Neck. He was Happy.

The Woman Continued Speaking and said, "Over there are Many of my People and we All Look Alike. All the Little Ones Look Alike, the Little Calves that are Still Yellow. You will be Told to Look for your Wife. My Father will be the One who will Tell you. My Father will Tell you to Look for your Son, too."

The Boy Spoke to his Father, "Father, when you Look for me I will Shake my Tail and Start for my Mother to Nurse. Then you can Say, 'this is my son.'"

The Woman then Spoke again, "When you are Told to Look for me I will Move my Right Forefoot just a little, and will Move my Right Ear."

Hawk spoke, "Your son, too, my little brothers, will go to his mother to nurse. And you will see the Spirit Tracks of your wife there, and you will hear the Medicine, when your wife moves her ear. These things will show you your Medicine."

Night Bear signed, *His Wife then Told him, "It is a long Way to where you Go Tomorrow and there is no Water Between here and there." His Son Told him, "As you Follow my Tracks Tomorrow, Father, Watch them Closely, and after we have Gone a long Distance you will See when we are Crossing a Dry Creek, where I will Turn Off. Follow my Tracks. I will Stamp on the Ground and Place a Rock Over my Tracks. Lift Up that Stone and you will Find Water to Drink."*

Hawk spoke, "Dry creek beds, my sons, are places where one can dig and find water. Think, my sons, of what this Sign of the Earth means. Seek this Sign."

Night Bear signed, *The Woman said, "I have been Sent this Way many Times and I have Brought Back Husbands, but Always they Became Frightened and were Overpowered. When you Come to the Top of the Great Ridge, you will See the Buffalo Scattered all Around. When you Get to this place Wear your Robe, Hair Side Out!"*

Hawk spoke, "As you plainly know, my sons, the Signs of the Medicines of the People and the Sun Dance are put upon their Robes. Put these next to your bodies, and show the hair side to the People. Give-Away all four of your Days of Power. Give-Away this great Medicine you will receive that the People may Give-Away, also."

Night Bear signed, *His Wife said, "Sit Still Upon the Hill and do not become Frightened. Hold Fast and Trust. My Father will Charge on you Four Times, but Do not Move. Hold Fast."*

Hawk spoke, "You too will be tested by the great Medicine, little brothers, from all Four Directions. From the North, South, West, and East. You, too, must hold fast, after your three days and nights. For these things you hear next you will experience in your fourth day. Your fourth day is twelve moons, or four seasons. It is one year."

Night Bear signed, *He Drank the Water and Sat there until he was Rested. After he Drank and Rested he Began again, and after a while he Came to the Ridge his Wife had Told him about. He Looked Over and Saw all the Land Covered with Buffalo. He Sat Down there and Wore his Robe with the Hair Side Out. When he Came in Sight, The Buffalo Began to Move About and to Go into a Circle. Many Buffalo Came from Every Direction to this Spot. They Came from the North, from the East, from the West, and also from the South. After a while, the Great Bull Came Out of the Herd and Walked Up Slowly Toward him. The Youngman Made Up his Mind that this was the One his Wife had Spoken about, and he Began to Get Ready and to have a Strong Heart. He Placed his Hands over his Eyes.*

Hawk spoke, "My brothers, we must give up our old Ways of perceiving at this time and only trust. We must put our hands over our eyes, also."

Night Bear signed, *When the Buffalo Came Near, he Pawed the Ground Making much Noise and Dust. He then Made a Ferocious Charge at the Youngman, and almost Touched him, but*

Veered Off. The Youngman did not Move. Then the Bull said, "Wheeey! Wheeey!, My Son-In-Law has a Strong Heart." Four Times the Bull Rushed the Youngman and the Youngman did not Move. The Fourth Time the Youngman was Rushed Upon and did not Move, the Bull spoke again. "My Son Truly has Medicine Power. Miaheyyun has Given him his Life." He Told the Youngman, "Now you can Stand Up and Go to your Wife." The Youngman Stood Up and Started Down Toward the Buffalo. After he had Gone a Short Distance he Saw a Great Lodge and Went Into it and Sat Down. The Lodge was Made of Two Lodges. It was very Large. His Mother-In-Law Gave him something to Eat. His Wife was not there.

Hawk spoke, "We now sit together inside a Lodge like that one."

Night Bear signed, *His Mother-In-Law said to him, "Four Days from Now you will Search for your Wife." Four Days later he Went Into the Middle of the Great Circle of Buffalo. He Wore his Buffalo Robe and was Painted Over his Whole Body. The Morning after the Fourth Night he was Told to Find his Wife Among All the Buffalo. The Buffalo Moved in their Great Circle, then Began to Run Toward the Middle. They Separated Naturally, the Suckling Calves Together, the Two-Year-Olds Together, the Cows Together, and the Bulls Together. It was their Natural Way of Running. And they Ran in Toward the Youngman. At the Sunrise all the Yellow Calves were Put into a Line and so were all of the Cows. The Rest of the Buffalo were Crowded Together by Age.*

Hawk spoke, "This will be your sunrise time also. It will be a new day for you. You will see the People gather in front of the Lodge and you will see the Powers of this world there, too."

Night Bear signed, *Contrary Now had to Find his Wife and Child. His Father-In-Law had Told him to Come Out and to Do this. "If you cannot Recognize your Wife and your Child," said the Great Buffalo Bull, "you will be Overcome."*

Hawk spoke, "You, too, my sons, must recognize your Medicine Gifts, your wives and your children, or you, too, will be overcome."

Night Bear signed, *When the Youngman Passed in Front of the Line he Went Slowly. He then Went Slowly Behind them. The Calves all Looked Alike. And as he Passed, he Looked Carefully as his Son had Told him. And at length One of the Calves Shook its Tail, and Moved its Head as if it Wanted to Nurse. The Man Put Out his Hand and Touched the Calf and said, "This is my Child."*

Hawk spoke, "You must write these things clearly upon your Shields, my sons. This is the Touching of the Calf. Who you are will be painted plainly on your Shields. These Signs will be your names. This is how you also Touch the People, for by these Signs they can plainly see you and can know you."

Night Bear signed, *When the Man Touched his Son, the Bull was Pleased and said, "Miaheyyun is Within our Son. He has Great Power." The Calves then all Scattered Out. The Youngman Saw his Son Hesitating as all the Calves Ran to Suckle their Mothers. The Youngman then had to Look for his Wife. By this Time some of the Calves had Reached their Mothers and were Nursing. When Contrary Got Behind the Line of Cows, he Walked Slowly. And pretty Soon a Calf Dodged in Front of him and Made the Motions his Son had Told him about some Days Before. It Shook its Tail as his Son had Done, and it Shook its Head to Try to Nurse. When the Calf Went in to Nurse, the Youngman Advanced Slowly and Watched the Cow's Ears and her Feet. The Cow Moved her Ear and her*

Foot, just as his Wife had Told him she would Do. He Touched her with his Hand, and he said, "Here is my Wife." The Great Bull was Pleased. Then the Buffalo Scattered Over the Prairie again, and the Youngman and his Wife and Child were Together.

Hawk spoke, "When the People go their own ways on the Prairie, they will recognize you, little brothers, when they meet you there. You will have your Shields, your Ways, and from these they shall know your names.

"Tomorrow I will sit with you all day," Hawk continued, "and we will talk. Come when you wish and ask your questions."

The young men came alone or in pairs the next day to talk with their Teacher. Singing Rock was one of the last to make his appearance, and he was accompanied by a young woman.

"My Father and I hunted together this morning," Singing Rock said as he sat down, "or I would have come earlier. This is my sister Red Star Woman. She wants to hear your answers."

"You have questions then?" Hawk asked.

The young man looked up at the sky and then down at the ground, collecting his thoughts before he spoke. "Truly, this Medicine Story has made my mind turn around. I thought for a while, when you were talking, that you were talking about the Double Lodge we were sitting in. Remember? You mentioned the young man was in a Double Lodge. And before that, you also spoke of our Fourth Day. Just before this, I was confused as to whether we were in the Great Lodge or the Double Lodge. The Story seems to go round and round. It has confused me. *Zahuah!"*

"You have answered your own question,"

said Hawk.

"Answered my question?" the boy frowned. "How?"

"You spoke it yourself," Hawk grinned. "The Story goes round and round. It goes around and around because it goes around the great Medicine Wheel. When you are in a circle of people and are walking in a circle, do you follow or are you leading? If you look behind you, the others appear to follow you. But if you look ahead of yourself, you are the one who is following."

"*Zahuah,*" the boy frowned.

"You will see, my son," Hawk said. "What I told you in the lodge were things to make you look. I opened some of the petals of the flower I have spoken of to you, but I opened them only in certain ways. It is for you to open them yourself in the other ways."

"You spoke of the Shields and of the Touching. Would you explain these things a little more to me?"

"Come," Hawk said, getting to his feet. There were a couple of trees that stood alone, not too far from the camp, and Hawk headed for these. It was a short time before they reached the trees, where they all sat down, glad to be back within the shade.

"It is a different world out there," Hawk said, sweeping his hand toward the endless prairie, "and another law prevails there, my children. When we are within the protection of our camp there are many hands to settle arguments, and to protect our lives. Out there it is different. When we step from the camp circle we are in a land so vast it staggers the mind to realize its greatness. Out there we are alone. If you were to meet another man out on the prairie and kill him, no one would know. He would never be found. No one would even suspect you if he was, because the elements there take many lives in natural accidents. What you do out there and how you dress there, even what you say there, is known only to you. The People will never know. No one will know except yourself.

"The prairie is a place of danger, but it is also a place of beauty. It is a place of adventure. All kinds of men visit the prairie. Some see only the danger. Some see only ugliness. Some seek victims to satisfy their own pleasures there. Some are timid, some fearless, some frightened, but all people who visit this place share one important thing. They share their aloneness. We face only ourselves on the prairie. We can discover ourselves there, or we can simply run with the animals of the prairie, blindly and at nature's whims. The prairie, my children, is life. This camp circle is a different place. Ultimately, a man's true Name and his Shield are clear to him out there on the prairie.

"Our People were given the Gifts. These Gifts were the great Medicine Wheel, and its Teachings. I wish to tell you a Story concerning these Gifts."

Hawk had carried a skin of water with him, and some food wrapped in a bundle. Now he unrolled the bundle of food and set the water beside it. "But first we will eat," he said.

They ate, and then Hawk began the Story. "This Story," he began, "is called The Star Water."

There was Once a Star, Way Out in the Universe, and it Fell to Earth. It Fell Upon the great Prairie, and when it did, It Shattered into Many Pieces. It was Scattered Over the Earth and for a long Time these Pieces Remained Glowing, like Parts of Stars. Gradually they Changed into Glowing Pools of Water, into Lakes. These Lakes Shone like Stars. There was a Beautiful Young Girl who Went Out to these Lakes. And From Each One she Took a Handful of the Star Water. She Brought these Back to the People. And she Gave One Handful to Each Person and Hung it Around his Neck, like a Medallion. These Medallions of Star Water Glowed like the Stars, and Each One of the People could See by them where Every Other One was. The People Lived like this, Until One Man Became Angry and Threw his Star Water Into the Fire. He then Went to Live Under the Ground, in an Earth Lodge. After this the Other People also Threw their Star Water Into the Fire, and also Went to Live in Earth Lodges Under the Ground. Only the Girl was Left with her Star Water. She Remained Above the Ground in a Beautifully Painted Lodge. The Beautiful Young Girl Took the Fire that Contained the Pieces of Star Water and Took them Back to the Lakes. She Took Back the Star Water that had been Thrown Into the Fire and Returned Each Piece to its Lake. She had One Piece Remaining, and at this Lake she Made Medicine.

A Great Elk Came to her at that Place and the Elk said to her, "If you Hang the Star Water Around my Neck I will Keep it for you. I will Give it Back to you when you Need it."

She Gave it to the Elk and she Returned to where the People were. She Returned to her Painted Lodge, and she Lived in this Great Lodge. The Rest of the People Continued to Live in their Earth Lodges. One Day the Elk Came to Visit her and she Fed the Elk and Ate with him. The Elk Left and Returned again. The Fourth Time he Returned he Spoke, saying, "You will be my Wife and I your Husband, and we will Live Together." They did, and they Hung the Star Water Outside the Great Lodge.

The Others of the People were Naked. They did not Know how to Live Together, and they had

KAREN HARRIS

Forgotten how to Live in Painted Lodges Above the Ground. The People Wanted to Remember how to Do this. The Great Elk Spoke to them saying, "Some of you Go to the North, and Others of you Go to the South, still Others of you Go to the West, and the Remainder of you Go to the East. In Four Years All of you Return to this Place. And you will Know how to Live in Painted Lodges again."

After Four Years, the People who had Gone to the North Sent Two of their People Back to Steal the Star Water from the Elk. The People who had Gone to the South Sent Two of their People to Trick the Star Water from the Elk. The People who had Gone to the West Sent Two of their People, and these Came Back to Take the Star Water from the Elk by Force. The People who had Gone to the East never Returned.

The Elk Resolved to Go in the Final Direction, the East, and so he Left, Taking the Young Girl and the Star Water with him. And Now if you Want to Find the Morning Star, you must Go to where the Elk is.

Hawk then took a hand drum from beside the tree he sat against and sang them a song. It was a Sun Dance song, and he sang it for them four times.

After he had sung this song he laid the drum back against the tree again, and said, "When you have found this Elk, little brother and sister, he will give you back the Morning Star Water because it is yours."

Singing Rock and Red Star Woman waited for the explanation, but none came. Hawk went on as if he had never told the story.

"If you were to meet a stranger out there, either a woman or a man," Hawk pointed to the prairie, "if you wished to talk with them, then you would have to speak in signs. Because they would not understand your tongue. It is also

this way even with your own People. They do not truly speak your own tongue either. Therefore you must use the signs with them, also. The great Medicine knew of this. He gave us a way to talk with all men, no matter what tongues they may speak. He gave us this way of signs. The greatest of these signs are the Shields, which are painted with the true hearts of men. The Medicine did this so that men would learn."

"Do you mean by this the sign language of the hands that every tribe understands?" asked Red Star.

"Yes," answered Hawk, "but I also mean much more. There are universal signs of love that women know well. It is when we hide these signs that we return in part to our earth lodges. There are other signs, too. Understanding is one. So are mercy, kindness, love, truth, joy, and many others. It is easy to throw the Star Water away in anger and to hide ourselves away in earth lodges. But it is more beautiful to live in truth above the ground. There we can learn and grow.

"Many men hide themselves in earth lodges of many sorts upon the great prairie. They believe that in this way they are made safe, but this is a selfish thing that will ultimately destroy them. These people will not grow. Soon they will forget how to live above the ground. And they will discover also that they are naked. And because they have hidden themselves, they will not understand the beauty of their nakedness. They will try to hide it and they will be ashamed.

"This is true with all things of men. But the Power has given us the Gifts of the great Medicine Wheel and its Teachings. The Power has

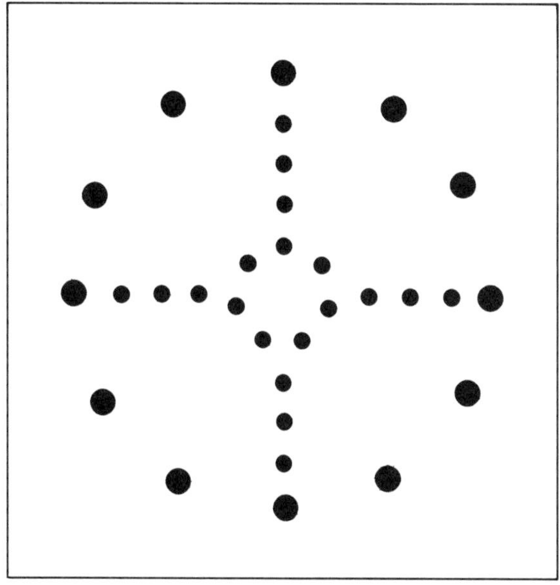

also given us the Four Directions. The most important of all these Gifts are the Shields.

"You, Red Star Woman, if within your being you have a love for people, then write this upon your Belt, the Shield of Women. It is one of your Gifts. Write the Signs of Truth in all things upon your Belt, and you will grow. Your sisters and brothers will see plainly your Name, and from their Shields you will also learn theirs. Your dreams and your fears should also be plainly written, because then you can receive Gifts from your brothers and sisters to help you become a Whole Woman. You will learn and they will learn.

"And you, Singing Rock, write who you are upon your Shield for men to see, and also for your sisters to know you. Men, little brother, for the most part mirror the women. If the women of the camp are without truth, the men of that camp mirror their unhappiness. Men are the striking arms of women. But, little brother, men are greater liars than women. Man is such a liar he even lies to himself.

"These reflections are the Forked Medicine Poles that make the Circle of the Great Lodge. One reflects and mirrors the other. The Medicine has made it this way that man might learn. Gather me some stones and I will teach you more."

Singing Rock and Red Star busied themselves picking up stones, while Hawk stripped down to his loin cloth and began to paint himself. After the two young people had gathered the stones, Hawk instructed them to place them in a pattern on the ground.

"What you see before you is a Sign of the Medicine Wheel," Hawk said. "It is the Sign of the Universe. One of the stones in this great

Wheel represents each of us. That one over there," Hawk said, pointing to one of the stones, "is you, Red Star, and that one over there is you, Singing Rock. You have been named for one of these Signs you see here. Your name is Singing Rock, and this means the stone in the Medicine Wheel that is within Harmony. This one over here is a Mouse. That one there is a Buffalo. This one here is all the Teachings of the Medicine Shields. All of these things are equal. And all of them are One. They are the great Medicine Wheel.

"In the middle of the Wheel you see Seven Stones, and they are right, they are in a Circle. These are the Seven Stars. They are also Seven Arrows. They are the Seven Natures of man and the Universe. Man is Mirrored within these Seven. Two of the Seven can be love and fear. The rest we must search out for ourselves because this is part of our learning. Seven Arrows always Reflects what we truly are.

"But the Medicine has given us more. There are also the Gifts of the Four Great Directions. These added to the other Seven become Eleven. The Gifts of the Medicine add to these of men that they might grow and learn. The Medicine makes Four times the Eleven and gives us the Forty-Four Great Shields of the Men of Peace, the Peace Chiefs. The Forty-Four Shields of the Ways of Peace are the Medicines that have been given to us by *Miaheyyun* so that we might all learn and grow. But, my children, these Gifts can only be understood by those who come from their Earth Lodges, and seek the Star Water. There are Four Ways that man will learn if he comes from his Earth Lodge. But remember that these Ways are multiplied for the Seeker, and are Reflections of men. They are the Seven again. And men must seek their fullness through these Ways.

"Wisdom is one Way of learning, but the nature of man's wisdom is to steal the Star Water. The second Way of learning is through innocence, but again it is man's nature of innocence to trick to obtain the Star Water. The third Way is looking-within, but men frustrate their own introspection and come for the Star Water by force. The fourth Way in the Story was walked by the People from the East who never returned. The fifth Way of learning is through the Mother Earth herself. She is also a Teacher of the Way to the Star Water. It was on her bosom that it first fell. And then there are the Stars and the Universe itself, where the Star Water came from, which can teach the Way to the Star Water. These are six. The seventh Way is through the Medicine itself. It is *Miaheyyun*. It is Truth. Men, many men, have found their Star Water through the understanding of these different Ways. But the last Way is the greatest. It is Truth. But it is also the hardest Way.

"The Elk in the Story is the Lightning Sign of the Sacred Mountains. There are many Ways to find the Elk of the Sacred Mountains. The great Medicine Lake, the Star Water, is also there.

"The Shields that men carry, and the Medicine Belts of the women, are called Mirrors or Hearts. These Mirrors are their Names and are the Morning Star. I am a Man of the Shield. It is my Medicine Gift to Teach in this Way, the Way of the Shields.

"If a man meets another man upon the great prairie, and he carries his Shield, then the Other Man may know him by his Signs, and be able to talk with him."

That evening Night Bear and Hawk visited the lodge of Little Wolf.

Tomorrow is the time for the Lone Dwelling Lodge, Night Bear signed as he sat down.

Tomorrow morning you can tell the camp crier to announce our needs. Those of the People who wish to give can counsel together. We will need twelve Forked Poles to form the outside circle of the Lodge, and twelve tall lodge pole pines from the mountains to reach from the others to the Center Pole. These are the hardest to get and the most people will be needed there. Others can bring the Forked Center Pole from by the river. It should be a cottonwood tree. Green chokecherry trees can then be cut by others on the day we will raise the Center Pole. These will be put around the Great Lodge to cool the Dancers.

I will do as you have instructed me, good father, Little Wolf signed his answer, and went on. *Have you and Hawk heard the talk today in the camp?*

No, Night Bear signed. *We have been busy with the Pledgers all day long. We have been talking of the Colors and the Painting.*

Part of what I have to tell you is good, and part of it is bad, Little Wolf signed. *First I will speak to you of what is beautiful. Green Willow Woman and Dancing Elk Woman, two of the most beautiful women of our camp, have asked to be the ones who will bring you the Gift of living with you. They know that both of you have been very lonely.*

Thank the People for us, Night Bear signed, *for we are grateful. We have indeed been very lonely.*

The other part of the news is bad, Little Wolf began. *We must move the camp immediately after the Sun Dance. Some of our young men have raided the whitemen for their goods. They have killed many of them. Witnesses among them said there were Brothers of the Shield with the whitemen, and they were killed, too. The raiders came to our camp late last night with their prizes, while you slept. These young men are from the camp of our brothers, the Medicine Hat People.*

"The Medicine Hat People?" Hawk asked out loud. Then, remembering Night Bear, he signed, *The People of the Medicine Hat were far to the east of us. How is it that some of them have come to our camp?*

These People of the Medicine Hat are no longer to the east of us, Little Wolf said with his signs. *The whiteman is in great numbers to the east, and they have driven the People of the Medicine Hat from those hunting grounds. This all has happened while you were living in the camps of the Little Black Crow. The ones who have visited with us have spoken of many strange things. They have told us that the whitemen have things that breathe fire and smoke and crawl up and down the rivers. The whitemen come riding these great things and kill our People and many of the buffalo.*

Crawl up rivers? Night Bear signed, *Zahuah, they must be terrible to see. But this is understandable to me after speaking with one of their talkers.*

There is more, White Wolf signed. *They have iron things that hold fire, and other things that they carry that burn in the night. And they have rolls-along-the-ground-on-hoops. Their horses pull these and the whitemen ride upon them. Some of the People have claimed they know already how to use these things, but I have never believed them. Here is a drawing one of the visitors made for me of the rolls-along-the-ground-on-hoops. See!* He held up a drawing made on deerskin.

The hoops look like Medicine Wheels, Hawk signed. *How very strange!*

Singing Rock lazily rode his pony, watching the prairie grass pass under its hooves. He and a few other young men had been given the responsibility of driving the herd of horses along with the moving camp. They had left the camp yelling and riding their ponies recklessly into the herd. The grazing animals, frightened by the charging young men, had exploded into a column of dust and swarmed across the prairie. But later this first burst of speed and excitement had died, and the day had become just a boring stroll for the herders.

Not Afraid Of Knowing turned his horse toward Singing Rock's, and pulled up his mount's head until it slowed to match the gait of the other pony. His horse threw its head around and danced as it came alongside, frightening Singing Rock's horse and bringing Singing Rock out of his reverie.

"You looked as if you were having a nice nap," Not Afraid Of Knowing laughed, "and I thought to myself, now why should my brother sleep so well, when I have to stay awake watching the herd? I will gamble you were dreaming about owning a new thunder iron, *Heyyaheh?*"

"That would not have been a bad dream at all," answered Singing Rock. "But in truth I was really thinking about the Medicine Man who Painted us in the Great Lodge. I was thinking of Night Bear."

"Night Bear?" Not Afraid Of Knowing's

voice squeaked. "By the Power! Why are you thinking about that stinking Little Black Eagle?"

"Stinking Little Black Eagle?" Singing Rock replied in surprise. "What sort of nettles have you been sleeping on? He is a Man of the Shield, a Peace Chief."

"Peace Chief! *Zahuah!* Starving Elk is a man of greater Power! He makes the Little Black Eagle look like a foolish child. You have seen the Shield of Walking Coyote, have you not?" Not Afraid Of Knowing laughed.

"Yes, I have," answered Singing Rock quickly. "He carries only a war Shield."

"Just a war Shield! It is not just a war Shield! It has been given special Powers!"

"But all the Shields have special Powers," Singing Rock replied angrily.

"The only special Powers of the Peace Shields I have seen is the one that says, 'Look, world, this is who I am.' But what is that? Can this stop the arrow point or protect against the thunder iron?" Not Afraid Of Knowing laughed.

"What in the tongue of the Thunder Bird are you talking about?" Singing Rock stormed.

"Little brother, you are a child." Not Afraid Of Knowing pinched his words. "If you did not hang around that Little Black Eagle so much you would learn something. There are warriors right here in our camp who have special Powers, written in special Signs upon their Shields. Crying Squirrel has one of these Shields, too. Starving Elk performed Medicine with him and gave him the special Power to dodge arrows. And it works! Many of the men will tell you so."

"There have always been one or two men who have carried the Shields of war," Singing Rock said, "and it is no secret that many of these men have had Powers that have spared their lives for them. What is so new about that? The People have always known of this. These men are to be pitied, not feared or envied, for this Power that they have."

"Say what you will and believe what you will then, Little Black Eagle lover, but I will choose this strong Power for myself, not the weak power of those dying Shields of Peace."

"Have you not listened to your Teachers?" asked Singing Rock. "The Shields are Gifts of the Medicine Elk, which is of the Golden Haired Woman."

"The truth," snapped Not Afraid of Knowing, "is that you have your head in dreams just as do those Teachers of yours. This is a world of striking first, before the things you have are taken from you. Many of the young men have talked about what we do now, and older men too. They say that in the days of the Shields, and of the Brotherhood of the Shields, the men were like women. They were afraid of their own shadows. The whiteman has taught us that this whole Way was a simple minded thing of old women."

"Whitemen! Whitemen!" Singing Rock snapped. "That is all anyone ever talks about now. What special Gifts do these whitemen have?"

Not Afraid Of Knowing doubled over on his horse with laughter. "The whitemen . . . the whitemen!" he yelled. "The whitemen have the whole world! And every Power in it, and everything else upon it!" He was still laughing as Singing Rock watched him ride ahead and down into a coulee out of sight.

Later the riders swung the long column of horses into a wide circle and brought them to a stop by a river for the night. Singing Rock wasted no time in removing the dust that had caked itself upon him, by jumping head first into the cool stream. He washed himself well

and drank his thirst away, then put on his fringed vest for the evening. He had torn a small hole in his leggings, which he was mending when Sees The Night Fire came up and sat down with him.

"Well, my brother," Singing Rock opened the conversation, "I see neither of us became lost during the day."

"I wished a couple of times during the hottest part of the day that I could have become lost," the man answered.

"What were you and Not Afraid Of Knowing talking about today? The Little Black Eagle?"

"Yes, we were. Why?"

"Because that is nearly all he ever speaks about. Not Afraid Of Knowing hates anyone who is not of his own tongue," Sees The Night Fire said.

Sees The Night Fire had been stricken with some illness when he was young, and it had left one of his legs partly crippled. He walked with a slight limp. But he was tall and powerful in every way, even with his limp. Because of his strong stature and bearing, he actually made his limp appear almost as something to be desired.

"I wish to talk to you about the Painting," Sees The Night Fire began again. "I do not quite understand it, and it is of importance to me that I do."

"What is it you want to know?"

"Everything."

"Night Bear, the man who Painted you, is of the People of the Four Stars. I asked him about this Sign on his Shield, and he told me about the Painting. I will tell you what he told me, and maybe you will be able to answer the question yourself," answered Singing Rock.

"He described a Shield to me that looked like this," Singing Rock said as he drew in the dirt.

Night Bear told me that this is One of the Shields of the Forty-Four," said Singing Rock. *"It is Called the Shield of the Four Stars. It is the most Colorful of all the Shields. The Four Stars are Separated here so Men can Learn from them. But these Four Stars are Actually only One.*

The Northern Star Upon the Shield is the Star of the Woman of the North. The Southern Star is the Sister of the Man of the South, the Gift Sister. The Eastern Star is the Golden Haired Elk Woman. And the Star of the West is the Black Haired Buffalo Woman. These are the Daughters of the Mother Earth, the Beautiful Young Girl in the Story of the Fallen Star Water.

Each Man, Woman, and Child Upon the Earth is a Living Fire of Power and Color. The Powers I Speak of here are Cold, Heat, Light, and Darkness. They are a Living, Spinning Fire, a Medicine Wheel. And these Colors from this Living Wheel of Fire can be Seen by all Men, and Each can Learn from them. It is very Simple to See the Colors of the Medicine. Any Man, Woman, or even a Child can See these Colors. But Before I Tell you how to See these Colors, Let us First Talk About them.

The Woman of the North Covers the Earth with her Colors of Winter. She Freezes Everything. This is the Coldness of Heart. The great Rivers are Frozen and Man cannot See the Water. The Woman of the North is very Beautiful. She Makes all the Colors Dance Within her Ice Crystals. She is Wisdom. But if Men Seek just the Wisdom of the North without also Seeking her Dancing Colors and her Forever Green, her Innocence, they may Visit her, but they will not Share Intercourse with her. These Men must Find the South Within the Sister of the North to Become Full.

The South is a time for the Water to Run Freely. The Whole World Becomes Green. It is the time of Innocence and Trust. This is the Time of the Give-Away. If Man Gives in Truth, Man then has Intercourse with the Woman of the South. These things are to be Found in Man.

If a Man Loves the Woman of the South, he is Loved by the Woman of the East. This Golden Haired Woman Loves her Sister of the South. What One Feels the Other Knows. The Golden Haired Woman is Eager to Know her Sister's Love of the South. It is a Mutual thing. For when Men have Intercourse with the Golden One of the East, the Sister of the South, too, Knows the Gift. The Colors of the East are Dancing Bright in their many Colors and Beauty. These things are to be Found in Man.

The Woman of the West is Sister to the Woman of the North. She Spreads her Colors and Unites them in her Evening Sky. When a Man has Intercourse with the Woman of the West, it is Shared with the Woman of the North. When Men have Intercourse with the Woman of the North, it is Felt by the Woman of the West. The Woman of the West Touches the Night. The Woman of the East Touches the Day. The Woman of the South Touches the things of Feeling and Heart. The Woman of the North Touches the things of Wisdom.

In the Time of the many Colors of the Earth, these all Come Together, and the Sisters Sit in a Common Lodge. And the Earth Dances with these Colors. It is a time when things are Equal, Hot and Cold, Light and Darkness. It is what Men must Strive for. They must Seek to Live Within this Lodge with these Four Women. This Lodge is the Great Painted Lodge. These Women, your Wives, will Feed you in this Lodge and they will Paint you and Teach you of the Painting.

Singing Rock paused and pointed again to the Shield he had drawn. "The Circle you see in the middle of the Shield is the Sign of the Spring, and also of the Painted Lodge of the Four Women.

"I told you that I would explain for you how to see the Colors. They are for anyone to see at any time. Take the water from a spring, any spring that comes from the earth. The water must be crystal clear. There are also some mountain lakes where this can be done. The face of the water must be calm, unmoving. Fast for three days and three nights. Then look into the water and you will see your Colors, or those of anyone else whose image you may also see there.

"There will be an aurora of Color around your body and head. Within all the Peoples of the earth these Colors are strong. You can see this within their faces. And these Colors are always changing, because they are the Seven Arrows.

"The Color of Red may be an angry Red, a Red of love, a Red of hate, or another completely different Red. But the Color that predominates in men and women is the Coloring of the Painting. The day my brother Hawk told me of the Fallen Star Water, he was Painted. One Half of him was Painted Red, and was striped with Black. The Other Half of him was Painted Yellow, and was spotted with Black. White spots were on his face and upon his chest and back.

"This is the Teaching. It is about the Blindness. When the People came from their Earth Lodges they were Blind to many of their Medicine Colors. If Half of a Man is Painted White, then he Perceives within Wisdom only Half of what he Sees. If there are Green Stripes or Spots upon him, then it is through the things of the Heart that he is Blind. He must strive to Understand these things to make him a Whole Man.

"If a Man is Painted all Black, and has Yellow Stripes across his Eyes, then it is of the things of the East that he is Blind. He must See Far to become a Whole Man. If a Mark of Yellow was drawn upon his Heart then he must be made Whole through the things of the East in his Heart.

"If a man is Painted Half Green and Half Black, then he is Half of these things. If there are Red Spots Painted upon the Half that is Green, then it is through the Spirit that he Sees Clearly in Innocence. If he is Spotted White on the Half that is Black, then his Blindness can be Overcome through the things of the North.

"Now, for the last thing. It is the Ice Hail Paint. This is the greatest of all the Paints. These Hail Marks that are Painted upon Men are the Dancing Colors of the North. The Hail Paint is of all the Colors and should be Striven for in Men.

"These things I have spoken of are all put upon the Great Mirror. The Colors upon this Shield are the Painting. These Ways upon our Shields are what we are, and are our Medicines. They are the Sun.

"Now, little brother, perhaps you have learned enough to tell me about the Painting of Hawk," Singing Rock asked.

"Yes, and you have helped me answer the question I asked," answered Sees The Night Fire. "I will ride with you again tomorrow and we will talk some more."

The next day the two young men rode together the rest of the way to the new camp.

It was a week later when Singing Rock and Sees The Night Fire were called to the lodge of Morning Star. When the two young men entered the lodge, they found Night Bear and Hawk sitting with Morning Star.

Morning Star spoke, "I have told my two brothers that you and your friend will be going soon with those of the People who will travel to trade their robes and furs with the whitemen. My brothers, Night Bear and Hawk, wish to go to the next camp of the People, which you will pass on your way. I have given them each two horses, but they tell me that they wish these to be Given-Away to the lodge of Blue Hair. So you two young men must go with them to bring back for Blue Hair the horses they will ride to the next camp."

The news was exciting, but the two boys tried hard not to show too much of their emotion.

Sees The Night Fire was the one of the two who finally spoke. He cleared his throat hard before he did. "We will bring back your Gifts, good fathers. We are honored."

"Just look at you," Night Bear chuckled to Hawk as they rode. "You look like a rich Medicine Song Bird raider sitting there with your new beaded vest and leggings. You do not look like the same poor Little Black Eagle who walked into camp a few months ago. And your stomach looks as if it had grown richer too."

"Me?" Hawk pretended to scowl. "You should see your own stomach. A spoiled, pampered Little Black Eagle! I saw your Gift Woman braiding your hair every day. *Zahuah!* I will bet you will not soon forget that camp."

"Where is this new camp we are going to now?" Night Bear asked, as he ducked under a cottonwood limb. They had been riding for about two weeks, and Night Bear had not yet asked about the new place to which they were going. It still seemed to be a small matter even now as he asked.

"I was wondering when you would ask me about that," Hawk called from the opposite side of the tree. "We are going to the camp of Blinds With The Arrows. He is of the People of the Throw Away Boy. This man, Shining Arrows, is also a Medicine Man. He is a dirty old Crow just like us. His People know him as White Clay. He married a Painted Arrow woman and has lived among the Throw Away Boy People ever since his marriage."

"You are as full of knowledge as Vihio," Night Bear grinned, as they approached a small stream. "Where did you learn all this?"

"The old man we are now going to see was Little Wolf's father's best friend. They were Brothers of the Shield. This man is Little Wolf's spiritual father, but Little Wolf has not seen the man since he was very young. In fact, he said he hardly remembers what he looks like. The woman the man married was Little Wolf's father's sister."

"Hoyeh! Hoyeh!" Night Bear called. "You certainly are a knowledgeable man. Are you sure that this man was not the father of the aunt whose cousin broke her leg when she married the uncle's. . . ."

"Zahuah!" Hawk howled. "Do you want me to break your arm?"

They were both laughing hard, when suddenly Hawk grabbed his arm, his face contorting with pain. The blood from an arrow wound began to spill down Hawk's arm just as a second arrow struck into a nearby tree, narrowly missing its target. Both men slumped low on their horses and kicked them into a run. As they rode Hawk heard the voice of a thunder iron crack, and he saw Singing Rock spin upon his horse and fall to the ground, limp. Then the whole scene turned into an insanity of dying brothers, dust, screaming, and milling horses and men. The ambush was over almost as quickly as it had begun.

Hawk was standing tied to a tree. During the attack Hawk had seen Night Bear's horse fall, and he had seen the horse trying to rise to its feet. His brother had still been mounted, but the dust and confusion had hidden whether or not he had escaped alive.

The man who had knocked Hawk senseless from his horse had tied him to a tree, and now stood in front of him. He was possibly a young

Comanche or Kiowa boy of about sixteen years. It was hard to tell because he was dressed partly in the clothes of the whiteman. He wore his hair in the Comanche way, but also wore a bandana headband that was of the Kiowa. The pain from the arrow still in his arm brought tears into Hawk's eyes, and he blinked both from this and from his confusion. He could not understand either the position he was in, or the strange young man in front of him.

Gradually more men came back to the place where Hawk was tied. They came by twos and threes. It was no surprise to Hawk to see that there were whitemen with them. The entire group of men that finally gathered around him looked like a mixed pack of angry animals. Hawk could tell by their unwashed appearance and their dirty clothes that they had been riding together for quite a while. Their gear was a confused mixture of the things of the whiteman and of many other Peoples. A bearded man separated himself from the group and approached Hawk. He looked at the man tied to the tree with the same distaste he might have shown if he had been forced to come close to a scabby dog.

"Haaannudfeiandaouttwhaaheissgoddamaamchhauaamppist," he bawled to another man, jerking his head toward Hawk. He walked a short distance from Hawk and sat down upon a stone large enough for comfort. He crossed one of his legs and draped his arms over it, and then looked straight into Hawk's eyes. Another man walked over to Hawk and stood in front of him straddle legged, studying him with his arms upon his hips.

"Hissaardtaaseaybuddiiudsssayheissagoddaumchrouuaorcheyeecchene," he said, still staring at Hawk.

"Tassheeirughsjtwjkhhe," the man on the rock answered. "You a People?" the man asked, addressing Hawk.

Hawk blinked some of the water from his eyes and answered, "Yes, I am one of the People. What is it you wish from me?"

The questioner turned to the man on the rock and said something to him. The man spoke a few words, and then the questioner turned his attention back to Hawk.

"More People yours near?" asked the man, as he spat something foully brown upon the ground.

"I believe you have killed all of the People who were with me," Hawk answered as he fought the pain that gnawed at his arm.

The questioner turned to the other man, again saying something. The man who sat on the rock bawled something and walked over to Hawk, slapping him hard across the face.

"Yeeagoddanmmaeingiefueackeindougyaoulltaulekereealse," the man roared, as he slapped Hawk again.

He then spoke in Hawk's tongue. "You heap shit foul dog, talk maybe," he said and made a sign of cutting Hawk's throat.

"What is it you wish to know?" Hawk answered as he spat the blood from his mouth.

"Where may be you shit foul people camped?" the other man asked.

"I have come from the camp of Little Wolf," answered Hawk. "His camp is three weeks of riding from this place."

Hawk turned to the group of his Plains People brothers who sat watching him. "Does anyone among you speak my tongue?" Hawk asked.

Hawk wished his hands were free so that he could sign his questions. No one said a word.

"Keehielatheaasaunouehabeietchaundletzegietaagoeain," the man bawled again, and swung up onto his horse. The others followed suit and climbed to the backs of their ponies. Then the man who was still standing in front of Hawk took his knife from his belt and thrust it deep into Hawk's belly. Hawk winced with the fire that tore into his body. Through his pain he dimly saw a small frog hop from the creek near where he was tied, and leap soundlessly toward his feet. It seemed to look up at him before the world turned into darkness.

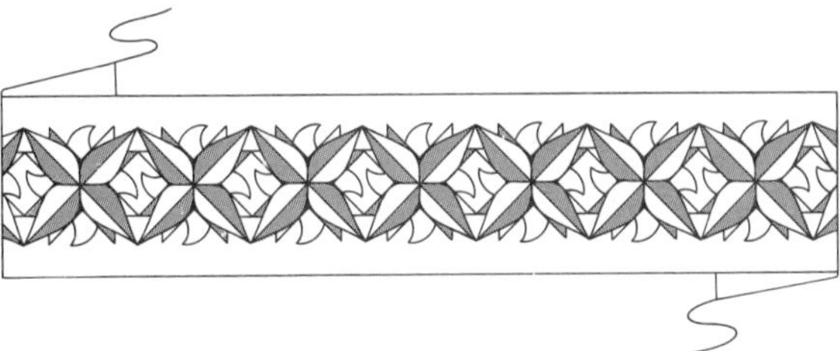

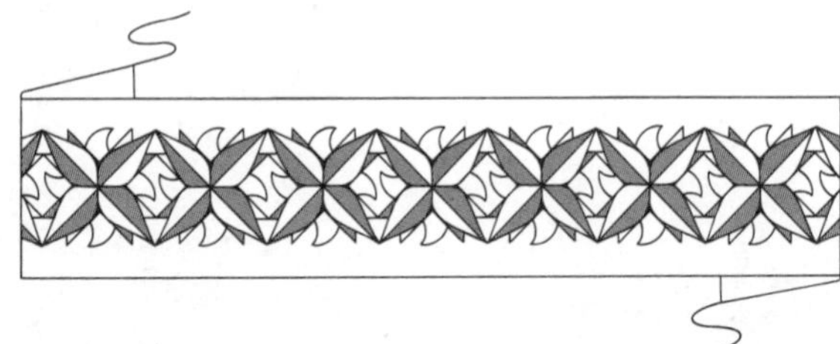

Night Bear's mare fell, pitching him partially under her. She lay on her stomach for a brief moment catching her breath, then clawed for her footing. Night Bear gripped the horse with all his might as she lunged to right herself. A white-hot pain seared his leg. Night Bear knew that it was broken.

Suddenly Tall Mountain appeared through the dust. He was walking his horse quietly as if he were going for an evening ride. Blood ran in small streams from Tall Mountain's mouth and from his stomach. He rode up to Night Bear, leaning forward and holding his stomach.

"Take this, good father," he said, pushing his thunder iron into Night Bear's hands. "I am too sick to use it. I think that. . ." He never finished his sentence.

Night Bear swung his horse down the creek and gave it its head. He rode hard until his horse was fighting for its breath, before finally letting it slow to a walk. Night Bear had seen, as he had ridden for his life, that their party had been badly outnumbered. Everyone that had been able to had scattered in every direction to escape the trap. Other than the thunder irons carried by Tall Mountain and Swift Eagle, there had been no weapons other than bows among them. These had been too little for defense against the raiders, most of whom seemed to have been equipped with the whiteman's irons.

Suddenly a rider came into view to Night

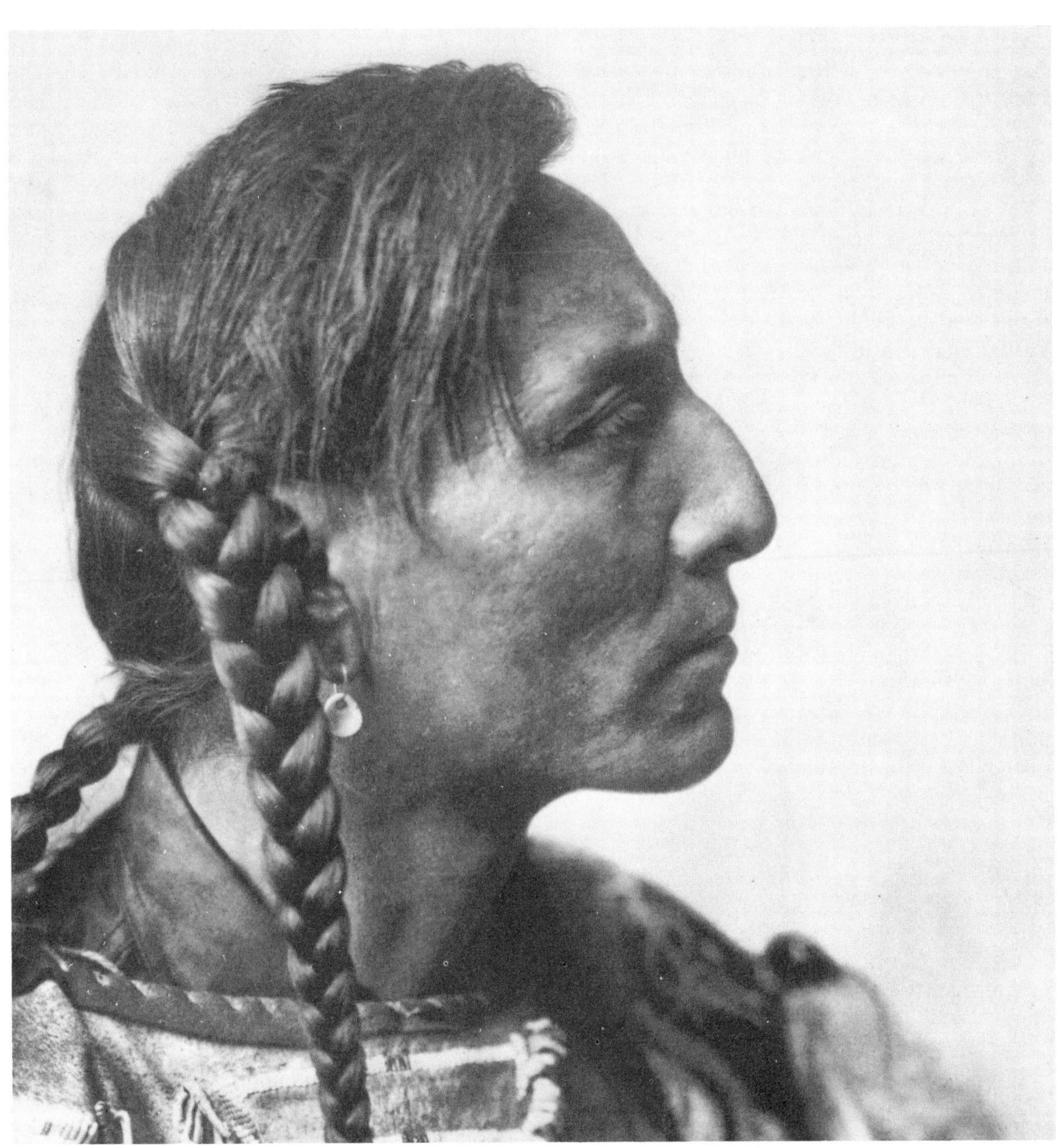

Bear's right. Night Bear started to kick his horse into another run, when he realized that the rider was Sees The Night Fire. He waited until the young man caught up with him, and then they rode together in silence for quite a while before either spoke.

They rode across an open meadow where the stream they had been following met with the prairie. The creek slowed here and began to meander. It was a perfect place to stop. Here they would be able to see approaching riders with enough warning to escape them. Night Bear turned his horse into the shade of some trees, and painfully dismounted. He took off his leggings and examined his leg. Sees The Night Fire also dismounted and tied both horses, leaving the reins within reach of where the two men sat.

"Your leg has a bad crack," said Sees The Night Fire as he examined Night Bear. "But it did not break completely."

Sees The Night Fire found an ash tree and made his companion a splint. Then they both settled down to wait for darkness.

As soon as the dusk had settled they mounted their ponies and made their way back to the place of the fighting. After traveling what they believed to be about half way to the place of the ambush, they tied their horses and continued on foot. Night Bear's damaged leg did not slow them, because their cautious pace would have been no faster even if he had been whole.

The moon was bright and full, making the return trip an easy one, but they knew that it would also illuminate their presence. They kept to the concealment of the brush and the trees by the river. They both knew that time was not important, because the possibility of their finding any of their brothers left alive was so remote.

It was not long before they reached the ambush spot and saw the truth of this. The sight that greeted them there was so ghastly Sees The Night Fire became ill and vomited. All of the dead had been stripped naked and scalped.

Night Bear hobbled to the tree where Hawk was still tied. Hawk was slumped over almost on his knees. His tied hands were the only thing that had held him from falling completely forward onto his face. Hawk's shield lay a few feet from him, partially in the creek. The blue Thunder Eagle on its face appeared to have a source of light within it, as it caught the reflection of the night's bright full moon. Night Bear picked up the Shield. The Shield seemed to pull the grief from deep inside him, releasing all of his pain. He stood, holding the Shield, and wept.

At sunrise the two men built scaffolds for the dead. Soon afterwards they headed west across the prairie, in search of the camp of White Clay.

White Clay turned out to be an older man than Night Bear had believed him to be. His camp was very small, consisting of only nine lodges. It was obviously a part of a larger camp circle that had been broken. It was hidden well, deep within a valley, and protected by a wall of pines. Even though the two men had known the camp was somewhere nearby, it had taken them a full eight days to find it. White Clay had retreated there in hiding with a small handful of his People, in the belief he could escape both the influence of the whitemen and of the rapidly changing Brotherhood.

The absence of old people in the camp was astonishing. There was no one within the camp over forty years of age, with the exception of Blinds With The Arrows. The greater part of the camp was made up of people who appeared to have reached less than eighteen winters.

The entire camp had turned out to welcome their two visitors, and when they had seen Hawk's Eagle Shield they had flooded Night Bear with invitations for the two men to live in their lodges with them. The joy and brotherhood of the camp was a welcome experience for Night Bear. At least two Shields hung in front of every lodge, and there were no war Shields among them. Night Bear began his stay in the lodge of Two Bulls Touching.

Two Bulls Touching was thirty-six years old and had two daughters, one fourteen, and the other fifteen. The wife of Two Bulls Touching was one of the most beautiful women Night Bear had ever seen. Her daughters, if it were possible, were even more beautiful. Night Bear's leg healed quickly, and it was not long before he was hunting with the other men. Winter was coming fast, and the whole camp was spending much of its time preparing for it.

There had been only one unusual happening in the whole camp in all the time they were getting ready. Sees The Night Fire's Horse had stepped into a prairie dog hole, and had fallen with him. As it turned out he had suffered only one small cut on his forehead, but nevertheless he had been doctored by almost every young maiden in the camp, including the two daughters of Two Bulls Touching.

One evening Pretty Weasel visited Night Bear. He was a man of about twenty-five years of age, and later he was to become Night Bear's closest friend.

Where are all of your grandmothers and fathers? Night Bear signed almost as soon as Pretty Weasel sat down. He had asked the same question of Two Bulls Touching, but they had been interrupted for a moment and Night Bear had noticed that the man had seemed to use the

break to avoid answering. *I have asked this same question of Two Bulls Touching, but he seemed unwilling to answer it.*

No, it is not that he is unwilling to answer that question, Pretty Weasel signed. *But it is painful for him. When the camps split, it was his father who made the most suffering for those of us who wished to leave. The father of Two Bulls was a man who had chosen the path of war, and this had become a constant sore between them.*

Yes, Night Bear signed his reply. *It is a frightening thing that is happening to the Brotherhood. I have been in camps where I have not been greeted as a brother simply because I spoke the tongue of the Little Black Bird.*

In the camp from which we broke away, signed Pretty Weasel, *there were three different tongues spoken. In this camp here there are also three tongues spoken. Yours now makes the fourth.*

Have you seen many of the whitemen? Pretty Weasel asked.

Enough, signed Night Bear. *What does this have to do with the tongues?*

Pretty Weasel laughed. It was a good laugh. *It is a complicated thing, my brother, but the tongues have much to do with it. Evidently you have been living in camps of the people that have had very little to do with the whitemen.*

That is true, Night Bear signed, *and I thank the Power for it.*

The whiteman has lived off and on within our camps for as long as I can remember, Pretty Weasel began. *I will tell you the story from the beginning. It began with the whitemen who wanted many beaver. Many of these men spent their entire lives trapping the beaver.*

Only the beaver? Night Bear asked.

I know this sounds very strange, but you must be

patient. These things and more will be clear to you when I am done, answered Pretty Weasel.

Night Bear settled himself for the explanation, one which he knew would be long. "What a very strange people are these whitemen," thought Night Bear as Pretty Weasel began his story again.

My father told me the trapping beaver men began to come to our village even when he was a little boy. Some of them lived among the People. Many of them married women of the People, and later even learned the tongues.

More and more of them came, some for the beaver and others only for talk. The talkers among them spoke of the Medicine Power that was called Geessis. This Geessis was a Power among them, a chief whom they later killed. He was not surprised that they killed him. After they killed him these men decided he was a Power, and they began to like him. He came back as a ghost and even now he walks among them invisible.

Night Bear could feel the hair rise on the nape of his neck.

This Geessis, Pretty Weasel went on, *is the greatest killer of them all. He kills all of their enemies. And he rewards those who follow his path with many things. Believe me, my brother, it is a very confusing thing, this Geessis.*

"I will never disagree with that!" thought Night Bear.

These talkers of the Geessis say that it is bad to do many things. And, believe it or not, killing is one of them. But, as clearly as I can understand it, this only means not to kill those who follow the warpath of Geessis. All others are to be feared and killed.

"By the Power!" Night Bear said out loud in his own tongue.

These talkers have convinced many of the People to take their path of war. They tell the People that the Shields are bad, and that the Way of the Sun Dance is bad. Their Power will burn to death anyone who keeps the Ways of the Brotherhood and the Sun Dance Way. These talkers were responsible for the split in our camp. Some whole camps of the Brotherhood abandoned the Ways of the Shields and joined this new Way of Geessis. Their Way became a simple Way. If you did not speak their tongue, you were their enemy. But many of the People also held hard to the Ways of the Shield, and soon they too became enemies. Everyone began to fear everyone else. No one knew when they might be attacked and killed, or who might do the killing.

Then one day White Clay came to our village. His camp had been attacked by people who had spoken his own tongue, and who had carried the Shields of Peace. No one had suspected them. White Clay's camp had been trading the beaver the whitemen like so much for many things, and they had become rich from this. These warriors came wearing a coyote's robe of peace. But in truth, they came to kill them and to steal their wealth. After the massacre only six of fifty were left alive from the camp of White Clay. He spoke of this in our council, and begged our people to give up this new Way of the Geessis warpath and to become strong again in the old Way.

There was great confusion in our camp for many days. Things became worse and worse with each day, until finally the people began to fight among themselves, and two of our brothers were killed. White Clay again called for a council. But it ended in disorder and yelling. A few of us went to him and told him we wished to keep to the Ways of the Shields, and that we would follow him away. He became angry with us and told us this was not right. "This is no way to have Brotherhood," he said.

He told us to join with others who believed as we did, and to help bring the camp together again. But many would not have it this way. The camp was broken up and many decided to go to one village or another. The people went nine separate ways, and soon there were only a very few left in camp. But things were better for only a week. Then Two Bulls Touching's father became enraged with him, and beat him. Two Bulls Touching never moved for three days, and everyone believed he would die. But he lived, and when he could travel again he brought us here with him. White Clay followed our camp.

"Zahuah!" Night Bear said aloud, then signed, *How will it all end?*

No one knows, Pretty Weasel signed his answer. *The whiteman kills everyone without compassion, and the Brotherhood now does the same. Also, they each kill the other. Only the strongest will survive!*

Let us go and seek out White Clay, Night Bear signed. *Would you mind if he, too, became a part of our talk? I have never yet had a chance to sit with him.*

That would be good, answered Pretty Weasel. *The old one craves company.*

When the two men were half way across the circle of lodges, Two Bulls Touching caught up with them. *Would another brother be welcome?* he asked in signs.

Yes, Pretty Weasel answered. *Between the two of us perhaps we can each twist one of Night Bear's arms and get him to tell us a Story.*

The two men playfully began pushing Night Bear, and as they entered White Clay's lodge all three of them were laughing.

I have been expecting you for quite a while, White Clay signed to Night Bear. *But I knew I would have to be patient because you are as young as the rest, and it is right that the things of the young are done first.*

I have been told that you possess great Medicine for healing, Night Bear signed.

The old man clapped his hands together and laughed. *Do you and your brothers here wish to learn of one of my Medicines? It is probably my greatest.*

"Yes, Yes, Yes," each man there said aloud in his own tongue, and also signed.

Then here it is, Shining Arrows began. *We will Talk about a People, for example, who Number One Hundred. My greatest Medicine is One of the Mind, and Body, and Heart. If you have One Hundred People who Live Together, and if Each One Cares for the Rest, there is One Mind. The Power of this One Single Mind is a Great One, and is a means of Keeping Sickness from Among them. If there are but One or Two Among them who Hate, there is little Threat to Any of the Hundred. But if Ten of that Hundred do not Care for the Rest of their Brothers and Sisters, then there is a Threat.*

The Threat is One of Sickness. I Know what you are all Thinking; that you have Heard of those who are able to make Others Sick, but this is not what I Mean. Nor do I Believe this is Possible. I do not Say that there has never been One who had the Power to Direct his Hate, Causing Illness to Another. This may sometimes have Happened, but I Think the Possibility of it is Remote.

The Truth of the Matter is this. The Hate these Ten People have Among the Hundred will Strike Out and Cause Sickness. We are Each a Living Spinning Medicine Wheel, and Each of us Possesses this Power to Destroy or to Create. When Ten of the Hundred do not Care, it Makes our Shield that much less Capable of Stopping Sickness. This Sickness Strikes out at Random, and can Hurt Anyone.

I am Sure you have Seen a little Child or a Person who is Gentle, Stricken with Sickness and sometimes Crippled by it. This Happens more because of the People not Caring than because of the Haters. If Twenty of the Hundred instead of Ten do not Care for the Rest of their Brothers and Sisters, there is Twice the Chance of the Sickness Affecting Someone.

Maheo! Two Bulls Touching signed. *You mean that not caring about our brothers is one of the causes of sickness?*

Exactly! answered the old man. *Not caring for one another has always caused sickness among a People. It is one of the means of the Medicine to teach man to care for his brothers. Caring is the only way to end sickness completely. Of course, it does not really make all sickness disappear. No! There are things in all men that may cause sickness. And they are endless in their naming. Even if all the hundred care, there are still the accidents of the great prairie. But these are not the same as sickness.*

You used an example of a hundred, Pretty Weasel signed. *Is the Power greater if there are more people?*

If there are ten, a hundred, a thousand, or just one, it is the same, White Clay signed. *It is not numbers, it is completeness. I am an old man, and I have seen clearly what happens when a People are not one. Before the whiteman began to destroy the unity of the camps, there was very little sickness. I had never seen a child born bad or dead. I never knew a man who was crippled by disease. Crippled men, yes! But they were crippled by carelessness upon the great prairie. This other is a carelessness much more deadly. It is the torn lodge, open to endless diseases. There are as many diseases as there are grasses upon the prairie, because there are many things of men.*

Do you mean to tell me that if all the People of

the world cared, there would not be one single person ill? Night Bear signed.

No, signed the old man. *I do not. There will always be minor sicknesses, because illness exists. But it would be so very weak a sickness by comparison that one would hardly notice.*

What if two camps of the People were to live close to each other, signed Pretty Weasel, *and in one of the camps there were those who were uncaring, and in the other camp all of them cared? Would one still affect the other, or does distance keep this from happening?*

Remember what I said to you? White Clay signed. *Sickness Exists in Random Places. Sickness has no Mind, and it cannot Seek Out Victims. One Camp, Ten Camps, or a Hundred Camps can never Stand Alone. Each Camp Affects Every Other Camp no matter what the Distance Between them. It is like the Teaching I have Heard concerning the Singing Stone. Both the Stone of Harmony and the Stone of Uncaring can be the Drums that Set the Rings of Water Into Motion Within the Dance of the Medicine Lake. One Ring Touches the Next until All is Within the Dance of the Medicine Lake. And it is the Last Leaf, the Tiniest Leaf, that is Set into Movement at the Edge of the Lake. This Leaf could be the Leaf that will Affect Everyone. If the People Care for One Another, then the Rings of this Dance are Harmonious.*

Then the answer is the same, signed Night Bear. *A People must care for their brothers and sisters to keep this from happening.*

Exactly! the old man answered. *This Teaching is the greatest of all my Medicines.*

What is your second greatest Medicine? signed Pretty Weasel. *Would you tell us of this one, too?*

My second Medicine is the Way of the Shields, White Clay signed. *This great Medicine is the healer of all men.*

But, Night Bear signed, *You also have Medicine herbs you give the People in times of illness.*

Yes, my son, I have, White Clay signed. *This is a great Gift of the Great Spirit. But it is small beside the other two.*

One week later, Night Bear was asked to tell a Teaching. Everyone in the camp was there to listen. A large fire was built in the center of the lodge circle, and everyone gathered around it. Pemmican, boiled meat, and dry meat were brought from each lodge and shared by everybody.

There are children among us, Night Bear signed, *and the Story I will tell first is for them. A mother, sister, father, or brother should watch my signs and put them into words for the little ones. The music of your own tongues is better for children than these soundless Thunder Bird Signs.*

Night Bear began with a very short Story of White Rabbit. Each time he finished signing, the circle quietly hummed in many tongues as the meaning of his signs was explained to the children. Soon he had finished.

Before I begin my second Story, Night Bear signed to the circle of people, *is there a Teaching anyone here wishes to discuss?*

Yes, signed Mouse Bear. *The talkers of the black robe have told our People that all men are bad. Even from the birth given us by our mothers we are bad, they said. Could you speak to us of this?*

Night Bear sat for a long time looking into the fire before he answered. *I have a Story that will untwist this knot. It is a Story I wish those talkers could hear, because this question has them tied to the ground. I will tell you two Stories. The first one concerns the talkers. It is a very short story, but one that is important.*

Night Bear began to sign: *There were Once Two Old Men who Lived Among the People. Both of these Men Possessed Great Gifts. One of the Old Men could Close his Eyes and he could See the Past. He had the Power to See the things of the Past and he could Build from them. The Other of these Old Men could Close his Eyes and he could See things of the Future. He was able to Build things from the Future. These Men Lived Among the People with these great Gifts. The People soon Gave these Men a Special Place and Cared for them. The Two Old Men, who Liked to Keep their Eyes Closed, Realized they would Get Special Care when their Eyes were Closed. And it was not Long before they were Keeping their Eyes Closed for Longer and Longer Periods of Time. This Went on for a very long Time until One Day the Two Old Men Realized that their Eyes were Stuck Closed. They could not Open them. They were Blind, and no matter what they Tried, they could not Open their Eyes.*

"What will we Do with them?" asked the People.

"That is Easy," answered the Two Old Men. "You must Care for our every Need."

There was a Little Boy in this Camp, and his Name was Mahko, which means Little Boy-Grandfather. He Told the People, "It will be Better if you Let the Two Old Men Learn. Let them Learn to Care for themselves and in this Way they will Learn."

The People Counseled with the Two Old Blind Men, and Told them that it would be Better if they Learned to Care for themselves. The Two Old Men Became very Angry.

"If this is the Way you are Going to Treat us, then Leave us by Ourselves," they said.

The People were Perplexed. "Why?" asked the People.

The One who could Look Into the Past Spoke First. "Because if something should Happen to the Camp it would be Better if we were Separate from the Camp and we would not be Killed. We are Blind and we do not Know which Way to Run."

The People then Heard from the Second Man. And this Man who could See the Future said, "And yes! Possibly if something from the Future should Happen to us, we would be Killed. It is Better we Live Separate from the Camp. We are Blind and do not Know which Way to Run."

The People Counseled Together and Decided to Do as the Old Men Said. They would Give the Old Men everything they Needed and would Hide them Carefully in the Trees Along the River. And if anything did Happen to the Camp, they could Run quickly and Help them.

The People Offered a Way to Set Up the Camp for the Two Old Blind Men, but they Became Angry and Told them how they Wanted it Done. "Take some Sinew and Stretch it from our Lodge Down to the River. Pound a Stake Into the Riverbed and Tie the Sinew to it. Then we will always Know where the River is."

So the People Did as the Old Men Asked, and the Two Blind Men Lived in their Special Lodge. They Cared for Themselves, and each Took Turns Cooking, or Getting the Water. One would Go for the Water at the River, and the Other would Prepare the Buffalo Meat that had been Given by the People in Exchange for Telling them of the things they could See either in the Future or in the Past. Each time One of the Old Men would Go for Water he would Follow the Sinew Down to the River and Back again to their Lodge. When the Water was Brought Back, they would Boil the Meat and Eat it Out of a Common Bowl. And they were very Content with themselves. It was much Better this Way, they Both Agreed. There were no Noisy Children, or Other things of the Common Camp Circle to Bother them.

"We are very Self-Sufficient," they said to Each Other.

Things were Going Along very Smoothly, until One Day a Raccoon was Walking Along the River and Spied the Sinew Tied to the Stake in the River. "What is this Strange thing Tied here in the River?" Raccoon Asked himself. He Examined it very Closely. He Followed Up the Sinew to See where it would Go. He Discovered that it Led to a Lodge, and he Looked In and Saw the Two Old Blind Men. Both of the Old Men were Lying quite Cozily, their Feet Near their Fire, the Coals of their Fire Keeping them Warm. "How very Strange," Thought Raccoon. "I Wonder what will Happen if I Move the Sinew while they Sleep?"

So Brother Raccoon Untied the String from the Riverbed. Then he Retied it to an Old, very Dry Tree that was almost Dead. It was a Forked Tree. And all that was Around the Tree was very Hard, Dry, Packed Earth. He Ran Back to See what would Happen.

The Two Old Men Woke Up and One said to the Other, "It is your Turn to Get the Water."

"Yes," said the Other, "I Believe it is my Turn," and he Yawned and Stretched. So he Grabbed the Old Buffalo Skin Bucket and Followed the Sinew. He Got to the End of the Sinew and Dipped his Bucket Down and Found only the Hard, Packed, Dry Dirt. He Followed the Sinew quickly Back to the Lodge and Exclaimed, "Brother, there is no more Water! While we Slept the River Dried Up!"

"Impossible!" said the Other. "It could not Possibly have Dried Up as we Slept. Here, Give me the Bucket and I will Go get the Water."

At this point in the story, Night Bear was laughing so hard with the rest of the People that he had to stop signing until he regained his composure.

Finally, Night Bear was able to continue. *But in the meantime, Raccoon had Untied the*

Sinew and Retied it Back to the Stake in the Water. The Other Old Man Hurried Along the String and Quickly Came to its End, where he Dipped his Bucket and Filled it with Water.

Both Men Grumbled to themselves as they Busied themselves Preparing the Meat. Raccoon Sat Among them but they could not See him. Each time the Old Men Prepared the Buffalo, they would Cook Four Pieces of Meat, Two for One, and Two for the Other. And when the Meat had Finished Boiling, One Took One Piece of Meat, One Another, but Brother Raccoon Took One Piece of Meat, Washing it Carefully before he Ate it. After a while One of the Blind Men Reached Into the Pot to Get his Second Piece of Meat and Found only One Piece Left.

"You must be very Hungry, my Brother," said the Blind Man. "You Ate Quickly. There is only One Piece of Meat Left."

"Hah!" said the Other. "It is you who Ate Quickly, because I have Had only One Piece of Meat!"

Raccoon Reached Over and Touched One of the Blind Men very Gently Upon his Face. The Man Flinched because he Thought he had been Struck by the Other Man. He Struck Out Blindly at his Brother and they Rolled and Fought each Other. But One of them Remembered the Fire and Called, "The Fire! The Fire!" and so they Stopped their Fighting before they Rolled into their Lodge Fire.

Raccoon in the meantime Grabbed the Last Piece of Meat and Ate it. Then Raccoon Laughed and Laughed Out Loud. The Two Old Blind Men Listened.

"Greetings, my Brothers!" Raccoon said.

"Sweet Medicine!" One Blind Man said to the Other. "This is no Good at All. Because these Raccoons are Endless and we will never have Peace. What shall we Do?"

"Follow your Own Sinew Down to the River," said Raccoon, "and I will Give you the Answer."

The Two Blind Men Followed the Sinew Down to the River's Edge and they Stood there Waiting for further Instructions.

"Listen to the Water," Raccoon said. "It will Give you your Answer."

But While they Both Listened, Raccoon Sneaked Up Behind them and Pushed them Into the River—and their Eyes were Opened.

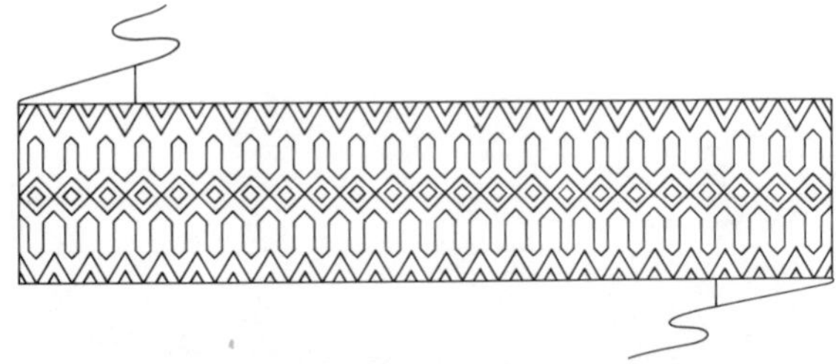

The wind whipped the rain into cold steam, obscuring the closest hills. It was almost evening, and Night Bear sat huddled with Green Fire Mouse in their shelter near a struggling fire they had made. The two men had volunteered to take pelts to the camp of Braided Hair Cane, to exchange them for salt. The entire journey to and from the camp they were now heading towards would take them a full six weeks. It was late fall, and the cold rain would soon turn to snow. They had five horses with them. One was a gift to Braided Hair Cane, two were pack horses, and the other two were riding ponies.

Green Fire Mouse was a tall, hawk-faced young man of about eighteen years. His black piercing eyes made him look like a young falcon.

We will have to take a different path, Green Fire Mouse signed without looking up. *There will be snow soon, and this path will be too difficult for the horses.*

Night Bear was busy trying to loosen the buckskin strings on his moccasins. The leather was wet and rubbery from the rain and needed to be hung for drying. His thoughts and hands were both struggling with the limp strings that resisted untying, making it impossible for him to answer. Green Fire Mouse took his knife from its sheath and handed it to Night Bear. But Night Bear ignored the knife, thinking it was offered for him to cut the already too short ties. He continued doggedly trying to unsnarl the strings.

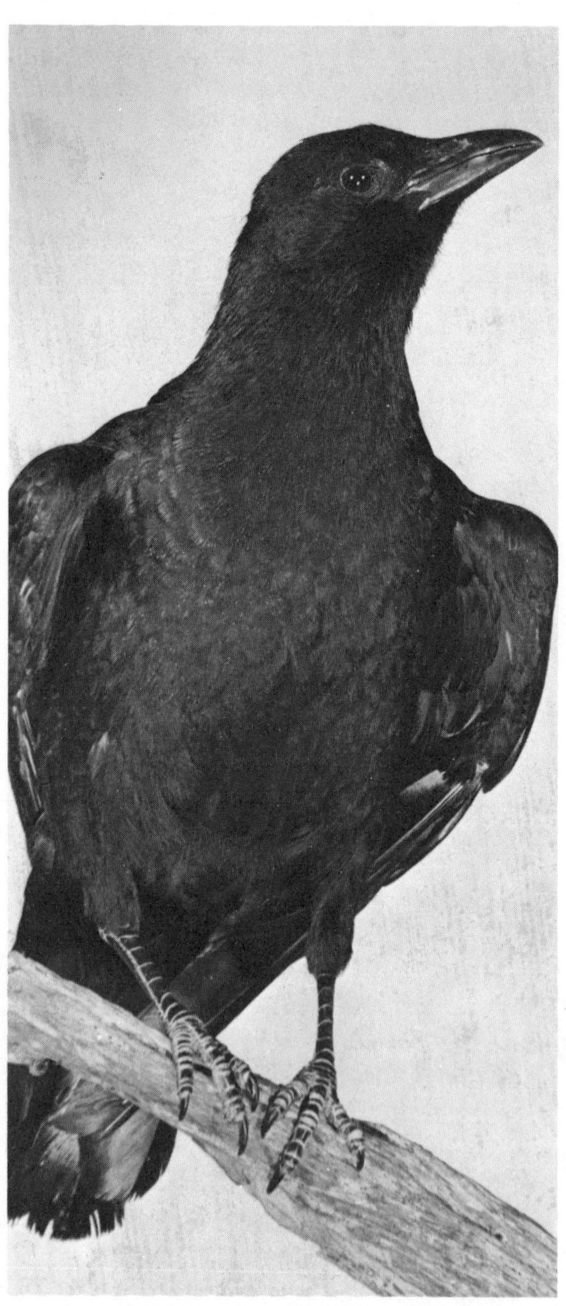

"Horns gut you!" roared Night Bear in his own tongue, his face livid with sudden rage.

"All you have to do is hook the end of the knife in the knot and it will come loose," Green Fire Mouse said smoothly in Night Bear's own tongue.

"How is it that you speak my tongue?" Night Bear asked in surprise. "Before this your talking to me has always been in signs."

"I assumed you were of the Painted Arrow People," answered Green Fire Mouse, "because until now I had never heard you speak in any other tongue."

"I am afraid that I know very little of the Painted Arrow tongue. I only recently visited their camps," answered Night Bear as he took the wet knot apart with his own knife. "Are you then of the Little Black Bird?"

"No, I am not," said Green Fire Mouse as he too removed his wet moccasins. "I am one of the River People. I have heard that your People are our cousins, but you are the first one I have ever met. We have given your People the name of the Mountains. How is it you call yourselves the People of the Little Black Bird?"

"There was once a man who lived among us who had the beginning name of Black Eagle. He was a great man. There was a trouble among the People at one time, and although no one remembers why the split occurred, there was war between them. Finally the man, Black Eagle, after a very long war, healed the two Peoples and brought them together again. His new Name from this was Medicine Crow, or Looks-Within Law."

"What do you suppose the trouble that broke their circle might have been? Have you any knowledge of it?" asked Green Fire Mouse.

"I spoke of this once with my father, a Chief named Hawk. He was one of the Painted Arrow

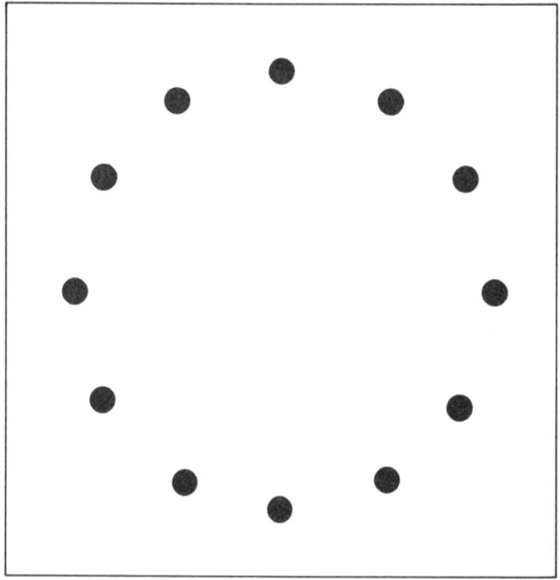

People, I think. He said he had known of the split, and in answer to my question he told me a Story. It was one he asked me to memorize. I can tell you of this Teaching if you wish, and my answer will then be your answer."

"Yes, I would very much like to hear this Teaching," Green Fire Mouse answered.

"The Story is called Bull Looks Back," Night Bear began.

The People used to Wander About the Prairie in those Days. The People were not yet One Song Together. Their Lodges were not One in the Great Medicine Circle. They were Hungry because of this, and Wandered About the great Prairie Seeking the Gifts, the Buffalo.

There was One Old Man Among them who Took his Wife and Family Away from the Main Circle of People to have his own Camp Circle, Alone.

Picking up a number of small stones, Night Bear placed them before him on the ground in the shape of a circle.

"Do you see this simple Medicine Wheel of tiny stones I have placed Here?" Night Bear asked. "The Circle was one of the first of the great Gifts, but as time went by the Circle became not One Harmonious Song, but broken pieces of a Blind Circle. This Reflection is a difficult thing for men to Perceive. As you already know by the name of the Story, the Name of the man who moved away from the Circle was Bull Looks Back. As you will see as the story unfolds, Bull Looks Back is the Old Gift. He is in actuality the Circle, but he is the Circle Looking Back upon itself. This is a Circle that only maintains itself and does not Grow. The Wife of Bull Looks Back represents the Marriage of the People with this first Gift, the Circle."

"That is more complicated than the Club of Winterman!" broke in Green Fire Mouse. "It makes my head spin like the Wheel that you speak of."

Night Bear laughed, "Do not try to understand it all at once, my brother. The Club of Wisdom can appear as a monster, like the striking arm of Winterman, only when we complicate that which is simple. Have patience, because the Story will unfold easily and you will understand."

"If Bull Looks Back is the Circle and his Wife is the Marriage with the People, then who are his Children?" asked Green Fire Mouse.

Night Bear laughed again. "There was the Marriage of the Circle with the People. The intercourse of these two things gave birth to two philosophies, or Ways. These are the Daughter and the small Son. The Children are the most important Signs of this Teaching. The Story is really about them."

Night Bear began his Story again.

He Remained Out with his Wife,
Daughter, and small Son for a very long time.
Then One Day Bull Looks Back Killed his Wife
and Deserted his Children.

"You see, Green Fire Mouse," explained Night Bear, "the Wheel had become a Fixed Wheel. It had become a traditional thing, and this is always the killing of the Marriage with the People. The Fixed Wheel of Tradition only maintains itself. It looks back upon itself, like Bull Looks Back. When this happens there are no new Gifts, and the People are Hungry. But remember, little brother, the Wheel is Bull Looks Back, and it is also the People. This Wheel looking back upon itself is a Blind Wheel of endless tradition, and it is always destined to destroy itself."

Night Bear went on.

The Orphaned Children Wandered About the Prairie Seeking the Comfort and Shelter of the Lodges of the People.

"This part of the Story should be clear enough," said Night Bear.

The Children Found the Lodges of the People and Went to them. The First Lodge they Came to was the Lodge of an Old Woman.

"The Old Woman is always the Sign of the Traditions of the Camps of the People," Night Bear explained again. "As you will see, these new concepts, the Children, face Tradition, seeking shelter and understanding within it."

The Children Asked about their Father, but the Old Woman would not Answer. Instead she Went to the Camp Crier, and Told him that the Children of Bull Looks Back were Asking about their Father. This Old Man Went Out and Spread the News to the entire Camp. Bull Looks Back was there Among the People, and he Came Running to the Crier Accusing, saying, "These Monstrous Children are Bad for the People. They have Killed their Mother and have Eaten her Flesh. That is why I have Orphaned them. Tell the People that even though they are my own Children, they should be Staked to the Ground and Abandoned."

Night Bear explained, "The Circle that maintains itself is an accuser, and it fears its own Children. Bull Looks Back does not ask the People to kill his Children outright, but still what he proposes means certain death to these new Gifts. Whenever any People stake these things down, fix them to the ground, they will starve them to death."

Green Fire Mouse shifted uneasily and stirred the fire. Night Bear, noticing his young companion's nervousness, got to his feet and went for more wood. He knew Green Fire Mouse needed a few minutes to settle whatever it was that he had in his mind, and the getting of wood was a good excuse for giving him the time he needed.

Night Bear returned with the wood, laying the dripping bundle down to the right of the place where he was sitting. Green Fire Mouse took two of the sticks of wood, and placed them on the fire. The wet wood steamed and hissed, but these were the only sounds in the night. Green Fire Mouse said nothing. Night Bear settled himself, cleared his throat and began again.

The Camp Crier Repeated all that Bull Looks Back had Said, Calling to the People that they must Tie the Children to the Ground and Move as Quickly as they Could. Because of what Bull Looks Back had Told them, they were not to Leave One Living Creature Behind with them, not even a Dog.

That Night the People Prepared Green Rawhide Thongs, and the Next Morning they Tied the Boy and the Girl to Sharp Stakes Driven Into the Dry Ground.

Night Bear explained, "Night is a time of rest, but it can also be a time of fear. In times such as these, it is a time when men do not see very far. Some of the things used for the tying are beautiful. The Color of the wet rawhide is Green, the Color of Innocence. It is mixed with Water, the Spirit of Life. But what the People intend will cause these things to Shrink and become Dry without Water, and they will turn Grey. It is the bright Illumination of the Sun, the Truth, that will cause these things to lose their Water and Color."

Night Bear began again.

The People Waited and Watched their Work until the Thongs had Dried and Tightened, and then they Moved their Camp Away.

"Why did the People do the bidding of Bull Looks Back?" asked Green Fire Mouse.

"Why did the People fix the Children to the

Earth?" asked Night Bear. "Because they were a fixed thing themselves. The Children were young and alive and growing, while the People were dying.

There had been in the Camp One great Black Dog. It had had Puppies, and it had Packed Buffalo Meat and Sinew for them in a Hole Near the Campsite. That Evening the Children Saw the Dog Come to them. The Dog had Seen them in the Camp and had not Wanted them to Die. The Dog Looked at the Children with the Eyes of a Dog, and then Began to Chew the Dry Rawhide Thongs until the Girl was Free.

"I know what the Black Dog is!" Green Fire Mouse said suddenly. "Those people meant by the Black Dog are the Dog Soldier people."

"They are truly the same," answered Night Bear. "These faithful creatures are vital to every camp of People, and the Buffalo Meat Sign is that of the Gifts that have already been given to the People. The Food of these things, combined with their Power to Build, which is represented by the Sinew, will help the Children to Live and to Grow.

The Girl then Untied her Brother. The Children Followed the Dog to the Dry Creek Bank where it had Dug its Hole, and her Puppies Brought Out the Meat and Sinew for the Children. These were their Gifts to Help them to Live. The Children Ate and Refreshed themselves. Water was Found for them in the Old Creek Bed by the Puppies.

That Night a Stranger Visited the Children, but the Girl would not Look Up at him. Even though the Stranger Spoke to the Girl First, she would not Look at him. Her Sorrow Kept her from Raising her Head to See. The Powerful Stranger then Spoke to the little Boy and the Boy Looked at him Immediately.

Night Bear explained, "The weakest Gift, and the prettiest to men, was freed of her bonds

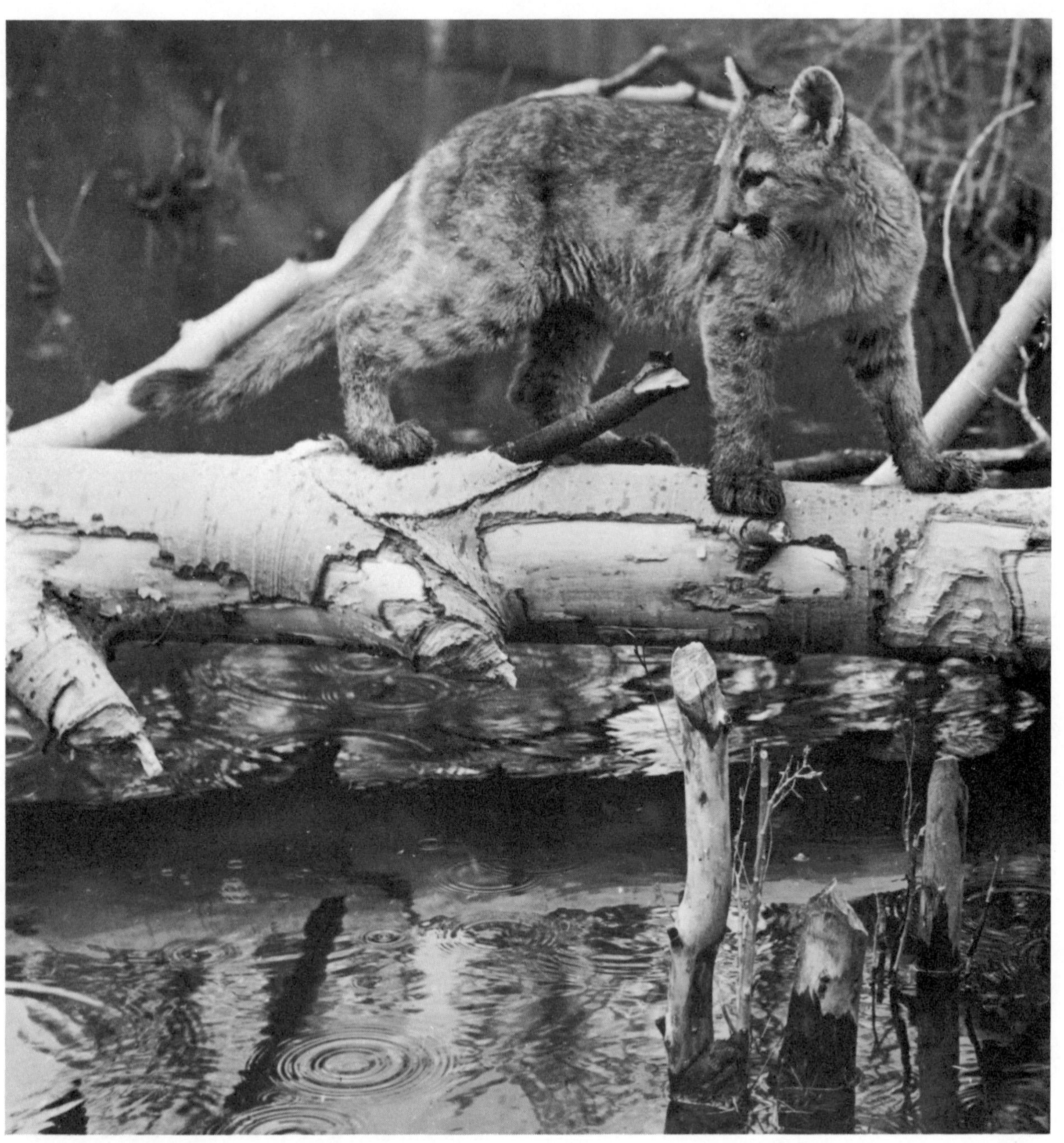

first. She then untied her Brother. But it was the little Boy who saw clearly the Medicine Stranger."

"Over there," said the Stranger to the little Boy, "You will See a Sweat Lodge and an Arbor. Go to them!"

"My Sister!" the little Boy said to her in Excitement. Finally she Raised her Head and Saw. She Saw that the Gifts were Good.

The Stranger then Spoke again. "Over there," said the Medicine Stranger, "is a great Herd of Buffalo. Look Upon them and they will be Food for the People."

"What is the meaning here of the words 'saw' and 'look'?" Green Fire Mouse broke in. "Are they the Perceiving?"

"Yes," Night Bear answered. "Whenever you hear the words, 'see,' 'look,' or 'saw,' or whenever the words even mention the eyes, this means the Perceiving."

"Then the little Girl, this new Concept, at first refused to Perceive the Gifts that were given them. Is this correct?"

"Yes, my son," Night Bear smiled, "You are correct." He began the Story again.

The Girl had been Given Medicine Power from the Man who had Visited there, even though she did not Know it. She Looked Upon the great Herd and the Buffalo All Fell Down, Ready to be Food for the People.

After this Give-Away, the Boy Brought his Sister Into the Arbor. A Bear and a Mountain Lion were Living there. The Stranger then Visited the Children again. He Spoke to the Boy. "Tell your Sister she must Make Use of all those Buffalo, and she must Save all the Sinew and Fat. A Big Black Crow will Come to her. It will Sit over there in that Forked Tree, and it will Look at her. Tell her to Give the Best of the Fat to this Black Crow. This will be the Third Day when the Crow will Come."

"The Children are growing fast, but their growth means a Spiritual Growing," explained Night Bear. "The Fat is the Healing of the People. The Sinew is the Sign of the Remaking or Building among the People. And of course it is the Black Crow, the Law of the People, who brings these things to the People. The Children, these new concepts, are Growing among the People. It is just this Healing that the People needed." Night Bear returned to the Story again.

The Girl now Believed in the Stranger, and so she Gave the Fat to the Black Crow. "Go," she said to the Crow. "Fly Through the Opening from the East and Drop the Fat in the Middle of the Circle. Tell the People that it is from the Children they Left Upon the Prairie to Die."

The People had been Starving for a very long time and they Counseled Amongst themselves, saying, "This Fat Means that the Children have Plenty of Buffalo for us to Eat."

Bull Looks Back said many things, because he did not Want the People to Go.

"Look," they told Bull Looks Back. "Our own Children are Starving to Death, and they must have Buffalo. We must Go."

Soon the Children Heard their Father Coming. As he was Walking, he was Singing Elk Songs. "That is my Father," the Girl Told the Lion and the Bear, "but he has Forgotten the Harmony of the Songs. Do not Touch him until he has Eaten, but when he Gets Up Ready to Leave the Lodge, Overcome him."

"The Bear is Natural Truth, or Looking-Within," explained Night Bear. Bull Looks Back must Look-Within to Perceive himself for what he is. The Lion is the Sign of the Earth. He is the mighty Hunter who keeps the Balance of all the Creatures of the Earth. The

Lion will eat Bull Looks Back so that there may be a New Circle.

The Girl Sent for the Children, the Women, and the Men to Come and Eat Together, for she had Prepared All the Buffalo. After the People had Eaten, the Girl Spoke to the Men. "With the New Sunrise, Bring your Lodges Into a New Circle. Chiefs will be Made in your Camp. My Brother and I have been Accused of Killing our Mother, but the Truth is we have Killed our Father through these Animal Signs. There will be a New Way. Hereafter if Anyone Kills Another with the Slow Death of the Heart he will be Banished from the Circle of People for Four Years."

"The most painful of all deaths is the one that is a Spiritual Death," said Night Bear. "If a man, woman, or child breaks the spirit or will of another and brings loneliness upon them, he not only separates these people from himself, he also causes separation and loneliness among all the People. This is the slow death. While Bull Looks Back lived, there was only one Way. But now we can learn of the many Ways. We will see the beginning of the Great Shields and the Brotherhood of the Sun Dance."

The Beautiful Maiden Instructed the People to Put Together Two Lodges for the Making of One Great Lodge in the Center of the Camp. The Lodge was to be Painted.

"This is the Lone Tipi, this Painted Lodge you speak of, is it not?" Green Fire Mouse asked.

"Yes, it is," Night Bear said. "The Lone Tipi now becomes the Center of Teaching for the People. But I want to show you more, because there is also the Teaching of the Shield that you will soon hear. Now we will complete this tiny Medicine Wheel that I began before,

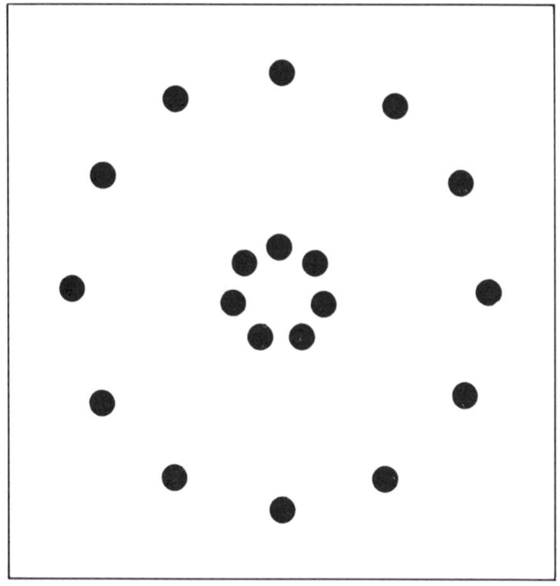

here on the ground at my feet. Before it was only a Circle, and the People believed that they were the Center. But they just ran around and around in their own Blindness. This Teaching will show you the True Center, the Sun Dance Shield."

Night Bear began the story again.

After the Lone Lodge was Constructed, the Maiden Took her Bundle and Walked Around the Lodge Four Times. Then she Entered. She Placed her Bundle at the North Side of the Lodge, and in the Center of the Lodge she Made a small Mound.

"This Mound of Earth," she said, "is the Sacred Mountain and Reflects the World." She then Placed Four Forked Sticks Around the Mound. "These are to be your First Chiefs," she said. "One is the North, One the South, One the West, and One the East."

She then Placed a Fifth Forked Stick in the

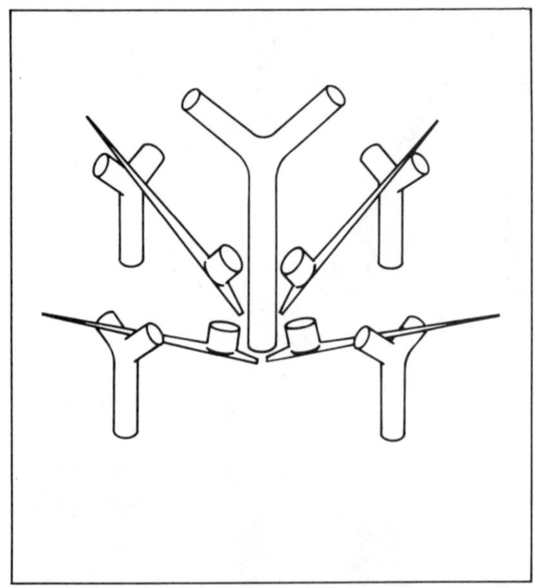

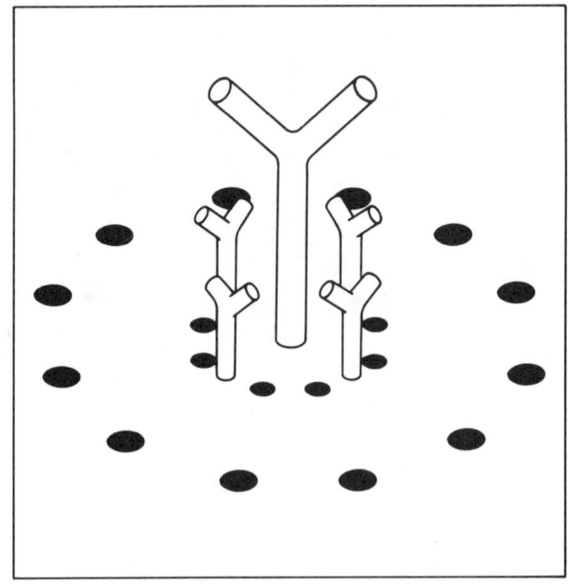

Middle of the Mound. "This is the Fifth Peace Chief," she added. "This Chief is the One all the Rest Dance to." A Pipe was Cradled in Each of the Four Outside Forked Sticks. The Bowls of the Pipes Rested Against the Middle Forked Stick. "In this Manner are the Peace Chiefs to Walk," she said.

Night Bear broke five forked branches from the wood he had brought, and placed the largest of them in the middle of the small circle of stones. He then placed the other four around the largest one.

"That is a Sun Dance Lodge," Green Fire Mouse said. "What does the circle of stones around the Lodge represent?"

"The outside circle is the world," Night Bear said.

"But is not the small mound in the middle also this Sign?" Green Fire Mouse broke in.

"It is," Night Bear said, "and it is also the People. And it is also the whole Universe of stars above our heads. And it is the Inner Man."

Night Bear then placed more stones in the wheel.

"These other Singing Stones," Night Bear went on, "are the many Ways given to each man to learn his own Name. The little Boy in the Story means the many Ways of the Singing Stones. These Ways lead to the Center of the Circle. Because there is now more than One Way, we are able to Sun Dance, each within our own Way, in Brotherhood and Peace within One Great Lodge. The middle Forked Tree in the Brother Lodge is the Great Shield. It is a Mirror of all Names and of all Shields. It is the True Center.

The Youngman, the Brother of the Maiden, then Made a Smoke with Sweet Grass and Cedar

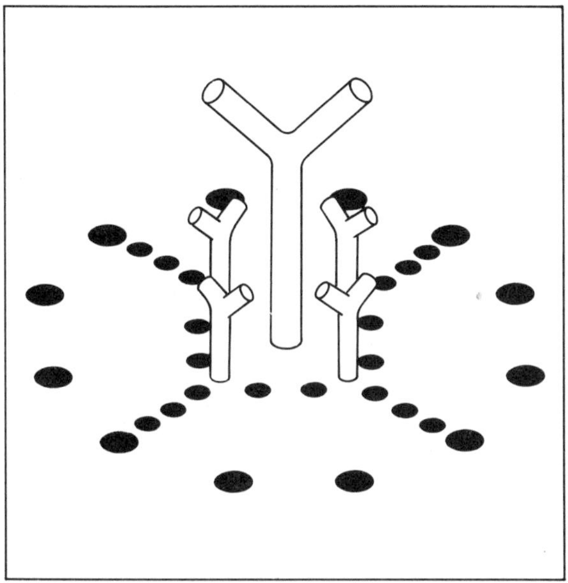

as a Sign of Prayer. The Youngman Walked Four Times Around the Camp, Meaning that every Four Years there was to be a Renewal of the Brotherhood. The Youngman then Constructed a Shield that was Polished so Brightly it Mirrored the Sun. He Carried this Into the Lodge. Other Men Walked in his Same Path, until there were Forty-Four. The Great Circle of Lodges then Became many smaller Circles. These were the Signs of the many Peoples and Tongues.

"Then was Medicine Crow, or Little Black Eagle, one of these men? One of the Forty-Four?" asked Green Fire Mouse.

"I really do not know," answered Night Bear, "because no one really knows which of the People this happened with first. Medicine Crow may have been a man who learned of this Way and Walked its Path bringing it to his People, or Medicine Crow may not have been a man at all. He may have been a Sign for the People."

The rain and wind continued into the night. Then toward morning it suddenly stopped. Even though the floor of their shelter was wet and deep with mud, the two men slept through the day. The next day was mostly grey and overcast, but in places the sky promised sunshine.

After changing into dry clothes, both men found spirit enough for joking.

They rode until noon, both marveling at the beauty of the colors that lay before their eyes as they began to descend from the mountains to the prairie. A herd of buffalo, numbering hundreds, moved across the prairie like a brown-red blanket, alive and molding itself to the contours of the land. An eagle that was circling high above their heads suddenly sang an angry note, then dived low across the prairie below them.

"The Old One is angry," Night Bear said to Green Fire Mouse. "His eyes are growing dim. See how he weaves along the river? He fears the water, the very place where he now finds his food. One day his angry blindness will be used by the Power to give him a good soaking in the river."

"That truly would be a horrible way to die," mumbled Green Fire Mouse.

"Horrible?" Night Bear laughed, "Never! It would be a new way for him to live. The Power would in all probability have him live again, as a young Otter."

"Would he then have memory of when he was an Eagle?" asked Green Fire Mouse.

"Yes," answered Night Bear. "Eagle would still have been his Beginning Name. He would perceive almost from his rebirth from the East. But his heart would now be of the South."

"*Zahuah!*" exclaimed Green Fire Mouse. "This would be a powerful name."

"It would be powerful," answered Night Bear, "but really no more powerful than any other of the Medicine Names. He would still have to seek the North, for he would be blind to the Wisdom of this Direction. And he would also have to marry the Woman of the West. This would be his hardest Way."

"Why would this be so difficult for him?" asked Green Fire Mouse. "He would live within the Medicine itself, the river."

"Yes, he would have an understanding of the Medicine," Night Bear said. "But he would only play within it. He must also follow the Way of the Jumping Mouse, he must visit the prairie."

"Would he then become Eagle again, as did Jumping Mouse?" Green Fire Mouse asked.

"No, he would not!" Night Bear laughed, remembering another Story. "He would dive below the waters of the Great Medicine Lake and almost drown because he would be a Buffalo."

Their conversation suddenly ended when Night Bear noticed a thin wisp of smoke to his left. They had come down from the mountains and were almost at the river. Night Bear touched Green Fire Mouse's arm for attention and quietly pointed toward the smoke.

I saw no smoke when we were coming down the mountain, Green Fire Mouse signed.

Neither did I, Night Bear signed his answer. *Let us dismount and approach the camp on foot. Or do you think we should put our horns to the ground and get away from here?*

Green Fire Mouse thought for a moment, then dismounted. Night Bear followed and they started for the camp. They had taken only about five steps when suddenly someone spoke from behind them.

"Greetings," said the voice.

"Peace," Night Bear replied, turning slowly. "I am called Night. . ."

"Bear," the voice finished.

Night Bear had never met the man who stood before them. He was dressed in leggings and vest. He held a painted Contrary Bow in his left hand, but his quiver was empty. His hair was unbraided and hung loose around his face.

"I am called Left Hand," the man said. "I am of the Brotherhood of the Mountain Turtle People. I have been searching for you since you left the camp of Morning Star."

"How is it that you knew we were here?" asked Green Fire Mouse, frowning. "And how is it that you speak our tongue?"

"I have been trying to catch up with you since I left your camp," Left Hand answered. "And I speak your tongue because I once lived among the River People."

"The River People!" Green Fire Mouse said excitedly. "Then do you know Stands Afar, my father?"

The man turned and motioned for Night Bear and Green Fire Mouse to follow him.

"Yes," he said as they walked. "I have met and spoken with your father many times. Your family is well. Their lodge is in the camp of Yellow Robe." He then looked at Night Bear. "And yes, everyone else is also well in the camp of Yellow Robe. It is about nine weeks ride from here, east of the camps of Morning Star."

"You speak of 'camps' when you mention Morning Star," said Night Bear. "Is there then more than one camp?"

"There are many camps," answered Left Hand. "They are circled in council for war."

"War?" Night Bear exclaimed in surprise.

They came to the clearing where Left Hand was camped. Four prairie hens were already roasting over his fire, almost ready for eating.

"I knew the rain would bring you down onto the prairie, so I waited for you here. It was only an accident, a good one, that you came out almost at my evening camp. I saw you coming and hunted for you, because I knew you would be hungry," said Left Hand.

Green Fire Mouse poked the chickens with his fingers and licked them. "I hate prairie chicken," he said grinning. "So I will eat only three of them."

All three settled themselves for the Pipe Night Bear was preparing, while they waited for the meal to finish roasting.

While they smoked, Night Bear began to feel restless because Left Hand still had not spoken

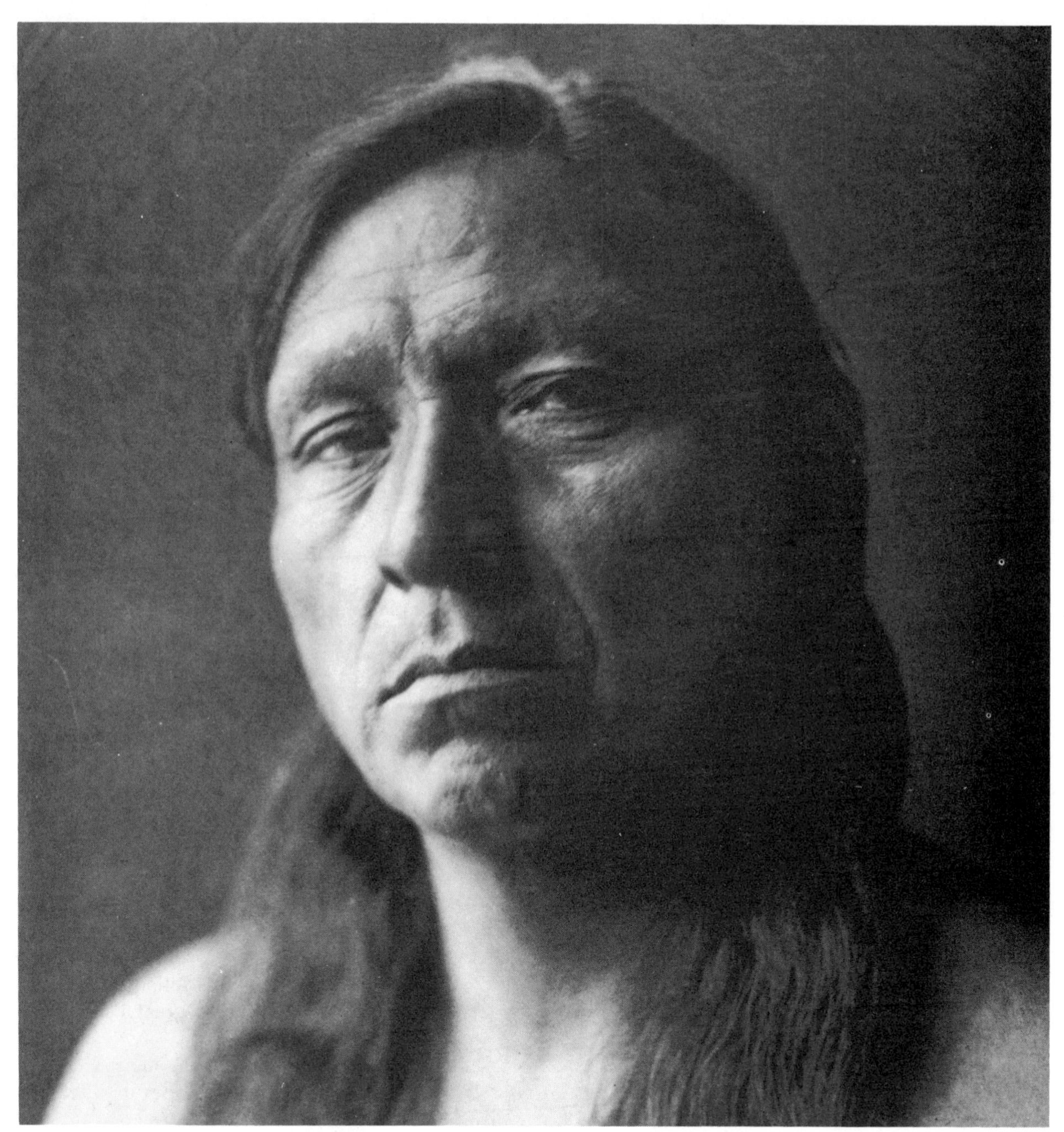

of his reasons for traveling such a great distance to find them. His patience had nearly all fled him when Left Hand finally spoke.

"My story is really one that is very simple. Curiosity was the first White Wolf that led me to the camp of Morning Star. I met a woman there with whom I wished to live, and I planned to remain with these People. But the wars have made this an impossible thing. The whiteman is becoming more mad with each day, and his insanity is spreading quickly. As you probably have heard, the Brotherhood is now only a thing of memory. Confusion, distrust, greed, and the new Way of the war god are destroying everyone. The North River of the Medicine Wheel, which the whites call the Missouri, was visited not long ago by whitemen who left great piles of robes as Gifts for the People who lived there. Word of the Gift robes spread quickly, and many of the People rushed to these places to get them. And the robes killed them."

"Killed by robes?" Night Bear said, unable to believe what he had just heard. "That is impossible!"

Night Bear saw that his brother's hands shook visibly, as did his voice when he continued.

"Yes, my brother, it does seem impossible," Left Hand went on. "But it is true. Hundreds died. Whole camps of the People rotted. The stink of the dead was unbearable. You could not even get close to these villages, there were so very many dead."

"But how?" Green Fire Mouse asked, his voice shaking. "What is this great Power that can make robes kill?"

"The whiteman somehow called sickness into the robes, little brother, and it killed for him."

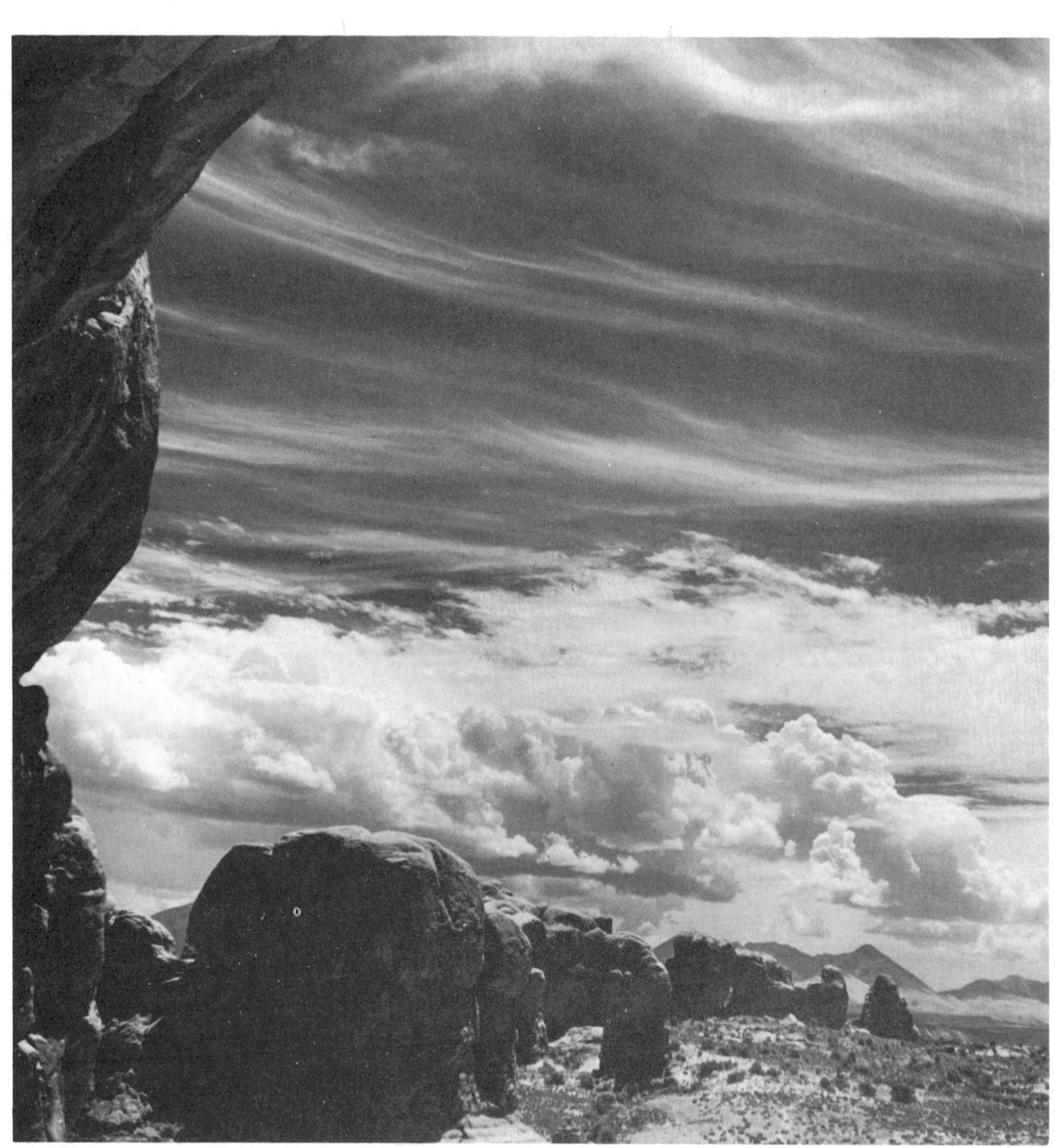

"They can command even the death of sickness," Night Bear whispered in awe. "Geessis is truly the most horrible of things devised."

"Geessis?" Left Hand frowned. "Is that the Power?"

"Yes," answered Night Bear. "The whiteman has named his terrible Power Way with this name. But tell us more of why you are here."

"The People," Left Hand went on, "are so overcome with fear and distrust that it is even becoming dangerous to be among friends in your own camp. When it is not the whitemen who are murdering, then more and more often it is the People themselves who are doing this terrible thing. The stinging water and the lust for rich prizes have caused whole camps to split and to fall upon each other in war. And there is even more."

"More!" exclaimed Night Bear. "It seems impossible that there could be more."

"Yes, there is more," Left Hand began again. "The whiteman has iron horses. Many of their people come in them, and many more come riding upon the hoops that roll along the ground. And they all kill. Did you see that herd of buffalo as you came out onto the prairie?"

"Yes," Green Fire Mouse answered. "It was a beautiful thing."

"The whitemen have killed whole herds even larger than that one just for the tongues and hides."

Night Bear held his head in his hands and rocked back and forth, unable to believe his ears.

"Why?" he said. "Is there no end to their gluttony and madness? What can they possibly do with so many tongues and hides?"

"No one knows," Left Hand answered. "But this killing of the buffalo has done strange things to the People."

"What strange things?" Green Fire Mouse asked. The fear that was in his eyes made Left Hand look down at his hands."

"It has made them even more afraid that they will starve," Left Hand answered. "They fear now that the whiteman will kill all of the buffalo, elk, and deer. There are even stories among the People that others of the Peoples further to the east have been killed by the whitemen like the buffalo, and that some of them were even eaten by the whitemen.

"There is only one answer then!" Green Fire Mouse shouted, jumping to his feet. "We must kill them! I see now why you have come here for us. You are on your way to gather warriors to kill the whitemen, and I will go with you!"

But Left Hand only continued to stare at his hands, not answering.

"That is not why you have come for me," Night Bear said, breaking the silence.

"No, it is not," Left Hand answered, still avoiding Green Fire Mouse's eyes. "Morning Star wishes for you and your father Hawk to hold a Renewal."

"A Sun Dance!" Green Fire Mouse exploded. "Are you as mad as the whitemen? I swear by my very life and Medicines that I will not let the whitemen kill my wife who walks with me, and my babies. It is a time for war, not for a Renewal!"

"You may do this if you wish, but I cannot," Left Hand answered, his voice full of emotion. "I walk the Way of the Shield. I can never talk for war. I must talk always for Peace."

"Then you are my father," said Night Bear. "But where is your Shield?"

"I have only the cover of my Shield, my brother," Left Hand answered. "I will make another frame for it. A young Medicine Song

Bird, who was maddened with anger by the killing of his entire family, smashed the Shield."

"Please, Medicine Fathers," Green Fire Mouse pleaded to Night Bear and Left Hand, his eyes full of tears. "Call the People together, all the People, and together we can stop the whitemen. You two have the power to do this. You of all the People in the whole world can do this."

"What you feel at this moment is not a real thing," Night Bear said to Green Fire Mouse. "You are looking out the door of your lodge, and this is always a narrow view. What you must do is to roll up the skins of your lodge upon their poles, so that you can see in every direction."

"In every direction is death," Green Fire Mouse mumbled and sat down.

"What you say may indeed be true," Left Hand answered. "But I believe it is equally true that the Power, the Power of Truth, will never allow the total death of the People. The Renewal of the Medicine Wheel and the Brotherhood are the only Ways. Is this how you also feel, Night Bear?"

"I do not know how I feel," answered Night Bear. "I understand what you are saying, but I am somehow unable to feel it right now. If Green Fire Mouse chooses to fight to save the lives of his children, I cannot speak to him against it. I have pledged as you have to speak for Peace, but at this place where I now sit, I lack the strength to do it."

"Then let us continue on your journey to trade salt," Left Hand said. Getting to his feet, he began to ready the four prairie chickens for their meal. "This will allow you the entire winter to think about it. It was my intention to leave immediately for Morning Star's camp, but I can wait. I, too, have been overcome with these things, and I have run blindly to search you out. I suppose in my heart I believed you would have answers that I did not have. I am afraid of what is happening, just as you are."

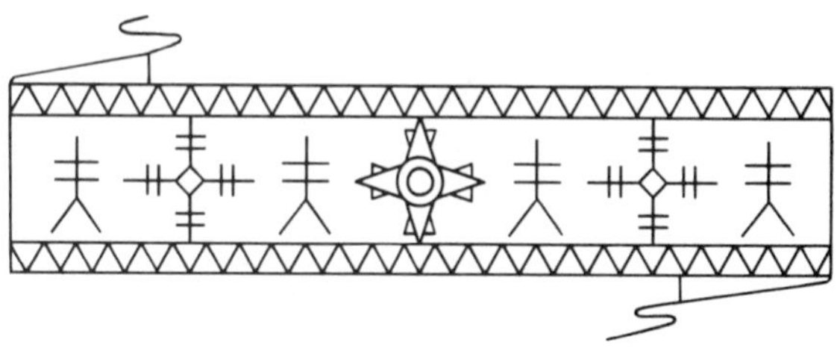

The winter was harder than any Night Bear had ever seen. But elk and deer were plentiful, and the people of the camp had a great deal of time for games and visiting. Green Fire Mouse sulked and brooded about Shining Arrows' camp like a cat, stalking the lodges of the other young men with talk of the coming wars.

One night he was sitting in the lodge of Coyote Runs In Circles, when Night Bear entered. At once Green Fire Mouse became silent and withdrew from the conversation. Suddenly he got to his feet to leave, but Night Bear grabbed his arm with an iron grip and stopped him. Green Fire Mouse turned slowly to Night Bear, his eyes slitted with anger.

"Let me go, you whimpering dog, or I will kill you," Green Fire Mouse said between clenched teeth.

"You must be reasonable," Night Bear said. But he had hardly finished his sentence when Green Fire Mouse hit him hard across the face. Night Bear reacted without thinking and knocked Green Fire Mouse to his knees. As the boy fell he reached out to protect himself, and he came down hard with both of his hands in the lodge fire.

Green Fire Mouse jumped to his feet and ran from the lodge. Coyote Runs In Circles ran through the door after him, calling for help. Night Bear's mind was a cauldron of confusion. He knew he had hit Green Fire Mouse out of fear and anger. His heart had been torn by the

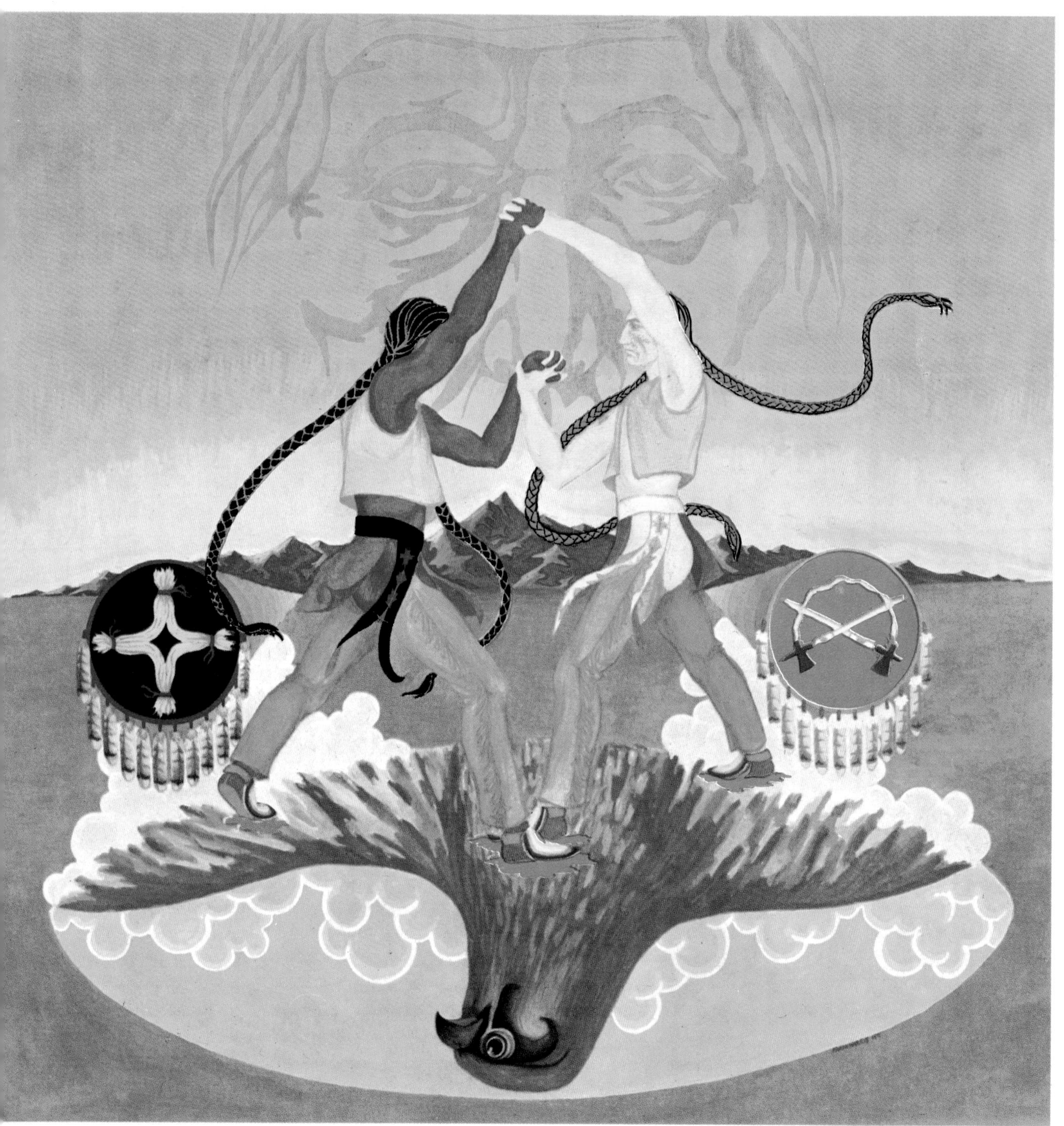

hopelessness he had seen in everyone in the camp. The thought of war had sickened Night Bear all winter long, but the thought of holding a Renewal without the participation of the whiteman seemed equally useless to him.

The following day a council was called to hear of the injuries that had been brought upon Green Fire Mouse and Night Bear.

All winter long I have been tormented, Night Bear began his signs to the council, *and last night my confusion caused terrible pain to my brother, Green Fire Mouse. I have sworn myself to peace and to the Shields, but these new horrors have been too much for me. I have been unable to understand even my own feelings, let alone to make decisions. Now I would gladly burn my own hands if it would heal the wounds I have caused within my brother, but even this would be futile. And so I tell you all here, that you may be my witnesses to it, I pledge myself to Green Fire Mouse. I snapped at him like a common camp dog instead of speaking as a Man of Peace. So I place my life and my bow, even if it means I must go to war, in the hands of Green Fire Mouse. I have spoken.*

Left Hand rose to his feet and began to sign. *I have not been lucky. There have been no brothers like Green Fire Mouse to help me see. In one moon I will leave for the camps of Morning Star. I leave this word with Green Fire Mouse. Come with me to the camps of the Painted Arrow, and bring along your brother Night Bear. Counsel with the People of the Painted Arrow. Then if you still see war, send your Dog, Night Bear, to this camp for any of the young men here who wish to fight. If instead there is to be a Renewal, then there will be no Dog that will bring the message for war.*

Pretty Weasel then signed, *I would say to my brother, Green Fire Mouse, that this is a Way that is wisdom. I would ask him to do this thing. I, too, will stand by his decision.*

What my brother Night Bear has done here just now has healed my wounds, Green Fire Mouse signed. *And I am humbled. I accept this Camp Dog, but I promise him my bow and all my heart until the day I am able to release him. As I sat here just now my hate melted like the snow, and became love. It has shown me a new Way.*

White Rabbit, Green Fire Mouse's wife, began to cry softly, hugging her children close to her. She began to speak in her own tongue. "I am so afraid," she said, her voice blurred with her tears. "These are men's games . . . something needs to be done . . . we must hide, or go someplace . . . I do not want my young ones to be eaten in their own nest." Then she broke down completely and began to sob helplessly. A few of the other women her own age came to her side and comforted her. But the look of fear in their own eyes unmistakably reflected that of their sister. None of the men in the council translated White Rabbit's words into signs.

The spring was unusually hot and dry. The three men had ridden across the Little Medicine Horn Mountains and down into the valley of the Greasy Grass, without having seen any signs of old camps. They had turned their ponies south at this river, and one week later they had arrived in country that was easy for riding and full of game.

"Since we left the village I have had a different heart," Green Fire Mouse said, turning to Night Bear. "Everything was pressing in on me in the camp. But here things seem less threatening. Somehow the whiteman seems farther away."

"It was I," Left Hand added. "I was so full of fear and apprehension that it affected everybody."

"Look!" Green Fire Mouse said suddenly, pointing. "Are those not men on horseback coming our way?"

Night Bear strained his eyes in the direction Green Fire Mouse pointed. The figures were so far away that at first he could not see them.

"They are People of the Little Black Eagle," Green Fire Mouse said, stretching his neck as high as he could.

Night Bear's horse backed nervously, feeling his rider's tension.

"How can you possibly tell at such a distance?" Night Bear teased. "You must have eyes like the eagle."

"You will see that I am right," Green Fire

Mouse answered. "Come, let us ride to meet them."

The three men touched their heels to their ponies' flanks and loped forward to meet the strangers. As the riders drew closer, it became clear that the other horsemen were People of the Perfect Bow, not of the Little Black Eagle as Green Fire Mouse had perceived.

Peace, good father, one of the men signed as the two parties met. *I see that You carry the Shield of the Sun Eagle.*

Peace, Night Bear signed the answer. *I am called Night Bear. This Shield I carry belonged to my father, who was called Hawk.*

Night Bear unrolled the face of his own Shield for the men to see

The Four Stars, another of the group signed. *We have one of your brothers in our camp. His name is Hides On The Wind.*

Then take us to him, Green Fire Mouse grinned as he signed. *I have grown so hungry that I am losing my appetite. Now only half a buffalo will fill me.*

Green Fire Mouse was answered by a whoop, as one of the youngest of the Perfect Bow warriors spun his pony on its heels and kicked him into a run, leading the way into their camp.

The camp was a temporary hunting camp, consisting only of a few shade arbors and three short, squat, hunting lodges.

A man came out from under one of the arbors and greeted the guests. His hair was snow-white, and hung in braids almost to his waist.

Peace, good brothers, the man signed. *I am called Hides On The Wind. Welcome to our camp.*

This man is your brother of the Four Stars, one of the young men signed.

Who was your father? signed Hides On The

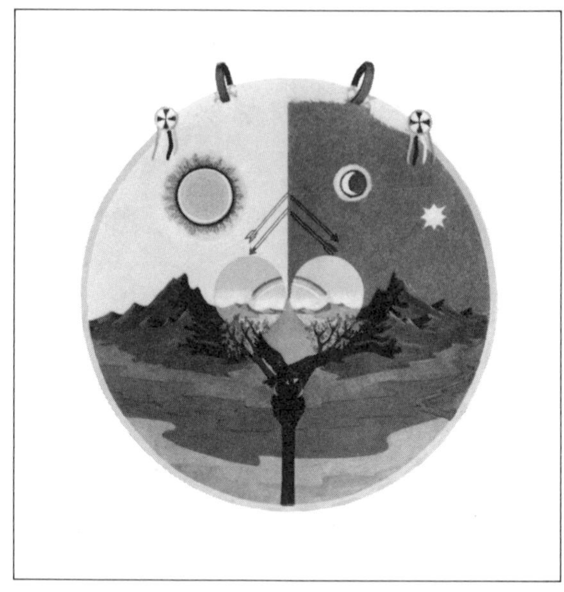

Wind.

Night Bear and the other men dismounted, and walked into the shade. Night Bear sat down and helped himself to a piece of dry meat before signing his answer.

My father's name was Hawk, signed Night Bear.

The Hawk. Hides On The Wind repeated the sign. *This name of the Great Sun Eagle is powerful. Was he also a Medicine Man?*

No, Night Bear signed. *He was not. I walked the Way of the Looks Into the Lake with my brother, White Wolf.*

White Wolf, Hides On The Wind smiled as he signed. *I know him well. He was born in the camps of the Perfect Bow. We were Kit Fox together there until he became a man.*

Have you seen him since he left your camps? Night Bear asked in signs.

No, Hides On The Wind signed. *He is only a memory. He left for the camps of the People of the Introspective Way, and I have never seen him since. Is your tongue of those People?*

No, Night Bear signed, and grinned. *I speak the tongue of the Little Black Crow. I was born into the camp of Yellow Robe. It was in this camp that I met and married the Teaching Way of my brother, White Wolf. The Song that White Wolf Painted for me was Looks-Within The Water of the Medicine. What was the brother called whose path you yourself now walk?*

He was called Running To The Camps With Singing, Hides On The Wind answered. *His beginning tongue was of the Medicine Song Bird People. He had four wives, and he hunted until his last days with the young men of the camp.*

The three men remained in camp for three days, and helped with the hunting. On the eve-

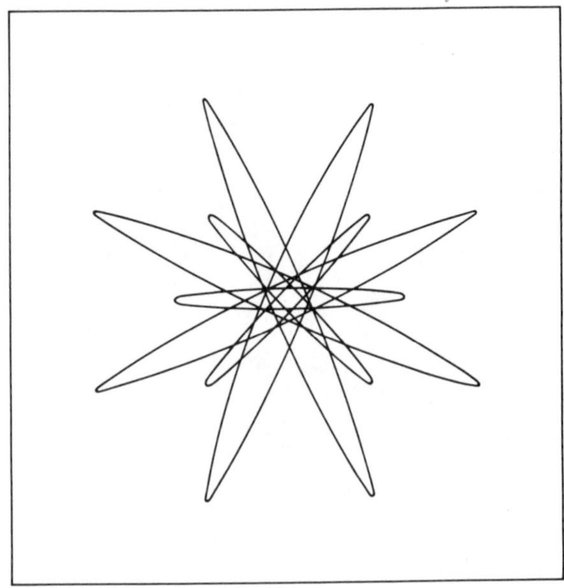

ning of the last day, Left Hand asked Hides On The Wind for a Teaching.

Yes, signed Hides On The Wind. *I think I can remember a Story.* He grinned and sat down in the small circle of men. *It is my favorite Song. It is called the Fallen Star.*

Once there was a Woman who Married a Porcupine. He Made her a Home in a great Cottonwood Tree. In the Fork of the Tree he had Built a Willow Reed Nest. And in these Willows the Woman Placed a Stone, and it was a Harmony Stone, a Singing Stone. This Stone was to Become Fallen Star.

And this is the Stone I shall place in the Medicine Wheel, signed Hides On The Wind.

Fallen Star was Orphaned and was in the Willow Nest all By Himself. A Painted Meadow Lark Came Flying By and Saw him there. She Took Pity on this New Son, Fallen Star. She Decided to have her Nest there and to Raise her own Little Ones with Fallen Star.

As the Baby Meadow Lark Birds Grew, so did Fallen Star. When they Perched on the Edge of their Nest to Fly, he Began to Walk. And they Grew Strong with Fallen Star. And they Danced Together the Wheel Dance, and Learned of its Colors.

Now I must draw you a Sign upon the ground.

Hides on the Wind drew the Sign upon the ground.

That is a Medicine Wheel, Green Fire Mouse signed.

Yes, it is, but it is made of Hoops. They are Hoops that are of many Colors, and they Spin among themselves. What we will do in this Story is to stop the Spinning long enough to examine them. But as soon as we take our hands from them they will Spin once again, or they will Die. They are a

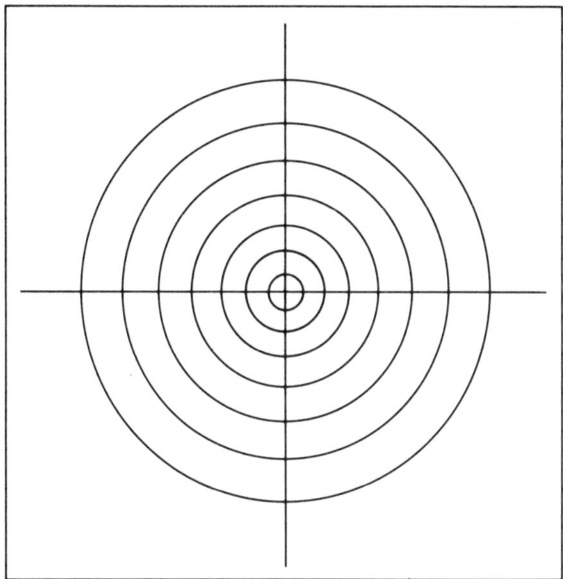

Teaching. We will Look at them from as many of the Great Directions as we can.

Here is this Freezing of the Water, the Painted Hoops. And Hides On The Wind drew another Sign upon the ground.

When I place this Stone within the Medicine Water it will make this Sign for us. It is the Singing Stone of the Fallen Star.

Hides On The Wind began the Story again.

One Day the Meadow Lark said to Fallen Star, "My Son, we are of the South and we must Return to the South. And my Other Children will Fly with me to this Place. But you are Different. Even though you are One of us, you must Remain Here." Fallen Star was Made Unhappy by this News.

"Can I not Follow you, my Mother?" he asked.

His Mother answered him, "No, my Son, you will have to Remain here in the North."

Fallen Star then Asked his Father if he could have Something Before he Left.

"Yes," his Father answered. "Anything. What is it you Wish?"

"Would you Give me some Arrows, a Bow, and a Quiver? I have my Knife for the Cutting of the Buffalo already from my Mother."

The Meadow Lark answered his Son and said, "Yes, I would be Glad to Do these things." And he Made him Arrows and a Bow, Using his own Tail Feathers to Tip the Arrows.

"Why do I have to Remain here?" asked Fallen Star.

"You have to," answered the Meadow Lark, "because your People Live right Over there. Right there Close to the River."

The Youngman Thanked his Father for his Gifts and Began his Journey to Find his People's Lodges. He Wandered for a while Upon the

Prairie, but after a while he Saw the Green that is at the Rivers. He Ventured Closer and Soon could See the Lodges. He Went right Up to the First Lodge, and an Old Woman Came Out to Meet him.

The Old Woman is tradition, Hides On The Wind explained, *and these things of the People are always the ones that greet the young man first.*

"Hello, my Grandmother," the Youngman said, "I am very Thirsty. Will you Give me a Drink of Water?"

The Old Woman Hung her Head. "Water is very Hard to Get, my Son. Only those who are Able to Run the very Fastest Near the River are Able to Get Water. Those who are Lame, or in some Other Way are Slow, are Caught by a Terribly Fearful Thing that Takes them Inside itself."

The Youngman Looked at his Grandmother and Felt Pity for her. He could See himself Reflected in her Deep Beautiful Black Eyes. Her Eyes were very Sad.

"What is this Fearful Thing, Grandmother?" he asked.

"We have No Way of Knowing, because it has many Faces," she answered. "But the People are very Afraid to Go Near it."

"Grandmother," the Youngman said. "Give me your Buffalo Skin Bucket, and your Horn Ladle. I will Bring you Water."

"Grandson, Grandson," she said. "There is a Terrible Fearful Thing there. Can you Run very Fast? I have Fear for you!"

"Do not Fear, Grandmother. I will Bring you Water." The Youngman Went Down to the great River. He Stopped at the Edge of the River and Looked Hard for the Fearful Thing that Lived there, but he could not See it. He Looked Hard Upon the Water. He Began to Dip the Buffalo Horn Ladle Into the Water and to Fill the Bucket. While he was Doing this, the Fearful Thing Suddenly Came Out of the Water. It Looked at the Youngman and Drew in its great Breath. The Youngman Tried to Grab Hold of Something, Anything, but Found only Air, and was Pulled Inside the Monster. When he Got Inside the Monster it was very Dark, and All the People were there who had been Trapped Before by this Fearful Thing. The Youngman had Held Fast to his Buffalo Skin Bucket when he was Drawn Inside the Fearful Thing.

The People were Crying, so the Youngman said in a Loud Voice, which was Almost a Whisper in the Great Monster Because of its great Size, "Do not Fear!" But he Cried himself, until he Remembered the Knife that his Mother had Given him. It was Upon his Belt, and he Cut Open the Side of the Monster.

Many of the People were Thankful and they Came Out from the Monster, but Others Thought that the Youngman was a Greater Thing to Fear and so they Remained Within the Darkness of the Monster. He Called to them, but they would not Come Out. The Others Took Water from the River and Went to their own Lodges.

I do not understand, Green Fire Mouse signed to Hides On The Wind. *Why did they not come out?*

Because, my son, answered Hides On The Wind, *these People are the Heart and Liver of the fearful Monster.*

Then was the Monster killed? another young man signed his question.

Killed? signed Hides On The Wind. *No. It was rendered Powerless for those who Went Out, but it still Lived.*

When the Youngman Returned to the Lodge of the Old Woman she Looked at him. She Looked very Closely. "Grandson," she said, "Who are you?"

"I am Fallen Star," answered the Youngman. "I am your Grandson who Made the Monster Powerless." He Sat Down and Ate with his Grandmother, and she Fed him Well, but she Watched him Closely.

"Grandmother," the Youngman said, "this Monster has Made the People Starve for Water for a very long time. That is why I Came here to Cut its Side. Remember that I am Fallen Star."

His Grandmother Became very Busy Fixing and Straightening this and that, Moving One Old Thing here and Another there, and while she Worked she Spoke to her Grandson.

"Here!" she said. "Marry One of my Granddaughters in this Camp, and you can Live here with us." She Poured some of the Water he had Brought into her Drinking Cup. It was Made from a Turtle Shell.

"No, Grandmother. I Want to Look for More of the People," said the Youngman. "Is there a Camp Near By?"

She Answered Quickly. "Yes," she said, "there is Another Camp Along the River."

The Youngman Thanked the Old Woman for her Food and Lodging and he Left.

The quiet of the Story suddenly was broken by a bee that began to buzz around Green Fire Mouse. He jumped to his feet, swatting at the bee, and ran a few steps from under the arbor, still pawing at his attacker.

Get a bow and arrow, one of the men signed to Green Fire Mouse. After the laughter died down and the bee had gone away, everyone settled down again to hear the rest of the Story.

The Youngman Traveled a long time. The Sides of the River were Covered with many things. Part of the time it was Easy Going, but at Other times it Became very Difficult. This Youngman did not have to Fear the Thing of the Water. Finally he Saw some Scattered Lodges in the Distance. He Went Straight to the First Lodge, and an Old Woman was in the Lodge. She Greeted him and Asked him to Come Inside.

"I have Come a very long Way, my Grandmother. Can you Make me Warm?" the Youngman asked.

"My Grandson, no," she answered. "I cannot Make you Warm. We have not Wood for our Fires."

The Youngman Looked at his Grandmother and Saw that she was Cold. "Why is there no Wood?" asked the Youngman.

"Because," she answered, "in the Trees and in the Places where Wood is Found there is a great Owl."

"Then does this Owl Keep the People from Gathering Wood to Keep themselves Warm?" Fallen Star asked.

"Yes," she said. "He Lives there and he Grabs the People who Go there and he Puts them in his Ear."

"Grandmother," he said, "Give me the Rope you have Braided and your Stone Ax and I will Go and Bring Back Wood for you."

"No! No! Grandson," she Cried Out Loud. "Do not Go. Stay Under the Robes with me and you will be Warm."

"No, Grandmother," the Youngman said. "I will Go and Get the Wood."

The Youngman Started Out to Look for Wood. It was not long Before he Saw Wood that would Make a Beautiful Warm Fire, and he Began to Busy himself Gathering the Wood. Suddenly he Felt the Presence of the Owl. The Owl Reached Down and Put the Youngman in its Ear. The Youngman Strung his Bow and Fitted One of his Arrows, Letting it Fly from his Bow Deep Into the Ear of the Owl. And the Youngman was Free.

He Gathered Wood and Returned to the Lodge

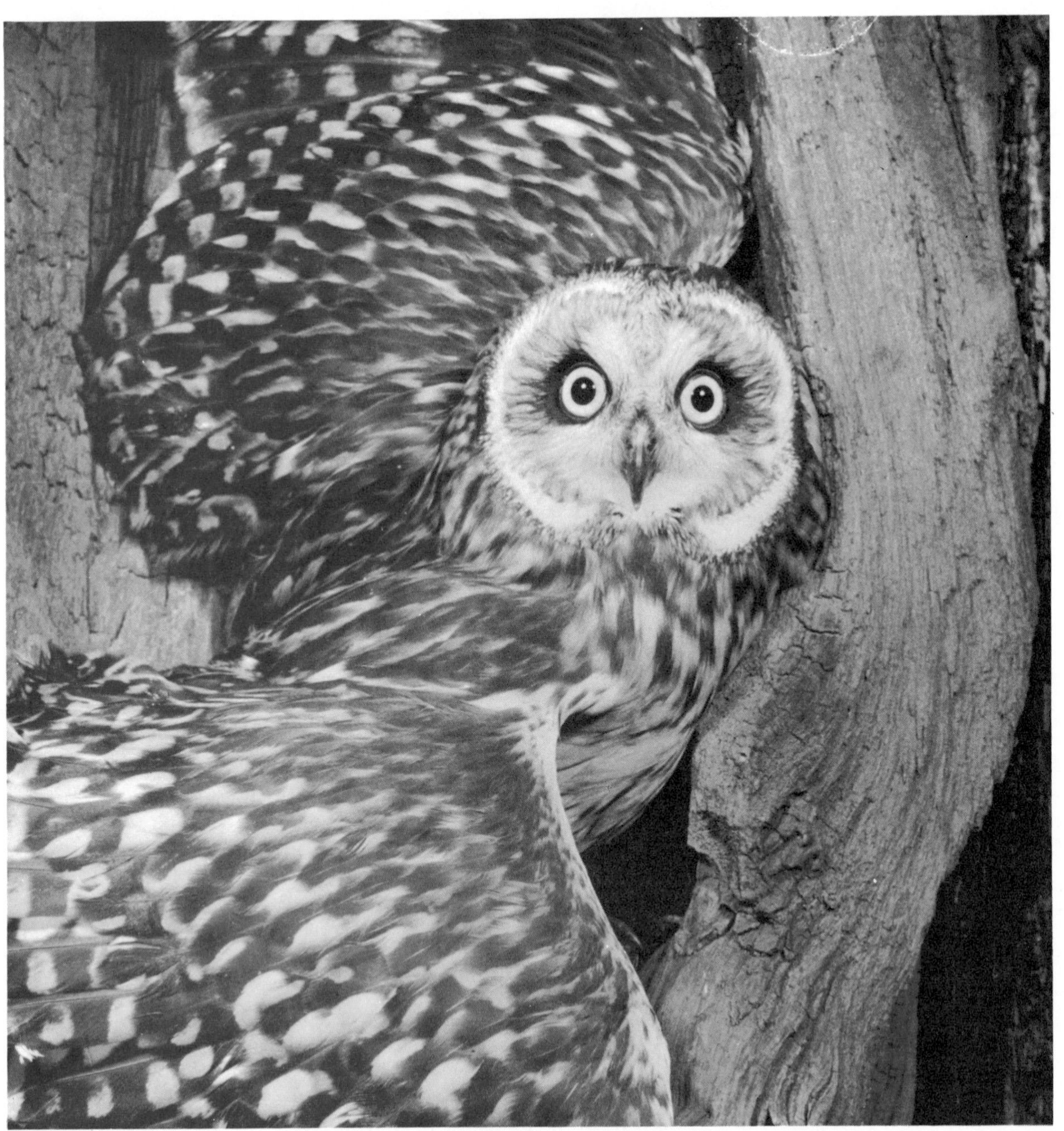

of the Old Woman. Many of the People Saw him Carrying Wood and Went to Gather Wood, too.

"Grandson! Grandson!" the Old Woman said when he Returned to the Lodge. She was Looking at him Closely.

"I have Shot One of my Arrows Into the Ear of the Owl," he said to the Old Woman, "and he will not Bother the People who Want Wood for their Fires."

The Old Woman Said Nothing of these things, and Immediately Gave him a Meal. He Ate with her. She Looked at the Youngman from the Corner of her Eye, saying, "Why do you not Stay here and Marry One of my Daughters in this Camp?"

"No," answered Fallen Star. "Will you Tell me if there are any Other Camps Near By?"

"Yes!" she answered, Smiling. "There is One Right Down the River from here."

Fallen Star Walked Along the River. The Way Along the River was Like the One Before.

Wait! signed one of the young men. *Who is the Owl?*

The other day, Hides On The Wind answered, *I was praying for you and a very strange thing happened. Something that still makes my skin feel cold. It concerns you and an Owl.*

Me? the young man signed, leaning forward. *What Owl?*

It is better that I should forget about it, Hides On The Wind signed.

Forget about it! signed the young man. *Forget about it? If you do not tell me, I will hang you up by your braids!*

Well, answered the old man. *If you insist, but it was not a good plume.*

Good plume? the young man signed. *What truth? Are you making a fool of my question?*

I am not making a fool of your question, signed the old man. *I am very serious.*

Then for the sake of my sanity, stop hiding, the young man signed back, *and give me the problem.*

While I was praying, the old man began, *I was holding my hands up for your blessing, touching, and an Owl flew over them. One of his plumes fell into my hand at the very time I spoke your name.* Sounds of exclamation and pity went around the circle of men.

Then I am going to die! the young man signed, *or some other terrible thing will happen to me.* His face was ashen, and he was visibly shaken.

May I ask you a question? signed the old man.

Yes! Yes! the young man signed. *Yes, anything! Is there something that can be done?*

What would have happened if instead of a plume falling into my hand it would have been Owl shit? Or what if the whole clumsy Owl had fallen into my hands? the old man went on.

The young man burst into laughter, and was joined by the whole circle.

I know who the Owl is now, old man, the young man replied, laughing so hard it was hard for him to sign.

The old man resumed his Story.

Finally the Youngman again Saw Lodges in the Distance, and he Approached them. An Old Woman Came Out of her Lodge and Walked to Meet him. "Grandson," she called, "Welcome to our Lodges."

"Grandmother," the Youngman said, "my Hunger is very great."

"Grandson," she answered, "I am Sorry, but I cannot Give you Food. Because there is None. There are no Buffalo."

"No Buffalo?" the Youngman said, Unable to Comprehend. "How is it there are no Buffalo? Buffalo are the Most Abundant Animal on the Earth. This Seems Hard for me to Believe."

The Old Woman's Eyes Grew Comically Large, and then she Frowned. "There is a White Crow that Warns the Buffalo whenever Anyone Comes Near. And our Best and Swiftest Runners are Unable to Touch even One of them with their Arrows."

"Grandmother," said the Youngman, "I will Go Get you some Buffalo. But I will Need Help. Are there Any of my Brothers here?"

"Yes," she answered. "There are a Few. There are Two Medicine Sons whose Fathers are Chiefs. They are our Swiftest Runners and they Wish to Hear of this New Way."

The Youngman Entered the Great Lodge of his Brothers, and they Sat Together in a Circle. "Give me your Oldest and Shabbiest Buffalo Hide," said the Youngman. He then Asked them to Follow him to the Prairie and they did.

When they were On the Prairie he Instructed them Further. "I will Circle the Herd of Buffalo, and will Follow Among them in this Old Scabby Hide," he said. "Come After me when you Go to the Herd. Run as Hard and as Swiftly as you Can. Shoot your Arrows Into me and Cut me me Open with the Knives your Mothers have Placed at your Belts. Act as though you are very Dissatisfied when you have Touched me, and then Leave me Lying there."

And so his Brothers Did. They Ran as Hard as they Could and Touched the Old Scabby Bull with their Arrows. Then they Left him Lying there.

I have a question, Green Fire Mouse signed.

What is your question? the old man answered.

I am a little confused, Green Fire Mouse began. *Does this mean that it was two Medicine Sons of the Shield who helped the Youngman?*

Yes and no, answered Hides On The Wind. *This is a Teaching concerning our Medicine Sons, and also our brothers who are not. All of them are help-*

less, because none of them can get the Buffalo. They sit together in the Great Lodge. The two Medicine Sons can be six, or sixty. What is important is simply the Teaching and its Reflection.

The old man began again.

The White Crow Came Near Fallen Star, Flying Low Over him. "Is this Fallen Star?" the Crow asked as he Flew By. The Second Time he Flew even Nearer. "Can this be Fallen Star?" he asked. The Third Time White Crow Alighted on the Ground Near the Scabby Bull, saying, "Can this be Fallen Star?" And the Fourth Time he Came right Up to the Scabby Bull, and he Spoke to All the Beings there. "Take Special Notice, All you who are Wolves and Coyotes. Your Way has Brought you here to these Buffalo. But the Eyes of this Bull must be mine. Because this Scabby Bull is Truly Fallen Star."

But Fallen Star Reached Out and Grabbed White Crow. The Youngman Took the White Crow Back to the Camp. Then he said to the People, "Now you can Hunt the Buffalo, because you have White Crow right Here Among you."

"We are Afraid! We are Afraid of him," the People Called.

"The Answer," said the Chiefs, "is to Hang Him Up in a Lodge. Hang him in the Smoke Hole and Smoke him to Death."

And they Took him Away to their own Lodge and Hung him there. But he Wriggled Free and Flew Out. The Young Men of the Camp were Angry because when they Chased the Buffalo, White Crow was there again, Making it Impossible for them to Touch the Buffalo with their Arrows.

What is this Sign of the White Crow? Night Bear signed. *Is it the same Sign as that of the Medicine Crow?*

It is the Law, Hides On The Wind signed.

The Law? Night Bear signed. *I am afraid I do not understand.*

The Way of the Law was a Gift to the People, the old man answered. *But whenever the Law becomes something to Get Around, then it is of no value. In fact it will Starve a People to Death. And as you see, the White Crow flew from the Smoke Hole of the Chief's Lodge. A People cannot Pray or Purify a Law to Death, because it is still not Understood. The Law should be made clear and easily Understood for all the People.*

Hides On the Wind Looked at the ground for a while and seemed to rest before he began the Story again.

The People were very Angry with the Youngman. "We have to Do it again," the People said Together with the Chiefs. "We have to Stay Out there again and Trick him."

"No," the Youngman said. "No. Follow me to the Lodge." He Went to the very Lodge that White Crow had Flown from and to the Men who had Hung him there. The Men who Stood there were Embarrassed, because in their Hearts they had not Wanted this to Happen.

"These are the Ones who Caused the Trouble!" the People Cried All Together and Wanted to Harm them.

"Do not Accuse yourselves," the Youngman said. "That is Useless. Here, Look! Here is One of White Crow's Feathers." He Told them to Take Sinew and to Tie it to the Feather. "Throw it Out the Smoke Hole," he told them. And they Did. "Now, Pull it Back, and Do it All Together."

The People Joined Together and Pulled On the Sinew, and the Men from Whose Lodge White Crow had Flown Pulled Harder than the Rest. White Crow was Pulled Back Into the Lodge.

Then the Youngman Spoke to the People, "You cannot Smoke White Crow to Death. It is you who will have to Put a Finish to him."

Then the Men of the Lodge Killed White Crow

and Gave One of His Feathers to Everyone.

The People were Happy, and it was Decided that they would have a Feast. "No! No! No! No!" screamed the Old Woman. "There cannot be a Feast! Because Upon the great Prairie there is still Another Thing." This made All the People Afraid.

"What is this Thing you Speak of?" asked the Youngman.

"It is Winterman," the Old Woman said.

"Come with me," said the Youngman. "We will go to Visit Winterman." But the Old Woman would not Go. He Took her by the Hand and Took her to the Prairie. She Made a great Noise and Dragged her Heels. All the People were Watching. Fallen Star Put an Arrow into his Bow and Let it Fly to Touch a Painted Buffalo Cow, and it Fell Down for them. He Gave the Best Parts to the Old Woman. These were the Kidneys and the Heart.

"Here," he said, "You may Have the Best Parts." But Winterman Came just as she had Predicted, and Demanded the Best Parts for himself. Winterman and the Old Woman Began to Argue. Then Winterman Turned to the Youngman.

"Why do you Give this Dried Up Old Woman the Best Parts?" Demanded Winterman.

"Because it will Make her Young again," answered the Youngman. The Winterman Became Angry and he Kicked at the Old Woman, but his Foot Flew to Pieces. He then Struck Hard at her with his Club, but it Flew Out of His Hands. He then Spoke things that would Kill her, but his Head Fell Off.

"Gather him Up," the Old Woman Ordered Fallen Star, "and Burn him because he Torments me. In this Way he can be Overcome."

"No, Grandmother," the Youngman said. "He cannot be Overcome this Way. "He then Asked the Old Woman where Winterman Lived, because Winterman had Put himself Together again and had Fled to his Lodge.

"Eat your Parts of the Buffalo," said the Youngman.

As the Old Woman Ate she Pointed her Finger, and Fallen Star Followed in the Direction in which she Pointed.

The Youngman Went Immediately to the Place where Winterman Lived. It was In a Cut Bank where Once there had been a Fine Sparkling Stream.

"Hello, my Uncle," said the Youngman when he Entered the Lodge of Winterman.

"You!" said Winterman.

"Yes," answered the Youngman. "It is I, Fallen Star." The Youngman Sat Down with Winterman. "Let me See your great Bow and your Arrows," said the Youngman. And when Winterman Handed them to Fallen Star, he Broke them. "Now Let me See your great Club," said the Youngman, and he Broke the Club.

"Why do you Do these things?" roared Winterman.

"Because I am of the South, and these Things are easily Broken by me!"

This so Frightened Winterman that he Took his Marriage and all his Children and Fled.

Grandfather, one of the young men signed to Hides On The Wind, *this confuses me.*

What is it that confuses you, my son? Hides On The Wind Answered in signs.

It is the Marriage of Winterman, the young man signed. *You have said that Winterman took his Marriage and all his Children and they fled. But many of these Medicine Signs confuse me. Would you explain them for me?*

Would any of you here like to answer this question for your brother? Hides On The Wind signed.

The Marriage is the one between Winterman and the People, Night Bear signed.

Then are the People the Wife of Winterman? the young man asked Night Bear.

Yes, Night Bear signed. *And the Children of this Marriage sometimes can be harsh Teachers. In many Ways these Children are the Coyote Children of the North.*

Yes, they can be, Hides On The Wind signed. *But you must remember, my sons, that the People will always have a Marriage with Winterman, because even though Winterman may appear cruel within his Ways, his Teachings still are a very important part of life.*

Would you answer still another question for me? the young man signed.

I will try, Hides On The Wind signed in reply.

Is not Winterman also the Great Drum of the Dreamer? the young man signed.

He is! Hides On The Wind signed and smiled. *His Teaching Drum is many times the Drum of the Dream. When Man visits the place of the Looks-Within, the Lightning Elk of the West Gives this Man Flashes as of the Lightning for his Illumination. But Man is stubborn in his Learning. He may See, may be given Illumination, but many times he will still refuse to Learn.*

Could you give us an example? Night Bear signed.

I will, Hides On The Wind answered, *but remember, my sons, that my example will turn in as many Ways as there are listeners.*

These things are like the Brother and Sister who did not know of the Planting. This Man and Woman Saw the Green Robe, the Corn we Eat and is Common now with all of us, but they did not have the Gift of Knowing how to Plant the Green Robe. They Saw and Collected the Corn of Green Robe whenever it Grew, but there were

times when these People were Without Corn and were Hungry. These were the times Winterman Struck at their Camps without Mercy and many Died. Many times the Man and Woman Sought the Marriage with Winterman, but each time they Failed.

One Day the Man and Woman Sat Together and Dreamed. The Coyote Visited them and Told them they would have the Marriage if they would Take Twelve Parts of the Corn and Hide them in the Ground. "Put these in a Circle," Coyote told them, "and Sing Four Songs of the Water." The Man and Woman did as Coyote Told them Within their Dream, and it was in this Way that they Learned of the Planting. The Woman and Man Now had their Marriage with Winterman and there were Children."

"Zahuah!" Green Fire Mouse said out loud. Hides On The Wind began again.

Fallen Star then Returned to the Camp. "Grandmother," the Youngman said as he Sat in the Old Woman's Lodge, "is there Another Camp Near By?"

"Stay here with us," the Old Grandmother answered and her Eyes Twinkled, "and Marry One of my most Beautiful Daughters."

"No," answered the Youngman. "I must Seek Another Camp."

The Old Woman Thought a long time, Trying to Remember. Then she answered. "Yes. There is Another Camp. It is Along the River, but in Between this Camp and the Camp you Seek are Scattered Out Lodges. These People are Alone."

"Scattered Lodges?" asked the Youngman. "Then they are not in a Camp Circle?"

"No. They Choose to Live Alone," answered the Old Woman.

Fallen Star Followed the Great River, and not

too Far Away he Saw some Scattered Lodges. While he was Going Toward these Scattered Lodges, he Saw a Man who was more Powerful than any Other Man he had ever Seen. Or maybe it was a Woman, he was Unable to tell. The Youngman Looked Hard at the Strange Figure. Around its Neck were Ears Strung like a Necklace. Fallen Star Went to some Pines and Cottonwood Trees that Grew Near By, and Shaped himself some Ears from the Green Moss that Grew Upon them. He Made Ears that were Identical to the Ears Carried by the Monster, and he Strung these Around his own Neck.

"Hello," the Youngman said as he Walked Up Toward the Monster.

"Hello, Monster," the Youngman Repeated as he Drew Nearer.

"Hello," the Monster answered. "How is it you Know that I am a Monster?"

"Because I am a Monster, too," answered Fallen Star. "Look, Around my Neck there are also Ears."

The Monster was very Glad to See that he had Company.

"I Know what Medicine Exists that will Overcome me," said the Youngman. "Do you Know what Medicine there is that will Overcome you?"

The Monster answered Quickly, "Yes! Yes, of course I Do."

"Tell me," said the Youngman. "Let me See if it is the Same as Mine."

"Mine?" answered the Monster. "Haugh! Mine is Simple. If Fat is Thrown Into the Lodge Fire and the Medicine Rattle Is Shaken, then I will Die."

I have seen this done, the youngest man there signed to Hides On The Wind. *It was performed*

one time just before a Give-Away and dance.

Yes, answered Hides On The Wind. *The Fat is the Sign of Truth and the Healing of the Gifts. It is also a Sign of the Fallen Star Fire. The Rattle is the Harmony of the People. One of the simpler Signs Given us here is that of the Ears. They represent gossip, but, of course, there is much more.*

Hides On The Wind continued his Story.

"Amazing!" said the Youngman. "Why are you Waiting here?"

"I am Waiting for the Ones who Live in these Scattered Lodges," the Monster said. "They are Simple, very Simple Prey. I will Take their Ears. I will Wait Until they have Fallen Asleep, and I will Bite their Ears Off. They will Make my Necklace even Greater."

"Wonderful!" the Youngman said, and Clapped his Hands Together. "That is Good. But Let me Go and Look First. I will Sneak Up Next to their Lodges, since I am much Smaller than you, and I will Look to See if they are Still Asleep. And then you, who are much Bigger than I, can Go In and Bite their Ears Off."

The Monster was Glad he had Company, and he Agreed.

So the Youngman Went to the Nearest Lodge, and he Entered. The Youngman Told the People who Lived in this Lodge, "If you Truly in your Hearts Want to End your Loneliness, and Want to Overcome the Monster of the Ears, then Hear me. When he Comes, Build Up a great Fire in the Middle of your Lodge, and Throw Fat Into the Fire. And then Rattle all of your Rattles Together, and the Monster will Die."

The Youngman Returned to where the Monster Waited, and Told it that the People were Fast Asleep. The Monster was Pleased, and Went Immediately to the Lodge. The Youngman Asked if it would Prefer for him to Go Inside First.

"No! No! No! No!" said the Monster. "I will Go First. I must Have their Ears for my Necklace."

So the Youngman Let him Go In First. But when the Monster was Inside, the People there Sprang Up from their Sleeping Beds and Built Up their Center Fire and Threw Fat Into it. They had Gathered the Wood Together for a great Fire. They Joined their Voices, Each Singing Louder than the Other, and Rattled their Rattles. The Monster Tried Desperately to Run from the Lodge, but the Youngman, Fallen Star, Held himself in the Opening of the Lodge like a Great Stone, and the Monster could not Escape.

"Now that you have Overcome the Monster," said the Youngman, "It is time Now for All of you to Go to the River." And they Went to the River Together. At this Place, the Youngman Built a Sweat Lodge.

"Take Off your Clothes, and Enter the Lodge and Sit in a Circle. Sit with your Hands Touching," the Youngman asked them. And they Did.

The Youngman Named Fallen Star then Heated Stones and Placed them in the Lodge. On them he Poured Water, to Make Steam. Then he Sang Four Harmonies, or Songs. He then Spoke to the People.

"Once Men Lived in Earth Lodges and were Blind to their Brothers. They Thirsted. The Medicine Water was All Around them, but still they Cried Out for the Water, Heaping more of it Upon the Heated Stones. And still they Thirsted."

Then the Youngman said, "Hold your Severed Ears to your Heads and Listen to your Brothers' Hearts, and your Ears will be Healed."

After they had Done so they Came Out of the Sweat Lodge and Ran to the River in the Bright Sunlight. There they Drank the Cold Sparkling Water, and then these People Went Back to their respective Camp Circles.

The Youngman Moved On, Following the River. After a While he again Saw Lodges in the Distance. An Old Woman Came Out and Greeted him, saying, "Welcome, my Grandson, Fallen Star. Your Marriage is here. Your Bride is in that Lodge right Over there." She Pointed to a Beautiful Painted Lodge.

"Who is it who Lives in that Lodge?" asked the Youngman.

"An Old Woman Lives there," she answered, "who has been Taking the Braids of the People. She has been Taking them by any Way she can Get them, Tricking the People and sometimes even Killing them for their Braids."

"What does she Do with All these Braids?" asked the Youngman.

"She Keeps them," answered the Old Woman. "She is Weaving them Into a great Robe."

The Youngman Went to the Painted Lodge and Entered it. The Old Woman was there, Sitting at the North Side of the Lodge. A Beautiful Young Maiden was also there.

"Grandmother," the Youngman said, "I See that you are Making a great Robe of Braids."

"Yes," she answered, "and I Need only Two more Braids to be Finished."

"Your Granddaughter has Beautiful long Black Hair," the Youngman said, as he Sat Down with her, "and she will be my Wife. And I, too, have Fine long Gold Braids, and I am your Grandson. Why, Grandmother, do you Make this Robe of Braids?"

"The Answer is quite Simple," answered the Old Woman. "When the great Robe is Finished I will be Able again to See Plainly, and I will be Able to Overcome the One who has the Necklace of Ears."

"And How will you Do this?" asked the Youngman.

"Simply," answered the Grandmother. "I will Learn his Name."

"What will Happen if you Learn his Name Before you Finish your great Robe of Braids?" asked the Youngman.

"I will Die," she answered.

"Grandmother," said the Youngman, "What will Happen if you cannot Get All the Braids?"

"If I cannot Get All the Braids, I will also Die," she answered.

"And you Need my Bride's Braids, and my own," said the Youngman.

"Yes," she answered.

"Then Cut my Hair First, Grandmother," the Youngman said.

But when the Old Woman Tried to Cut the Youngman's Hair, she Found that it was Made of Stone. And she could not Cut it.

"Your Hair Braids are Stone," the Old Woman exclaimed.

"Yes, my Grandmother," answered the Youngman, "because I am Fallen Star."

The Old Woman Looked Hard Upon her Grandson, but her Eyes could not See him Clearly.

"Grandmother," the Youngman went on, "the Monster of the Ear Necklace is Already Overcome."

"Overcome?" she asked. "How is this Possible?"

"It was I who Tricked him, Grandmother," answered the Youngman, "and his Name was Double Eyes."

And the Old Woman Died. The Youngman then Went Out to the People. "Go In!" he called. "Go Into the Lodge and Get Back your Hair Braids."

"No, no!" answered all the People. "We are Afraid of her."

"You have Nothing to Fear," answered the Youngman. "The Old Woman is No More. Go In and Get your Hair."

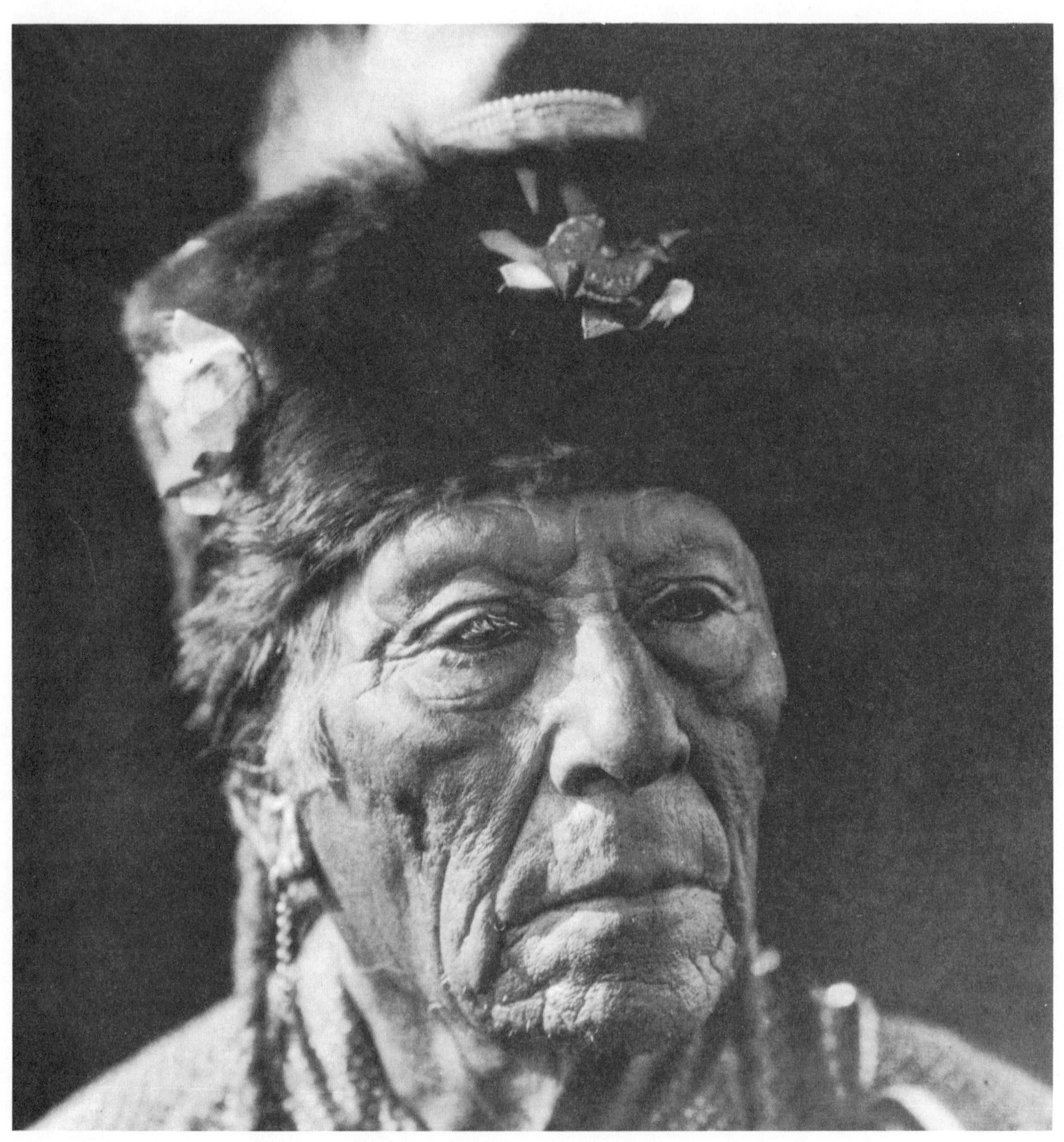

Sunday
March
1987

8

nd

67/ 298 Sunday, March 8, 1987

And that cuts it off! said Hides On The Wind, clapping his hands together loudly. *Can you tie any new Arrows that are parts of yourselves to this Teaching?*

Will you tell me the Sign of the Hair Braids? signed Left Hand.

There is a paradox here of which I will speak to you, Hides On The Wind answered, *but it is for you to open the Petals of this Flower yourself. The Braids represent the Experience of People. Many Peoples have Braided and Woven the Power of their Traditions together, but the problem is this. Each Generation of Children have their own Hair.*

This Teaching is difficult, signed Left Hand.

Yes, signed Hides On The Wind, *but you now have a good beginning, and remember, this Teaching will Grow as you Grow. I am still learning from the Story of the Jumping Mouse. I suppose that in twenty years more I will also be more illuminated by this one.*

"That is a horn in the gut," exclaimed Green Fire Mouse in his own tongue to Night Bear. "I thought I had almost untangled this Teaching! But if this old man has been seventy winters unfolding it, then my learning will require two hundred!"

You are too modest, signed Night Bear, to let the rest see the conversation. *Your learning will take five hundred years instead of the two hundred of which you speak!* Everybody laughed.

The next morning the three men resumed their journey to the camp of Morning Star. The first part of their journey was uneventful, and the riders saw nothing. Night Bear, Left Hand, and Green Fire Mouse were anxious to reach the camps and to see their brothers.

"I have seen signs all morning of horses," Green Fire Mouse said lazily to Night Bear. "According to these signs we should not be more than a half day's ride from Morning Star's camp circle."

"The People of the Perfect Bow told us they believed his camp to be little more than an eight day's ride, but we have already been riding nine days," said Night Bear, "and still we have not reached it."

"That is true," answered Left Hand. He was about to say something more, when suddenly they were surrounded by warriors from the camp of Morning Star.

Night Bear and Left Hand were recognized and greeted.

Peace, good father, one of the young men named Braids The Wind signed to Night Bear. *Welcome to the camp of Morning Star.*

Where is your camp? Night Bear signed.

It is hidden over there in the ravine, Braids The Wind answered.

Are there other camps of the People joined with that of Morning Star? signed Night Bear.

No, Braids The Wind signed his answer, as the party of men moved off toward the camp. *The lodges that had joined us here in council for war have all moved away for the winter.*

The camp of Morning Star was still humming with talk of war. The new Way had made so many changes among the People that the camp

was almost unrecognizable to Night Bear. Brother Shields had almost entirely disappeared. Many had been replaced by the Shields of war. In other cases, Shields had simply been discarded completely. The startling newness of the People's lodges was the thing that seemed strangest of all to Night Bear, who asked Little Wolf about it.

Yes, Little Wolf answered him in signs. *It does seem very strange even to me. The lodges seem naked. But we have moved many times since we saw you last. There has been little time for the painting of the lodges, and fewer and fewer of the People still care to do this. As you can see, other than my lodge and Morning Star's, there are only three that are painted.*

After only a few weeks in camp, Night Bear had already noticed the coming and the going of many whitemen among them. He carefully avoided these visitors, but still he found that even their presence nearby caused him a great deal of discomfort.

This constant coming and going of the whitemen is maddening, complained Night Bear one day to Morning Star. *"Does it not bother any one here besides me?"*

"I know exactly how you feel," answered Morning Star. *"But it is a thing one becomes used to. It must seem an insane thing to one who is not yet used to it."*

It is insane! Night Bear said, feeling his emotions welling up inside of him.

Insane? said Morning Star. *It is more than insane. We are fighting for our very lives with these whitemen, and yet at the same time we trade with them.*

But why? Night Bear almost hurled his signs at Morning Star.

Because it will do us no good to run from them, a man signed as he entered the lodge. He appeared to be a man of about thirty, average in his height and weight. He was a plain man, but clearly a man of deep feeling.

"I am called Lightning Thunder Bow," he now said in Night Bear's tongue as he settled himself, "and I am your brother. If the People do not stand and face this new thing, the whiteman, they will die."

"It seems to me that they will die anyway," Night Bear answered him.

The man laughed a deep warm laugh before he spoke again. "The Power knows I have felt just what you are feeling now," Thunder Bow answered, "but this feeling is only an Owl."

"Only an Owl!" Night Bear exploded, then checked himself from saying more.

"Come, my brother, and walk with me." The man got to his feet and walked out the door of the lodge. Night Bear grudgingly got to his feet and followed.

"*Zahuah,* what a fool!" thought Night Bear as he followed the man from the lodge. "It really takes all Medicines."

"I know what you are thinking," the man began as they walked. "You probably think I am a fool. Well, maybe I am, but I have visited a place where I perceived differently." He looked at Night Bear, noticing that he seemed to want to hear more, before he spoke again.

"As I walked, I began from the West. When I looked inside myself, I saw a whiteman," Thunder Bow began. "The image there frightened me. It was almost like seeing a wolverine, but I followed the Gift to see where it would lead me. I saw the whitemen's children, and felt their seeking. And I heard their god roaring in

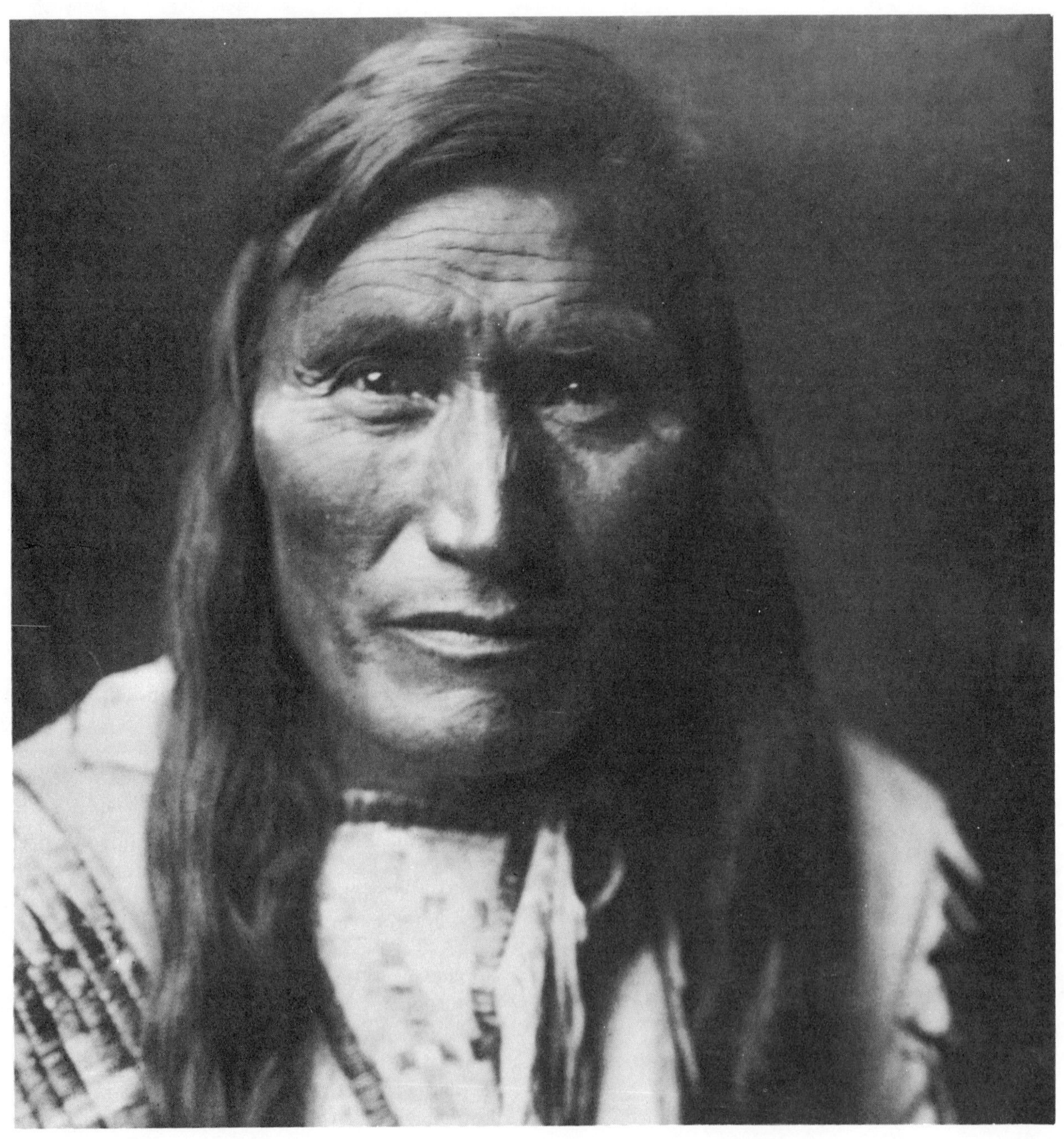

their ears. I saw through their own eyes their great Gifts. I saw some of the whitemen trying to use these Gifts to fill a great void that was in their hearts. I saw others marvel and take pride in the Gifts, believing that they had created them. I saw still others try to escape from them. Then suddenly I heard their god again, this time speaking from around the Medicine Wheel. Its voice came first from one Way, and then from another. Sometimes it sounded as a screaming, but at others it seemed as a whisper. And many times I heard it as a pure song. And even as a gentle Touching."

"That is incredible!" Night Bear said with emotion crowding into his eyes. "It seems impossible."

Suddenly Thunder Bow appeared to him to be truly the Coyote, the Trickster. But then Night Bear remembered Hawk, and instantly he knew that what he had believed had been only his own Reflection. Because this man Thunder Bow was a Man of the Shield, a man given the Medicine and also the problem of being the Mirror. Night Bear looked at him again, but this time with his heart, and he saw the man clearly. His face was sincere, and one that spoke the truth.

"Tell me, Shield Maker," asked Night Bear, "how can this be? Is not their god one of war and destruction?"

"Almost everything they say and do leads one to believe this, but somehow I think there is more," answered Thunder Bow.

They had left the camp circle and were now near a small stream. Both men made themselves comfortable under a large cottonwood tree. Some of the children from the camp were wading and splashing in the stream. The young girls who were watching the children sat along the banks, adding the music of their laughter to that of the children. No one paid any attention to the two new arrivals.

"This is a good place for us to sit," Thunder Bow said as he made himself comfortable.

"I could go on and on about my own feelings," Thunder Bow began again, "but instead, I believe it would be better if you were to learn of one of our Teachings."

"Will it explain the whiteman's war god?" asked Night Bear.

"There is no way to explain anyone's personal Reflections of the Universe, little brother," answered Thunder Bow with a grin, "but maybe this Shield Sign, one of the Forty-Four, will give you the same understanding it has given to me."

And he began his Story. "This Story is called the Wolf Stick, and it is very old.

The People were Once Camped Near a Great River. There was a Youngman who Lived with them there in his Lodge. He Lived with his Grandfather, Father, Mother, and his Four Sisters. He was One of the Smallest of the Young Men in the Camp for his Age. All of the Other Young Men could Outrun him, Out-Throw him, and Out-Wrestle him. His Sisters were very Beautiful. Soon the Young Men of the great Camp Began to Compete for the Hands of the Girls in Marriage. The Situation Quickly Grew Ugly, because the Young Men Began to Dispute Among themselves, and eventually there was Violence.

Soon the Lodges Divided into Smaller Camps. They were Built this and that Way, and some of them were Alone. Then Finally some of the Men Decided that they were Going to Solve the Disagreement by Coming and Stealing All of the Girls during the Night. Two Different Camps, Unknowing of Each Other, had Decided Upon this same Action in the same Night. And when they Came Together they Found themselves First in Argument, and then in terrible War. The Result of this Conflict was the Death of the Father, and the Wounding of the Grandfather of that Circle.

The Next Morning All the People Hung their Heads in Shame, and could not Look at Each Other. Then Suddenly they Noticed that the Camp Dogs were Snarling and Barking and Rushing Together at something in the Middle of the Camps. No One had Noticed that during the Night Someone had Entered the Camps, and Now Sat not too Far Away Near the River. The Dogs Rushed Growling and Barking at the Figure, but he Sat there Unmoving and quite Alone. He Carried a Contrary Bow, and was Painted with Hail Signs that were White and Red. His Arms and his Legs were Painted Black, and he Wore an Owl as a Headdress. The Young Men Made a Circle Around the Figure, and Drew Their Bows and their Arrows Against him. And they Loosed them at him, but their Arrows Fell Short Into the Ground and Broke. They Became very Afraid then, because they Realized this was a Medicine Person. The Chiefs of the People then Came, and they Made a Ragged Circle Around the Figure.

"What is it you Want?" they asked.

The Figure's Face could not be Seen Clearly by the Chiefs. Even his Eyes were Painted the same as his Body and his Face.

"I have Come for my Granddaughters," he told them, "and for my Grandson."

So the People Gave the Grandson, Granddaughters, and even the Father who had been Killed to the Stranger. The Stranger Helped the Family and Painted them a New Lodge. Each Day he Worked with them. He Brought them Firewood, and Hunted Buffalo for them. When he Brought them Buffalo, the Sisters Made the Hides Useful. And they Saved All the Sinew, and

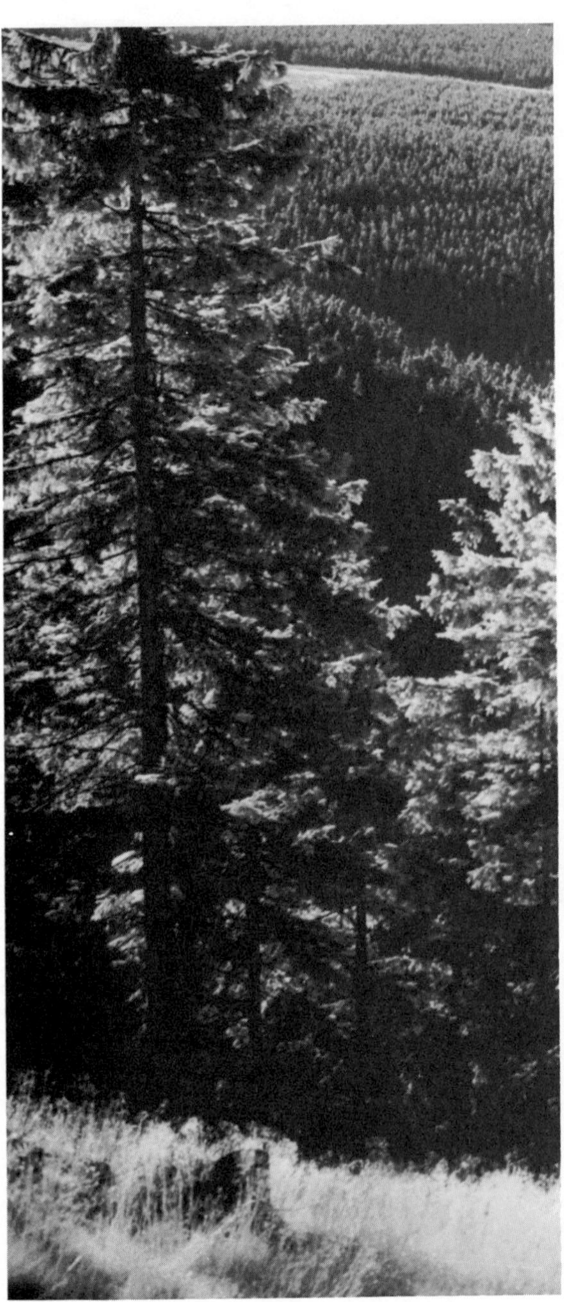

Prepared the Buffalo for Eating. The Old Man's Wounds slowly Healed.

The First Day the Stranger was there he Made them a Pipe. He Set the Pipe Outside the Lodge Upon a Forked Stick, and he Told the Youngman to Care for it. The Second Day the Stranger Made a Thunder Bow, and he Set this Outside the Lodge with the Pipe, Telling the Boy to Care for it. The Third Day the Stranger Made a Headdress that was Shaped All in One Straight Line, Made of Eagle and Hawk Feathers and their Plumes. He Set this with the Rest, Instructing the Boy as he had Before. On the Fourth Day the Stranger Made a Lance which had a Dull Point, and he Put this with the Other Things Outside the Lodge.

Then the Stranger Called the Boy and the Family to him. Because the Man had been very Kind and had Showed them How to Hunt the Buffalo, and How to Care for them, Tanning the Robes and Using the Sinew, they All Loved him and Believed him.

"Sit here in a Circle with me," he told them, "Around these things." He Seated One of the Sisters to the South, One to the North, One to the East, and One to the West. He then Asked for the Old Man's Robe. The Old Man Gave the Stranger his Robe. He Placed the Robe Upon the Ground Over the things he had Made.

"You must Go and Find our People," he told the Youngman, "because they are Scattered Upon the Prairie and they are Hungry. Find the People and Bring them Together here. Take this Bundle of things with you, and Make a Gift to Each of the Camps. I will Wait for your Return. I will be Camped just Across the River from here. Bring the People to this Place, and Tell them they will not be Hungry because there will be a great many Buffalo here."

The Youngman Wanted to Do these things, because he Loved the Stranger. The Next Morning he Began his Search for the People.

"Was this a dispute concerning the Way of the People?" asked Night Bear.

"In a roundabout manner, yes," answered Thunder Bow, "but instead of giving you a simple answer to your question, let me say this. The Girls in this Story are things that are New and Beautiful to Marry. The Father is all the things the People were before, the Old Circle. The Old Man is the Tradition of these things."

"And the Boy?" asked Night Bear.

"The Boy?" laughed Thunder Bow. "We will see." He began the Story again.

The First Day of the Boy's Search Brought him Among a great many Trees. They were Pines, and his Journey Became Steep and Difficult. He Sat Down to Rest because his Bundle was very Heavy for a little Boy. While he Sat there he Realized he was completely Lost. He did not Know which Way was South, nor East, nor North, nor West. He did not even Know which Way he had Come from. He Cried Out in his Loneliness, and he was very Hungry. A Coyote Heard him and Visited him there.

"Hello, little Brother," said the Coyote.

"Hello," answered the Youngman.

Coyote said, "What is the Matter?"

"I am completely Lost," said the Boy.

"I will Help you," said the Coyote, "but you must Hunt with us. And you must Make me a Gift, also, of One of the things you have in your Bundle."

The Youngman Agreed, and Coyote Led him Out of the Trees. He Took him to a High Plateau in the Mountains. There he Hunted with the Coyotes and they Taught him Four Harmonies, or Songs. After the Youngman had Learned the Songs, the Coyotes Told him it was time for him to Leave.

"One of us will Go with you," said Coyote.

The Youngman was very Glad. He Picked the Oldest Among them to Go with him, because this Coyote had been his Father.

"Now it is time," Coyote said, "for us to have our Gift."

"Which One of these things in my Bundle do you Wish?" the Youngman said.

"Give us the Pipe!" answered Coyote.

The Youngman was very Sad, because Now he would not be Able to Make a Gift to One of the Four Camps.

"But what Gift will it then be that I can Give the First Camp of People?" asked the Boy. "You Now have what was meant for them, the Pipe."

His Father answered, "You can Give them yourself, and I will Give them my Robe."

The Youngman was Happy, and he and the Oldest Coyote Continued Upon their Way. As they Traveled Looking for the People, Coyote Hunted Food for him. But he was Old and it was very Hard Hunting, so the Boy did not have too much to Eat. Coyote's Eyes were Getting Weak and he could not See too Well, so the Youngman had to Do all the Looking for the Lodges. Soon they Found themselves Upon a great Prairie, and they Walked for a long time. It was not long before it became Apparent that they were Lost. It was the Second Day.

"Old Man Father," the Boy said to the Coyote, "which Way have we Come? Was it from the East, West, North, or South?"

Coyote Ran Around in One Great Circle Searching for their Tracks to See from which Direction they had Come, but his Nose was Old and he could not Smell.

"I cannot See nor Smell the Direction from which we have come," said Old Coyote, "but I will Hunt for you."

The Youngman Sat Down Wearily, and he did not Know what to Do.

"Let me Go to Find our Brothers," Old Coyote said, Pricking up his Ears. "They Will Help us." And he Left.

The Youngman soon Became Lonely and Sad. He Cried. A Wolf Heard him Crying, and Came to him and Sat like the Boy, not too Far Away. The Wolf was very Powerful and Strong.

"Why are you Crying?" asked Wolf.

The Youngman Looked Up and Saw him.

"I Cried Out because I am Sad and Lost," answered the Youngman. "I do not even Know what Direction I have Come from."

"I will Help you," said the Wolf, "But you must Come and Live with us, and Hunt with us, and I must Have One of your things from the Bundle."

The Youngman Agreed, and he Went with White Wolf. White Wolf Took him to a small Stream where the Wolves Lived Upon the Prairie. They Taught the Youngman how to Hunt the Deer and the Elk, and they Taught him Four Harmonies, or Songs.

"Now it is time for you to Leave," said the Wolves. "And you can Take One of us With you."

The Youngman Looked at his Brothers and Thought.

"I will Take the Youngest," answered the Youngman.

"Good," answered the Wolves. "Now we will Have our Gift."

"What will you Have?" asked the Youngman.

"We will Have the Bow," answered the Wolves all together.

"But what will I then Give as a Gift to One of the Camps?" asked the Youngman.

"Give them your Grandfather," answered the

White Wolf. "And we will Give them this Wolf Robe."

The Youngman was Happy, for Now he Had a Gift for the Second Camp and he Left With his Young Brother. His little Brother Hunted for him, but since they were Both very Young, they were Able to Find Only the Smaller Animals as Gifts for Food. They had a great deal of Fun Together and they Played.

One Day while they were Playing, they Both Fell Into a Deep Hole.

"Now what are we Going to Do?" the Youngman asked his Brother.

"Lift me Out of the Hole," answered the Wolf Pup, "And I will Run to our Brothers for Help."

The Youngman Lifted the Young Wolf Out of the Hole, but he Knew it would be a long Wait.

"Why, oh why, did I Fall in here?" the

Youngman Cried Out.

An Otter Visited him, Looking Into the Hole. "Why are you Yelling?" said the Otter to the Youngman.

"Because I cannot Get Out of this Hole," answered the Youngman.

"I can Help you Out of that Hole," said the Otter. "But you must Come and Live with us, and I must Have One of the things in your Bundle."

Otter Began Handing Down Dry Wood for the Youngman to Pile Up and Stand Upon, and soon he was Out of the Hole. He Went to Live with the Otters. He Swam with them and Splashed in the Great River where they Lived, and they Taught him Four Songs.

"It is time for you to Leave us," the Otter Told the Youngman. "You can Take One of us With you. Which One will it be?"

"I Think I will Take One that is neither Old nor Young," answered the Youngman.

"Good" said the Otter. "Now it is time for you to Give us our Gift from the Bundle."

"What is it you Wish?" asked the Youngman.

"Give us the Straight Line of Headdress Feathers," they Told him.

"But then what will I Give the Third Camp of People as a Gift?" the Youngman asked.

"Give them your Sisters," answered the Otter. "And we will Give them an Otter Robe."

The Youngman was Happy and Went On his Way with the Otter that was neither too Old nor too Young. They Swam and Played in the Great River, Looking every Once in a While for the Lodges of the People. They Followed the River, and the River Became more Swift as they Went Along it. This was the Third Day.

Finally the Current Grew so Swift it Carried them Away Down the River. Soon the Youngman

Grabbed Onto a Rock and Climbed Upon it to Save himself from Drowning. But Now he was in a Deep Canyon. There was no Way to Walk Along the Banks of the River, and if he Tried to Swim he would Drown.

"What are we Going to Do Now?" asked the Youngman.

"Let me Go and Swim for Help," answered the Otter. "Our Brothers will Help us." And the Otter Swam Away.

"Zahuah!" the Boy exclaimed. "Now what am I Going to Do?"

Just then an Eagle Alighted on the Canyon Rim Above him and Spoke to him.

"I can Help you," said the Eagle, "but you will have to Come and Live with us. And I must Have One of the things in your Bundle."

The Youngman Agreed, and the Eagle Flew Down and Carried him Up and Over the Trees and the Prairie to the Mountains.

The Eagle and the Other Young Eagles Taught him Four Songs.

"Now," said the Eagle, "there is something you must See. That, Over there, is the East. This Way is the West, and Over there is the North. And that Way is the South." The Eagle also Showed him the Night Sky and the Day Sky. And he Talked to him About the Half and Full Moon. Finally the Eagle also Told him that it was time for him to Leave, and that he would Fly him Back to the Prairie. The Youngman could easily See Now all the Scattered Lodges of the People.

"Now it is time for me to Have the Gift from your Bundle," the Eagle Told him.

"But what will I then Do for a Gift to the People?" asked the Youngman.

"Over there," Pointed the Eagle, "is where the Stranger Waits for you. This is your Gift to the People." And the Eagle Flew him Back to his own Lodge, where his Grandfather and his Sisters

Waited for him.

Thunder Bow stretched and rose to his feet.

"Night Bear, my brother," Thunder Bow said, looking toward the camp, "The smell of cooking back in the camp has become too much for me. The rest of the Story will have to wait until I have eaten something."

"I am nearly half starved, too," Night Bear said. "Your idea is a good one."

They walked back to the camp and stopped at the first lodge they came to. It was the lodge of Red Prairie Grouse. He had arrived at his lodge a short time before them, and was removing two fine buck deer from the back of his pack horse.

"Tell your wife to cook only one of those deer," Thunder Bow said as he walked up to the fire. "Night Bear can only eat one today," he teased.

"I will tell her to cook both," Red Prairie Grouse grinned. "I will be the other half of that hunger."

While they ate, they began to ask Thunder Bow questions about himself.

"Me?" said Thunder Bow, suddenly turning very serious. "Yes, I will tell you about myself. The Power made his first mistake with me. I was born nothing but hair. It really upset my mother, and she had a hard time feeding me." Thunder Bow had noticed that they had been joined by two children. This explanation was for their benefit. He pretended not to see them, and continued. The children's eyes began to grow, as did the story.

"Finally," Thunder Bow went on, "she decided to cut off all the hair so that she could find me." At this point, Night Bear and Red Prairie Grouse were both wondering about the sanity of the man who sat in front of them.

Thunder Bow went on, "She cut and cut, but finally there was no more hair to cut. But there was still no child to be seen, either. She could hear me crying, but she could not see me. Things like this are difficult for a wóman with her first child. Do not tell anyone," Thunder Bow said, sounding secretive and looking around, his eyes avoiding the place where the children sat, "but she had married a toadstool. In fact," he said, his eyes growing wide, "the very one that little girl right there is now sitting upon!" And he pointed to one of the little girls.

"You are silly," one of them giggled.

"I am going hunting again this afternoon," Red Prairie Grouse offered, changing the subject. "Will my brothers join me?"

"That will be just fine!" Thunder Bow said, his face lighting up. "But I must finish a Teaching first."

"Is the Story almost finished?" Red Prairie Grouse asked.

"It is," answered Thunder Bow. "However, I will go get the horses and our bows ready and my brother can give you the beginning of the Story. I will be back shortly, and we will continue the rest of it together."

It was not long before Thunder Bow began the Story again.

His Sisters Came Out of their Lodge and Hugged him. It was the Fourth Day.

"Come," the Youngman said, "Let us Go Across the River where the Stranger Told us to Meet him."

They Followed him Across the River. When they Crossed the River, they Saw a great Herd of Buffalo. It was just as the Stranger had Promised. The Prairie was Covered with Buffalo as Far as the Eye could See. They Looked Everywhere for the Stranger, but they could not Find him. That Night when they Lay Down to Rest, they Suddenly Saw a Great Lodge. The Youngman Got

Up from his Sleeping Robes and Went Toward the Lodge. The Youngman Looked Inside the Lodge and Saw a very bright Light. The Light was in the Middle of the Lodge. It was Bright to the Point of Blinding the Eyes.

Within the Great Lodge were Four Beautiful Young Women.

Each of the Young Women had hair of a Different Color. One of the Young Women's Hair was as Green as the Spring Grass, and Another had Hair the Color of the Whitest Snow. One had Hair the Color of the Bright Morning Sun, and the Other had Hair Black as the Night. Each of the Young Women was Wearing a Medicine Belt. The Woman with the Hair as Green as Grass had a Medicine Belt that was White and Red, with the Signs of the South. The Young Woman with Hair the Color of Snow had a Medicine Belt that was Green and Blue, with the Signs of these Ways. The Young Woman with the Hair as Bright Gold as the Morning Sun Wore a Belt of Black and White, and was Covered with the Signs of the East. And the One whose Hair was the Color of the Night had her Belt Colored with All the Colors of the Setting Sun, with Gold, and had the Signs of the West.

When the Youngman Entered the Lodge, they All Greeted him and he Ate with them. They Hugged him, for they All Loved the Youngman. The Youngman Stayed in this Lodge for Four Days. The Night of the First Day he Slept with the Girl of the South. The Second Night he Slept with the Girl from the North. And his Third Night he Spent in the Bed of the Girl to the East. His Last and Fourth Night was Spent with the Girl of the West. On his Fourth Morning the Lodge was Gone, and he was Lying Alone on the Prairie. In the Places where his Wives had Been, there were

Now Four Robes. To the South was the Robe Coyote had Given him. To the West was the Robe that Otter had Given him. To the North was the Robe that White Wolf had Given him, and to the East was the Great Bundle he had Originally Begun with.

And Sitting in the Middle of these things was the Stranger with the Owl Headdress. But Now he was Painted completely Blue.

He Spoke to the Youngman, saying, "In Each of the Robes is the Gift for the Four Camps of People. Call them Together here and Give them to them because Now they are Able to Hear you. They are very Hungry, and that is why they can Now Hear."

The Youngman Called All the People, and they Came Together Making a great Circle.

"Build a Great Lodge here," he Told the People. "Build it Around these things you See here."

They Built the Great Lodge and Followed Each Other Into it with the Youngman. The Door of the Lodge was Open to the Rising Sun.

"Those of you who were Camped to the East, Now Camp to the West," he Told them. "And those of you who were Camped to the South, Now Move to the North. Those of you who were to the West Now Go East, and those of you who were to the North Now Camp to the South."

The Youngman Took the Great Bundle and Removed the things from it in Front of All the People. The First thing Taken from the Bundle was a War Ax. The Second thing was a Contrary Bow of War. The Third thing Taken from the Bundle was a Lance of War. The Fourth thing was the Headdress of War with its Feathers in a Straight Line.

The Youngman then Asked his Four Sisters to Enter the Lodge. They were Carrying the Coyote

Robe with them. They Gave it to their Brother. The Youngman Opened the Robe and Removed Four Arrows from it. He Gave One to Each of his Sisters. His Sisters then Chose where they would Sit. One Went to the North and Sat with the People there. One Sat with those of the South, the Next One with those of the West, and One with the People of the East.

"These, my Sisters, are my Gifts," he said, "and these Arrows are also your Gifts."

The Youngman then Covered those things of War that were in the Middle of the Lodge with the Coyote Robe. He also Placed the Robe that White Wolf had Given him, and the One from Otter, Under the Coyote Robe.

"Under Coyote's Robe is a Gift for Each of you," he Told the People. "They are for you who Sit in the North, the South, the West, and the East. Under Coyote's Skin are the things that will Give you Buffalo. You will not Hunger, nor be Alone, nor Lost."

The Youngman then Told those who Sat in the Four Directions to Pick their Gifts from Under the Robe.

"I will take the Ax," One said.

"And I the Lance," said Another.

"I will Have the War Bow," said still Another.

"I will Take what is Left, the War Headdress," said the Last.

The Youngman then Asked the Grandfather to Uncover the Robe of Coyote, and to Give Each of them their Gifts.

The Old Man Lifted the Robe of Coyote.

But the War Ax was Now a Fragile Pipe Stone, Shaped like the Pipe of Peace. The Lance was Now Covered with the Wolf Skin and that of the Otter, its Point Broken, a thing that could not be Thrown. The Last thing was what had Once been Two. It was the Contrary War Bow Now Strung with the Straight Line of Feathers. The Eagle

Feathers were Now the Single Brother Feather as is Worn in the Hair. And the Bow was Now One of Peace. It was the Thunder Bow.

"Which of you Now Wishes to Possess for himself the Gifts you See in Front of You in this Brother Lodge?" asked the Youngman.

They All Hung their Heads because they Recognized these things.

Each of them in his Turn Asked the Sister who had been Given to him to Place their Arrow as a Gift Together with the things of the Coyote Robe.

"Now there are Four Things," said the Youngman. "They are the Wolf Stick, the Thunder Bow, the Pipe of Peace, and the Brother Arrows. Now there can be a Renewal."

And they Danced in the Brother Lodge Together. And there were Buffalo Given to them. This Youngman's Name was Sweet Medicine.

"What is the Sign of this Shield of the Forty-Four?" asked Night Bear. "Could you draw it for me?"

"I can do better than that." Thunder Bow grinned a broad smile, "I will show you mine." And Thunder Bow took his Shield from the side of his horse and showed it to Night Bear.

"I still do not see what connection this all has with the terrible god of the whiteman," Night Bear said.

"There is a great deal to be learned from this Story, little brother," answered Thunder Bow. "But what it has taught me is this, especially after I walked the Way of the Bear and looked inside. The coming of the whiteman and his Gifts is like the Story of the Four Sisters. In this Story, some of the men simply wanted to get rid of the Girls. There were also those, no doubt, who wanted only what they could get from the Girls. And there were also those people who never did understand anything of the four Girls at all. And of course, there were those who loved them. It is the same way now."

"This could make sense in the light of the Gifts," Night Bear said. "But surely you cannot mean this concerning their war god."

"You keep seeing shadows, my brother," Thunder Bow answered.

"Shadows?" Night Bear said suddenly finding himself angry. "The things I have seen and heard are not shadows. These whitemen are vicious killers! They are mad dogs, and their talkers are men who are blinded by their Way."

"You mean those frightened black-robed mice who visit our camps?" Thunder Bow asked, raising one eyebrow.

"These old men you call frightened mice are more vicious than the Pony Soldiers!" Night Bear slammed the words at the man across from him. "They are tearing our whole world to pieces. How can you talk this way?"

"Do you wish for me to run blind with emotion as you are?" answered Thunder Bow. "Or will you hear me out?"

"Speak then," Night Bear said. None of the fire that roared inside him was quenched.

"It is not possible for the Medicine to be a Power of war," Thunder Bow began. "Because if this were true, then our own Power would be one of war. Why would this be true? Because many of our People wish to see this same Power Reflection that the whiteman perceives. Many times the Reflection of the Power is twisted by those who wish to justify some wrong, but this Way is only a Begging Way. It is used simply for personal satisfaction. And so it is with the understanding the whitemen have concerning their own Power."

Night Bear felt himself wince at this piece of truth. Thunder Bow went on.

"Was it the whitemen who threw away the Brotherhood of the Shields? Look at the Shields of war our own People have made. They are all around us. This is what truly is crushing you, not this Sign the whiteman has become for you."

"What you say is real," Night Bear answered, feeling his hands unclench. "But why is this happening? Is there no Way for Peace?"

"Yes!" Thunder Bow grinned. "Yes, there is. This Way is found in the Lodge of the Brotherhood. These same Sisters of the Wolf Stick Teaching who have caused the tearing apart can also be the Gifts. If the Men of Peace can themselves grow and learn as Sweet Medicine did, our People can be healed. You see, while I walked with the Bear of the West I saw myself as a whiteman. And I saw how they had frozen their Medicine Wheel. This frozen thing caused them to see their own Power, twisted within its Reflection. The freezing of the Medicine Wheel Water has caused their blindness and their wars."

"Then the answer is always the same," said Night Bear. "We must grow and seek the Four Directions and the Brotherhood. There must be a Renewal, a Renewal of the Sacred Arrows."

"Yes," answered Thunder Bow.

Night Bear hurried into the camp to look for Green Fire Mouse, eager to tell him of his new illumination. He saw Touches The Enemy coming toward him. "He will know where Green Fire Mouse is," thought Night Bear. "He has been with him every day since we have been in the camp."

"Have you seen my brother, Green Fire Mouse?" Night Bear asked the man as soon as he was close enough to be heard by him.

"Yes," answered Touches The Enemy. "He is two days ride from here in one of the camps of the Brother People. They are there in council for war against the whiteman."

Night Bear had already caught his horse and was preparing to leave, when Lightning Eagle came riding up to him.

"Where are you going?" Lightning Eagle asked, pulling his pony to a stop.

"Come with me and I will explain it to you as we ride," Night Bear said, kicking his horse into a trot. "We are off to see our brother, Green Fire Mouse."

As they rode, Night Bear explained the reason for their journey. They camped together that night, and the next morning they set out again. It was hot and dusty, but the smoothly rolling prairie made their riding easy. It was almost midday when both men saw a small stream. The grass and green trees that grew along it promised them both shade and a cool swim.

Night Bear kicked his horse into a run.

"The last man into the water cooks the supper," he called as he raced for the small creek.

"Then prepare yourself for the cooking," Lightning Eagle laughed as his pony inched past Night Bear's.

Then the air suddenly exploded with the roar of thunder irons. Night Bear clutched at the fire that seared his stomach. He dimly saw Lightning Eagle spill from his horse just before another bullet hit him in his head.

Thunder Bow met Green Fire Mouse as he rode into camp. The party of warriors he rode with scattered to their respective lodges, leaving Green Fire Mouse alone with Thunder Bow.

"Where is your brother?" Thunder Bow asked.

"Dead," Green Fire Mouse answered flatly as he dismounted. "They stumbled into a camp of whitemen and were killed."

At the next sunrise, Morning Star called Thunder Bow to his lodge.

"After we have eaten," Morning Star said as soon as Thunder Bow had made himself comfortable in one of the back rests, "We will discuss the Renewal."

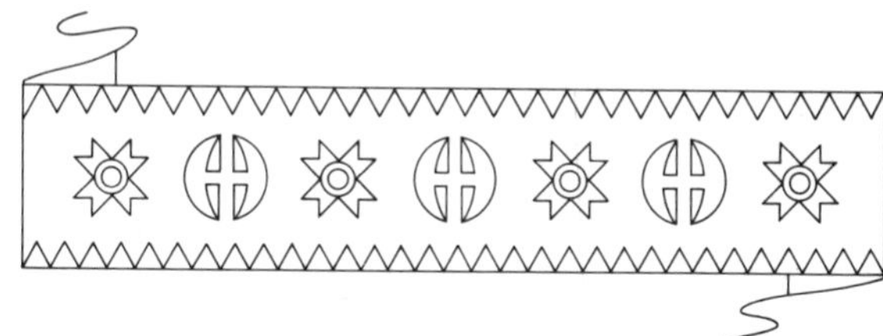

Green Fire Mouse rode alone, impatient to reach his own People. In his mind he envisioned himself riding into his own camp, greeted by his People as a hero come to gather warriors against the whitemen. Each time he lived the vision it loosened the knot that turned inside of him, and each time his appetite for greater numbers of warriors grew larger. His dream had begun with a large force of two or three hundred, and then it had grown to become an unimaginable two or three thousand. Over and over again he dreamed the dream, watching the whitemen flee before the overwhelming force of his People and retreating forever.

But gradually the dream faded, and he realized that he rode alone. He felt crushed. The dream had died with Morning Star's decision for Renewal.

Green Fire Mouse turned his pony down into a small ravine with the intention of dismounting there, giving his horse a rest, and relieving himself. His physical need and the thought of resting himself brought a temporary turn of thoughts which eased his feelings, and for a moment the young man drifted with a neutral mind.

"Green Fire Mouse!" a voice called suddenly from nowhere.

Fear and surprise shocked Green Fire Mouse's mind and body into immediate alertness. His sudden tension was telegraphed to his horse, causing it to start with a quick jump. The young man jerked the pony's head around to face the voice, nearly bringing him to his knees with the sudden turn. Green Fire Mouse's legs clamped around him like a vice, and his pony jumped again, ready for a hard run.

"Wait," the voice called again, just as Thunder Bow rose into view from a small hollow in the prairie. Green Fire Mouse's horse backed and wheeled as Thunder Bow brought his own pony to a sudden stop beside him.

"You dog!" Green Fire Mouse growled. "I might have killed you in my surprise! Never do that to me again."

Thunder Bow dismounted almost immediately, and grinned up at Green Fire Mouse through the dust his horse had made.

"My brother," Thunder Bow laughed, "you must have been deep within the world of dreams, because I have been calling you for quite a while. In truth, I could more easily have killed you." He laughed again.

"Owls sit on your head!" Green Fire Mouse growled, returning the smile stiffly. "Yes, I was truly in another world. I had planned to stop and quietly relieve myself here, not to escape from some insane rider who would try to run me down with his horse!"

Thunder Bow led his pony down into the wash, to the shade under two small trees. Green Fire Mouse was still mounted and had not moved.

"What is the matter?" Thunder Bow asked as he hobbled his horse. "Is there something wrong?"

"No," Green Fire Mouse frowned. "It is just that I suddenly felt strange, as if I should be somewhere else instead of here. He shrugged and then grinned. "It was probably just because of your scaring me the way you did."

"The sky is clear and the moon will be full tonight," Thunder Bow said, taking the robe from his horse. "And it is silly for us to ride in this heat. Let us eat a good meal and then sleep until it is dark."

Green Fire Mouse dismounted and led his horse into the draw, then hobbled him. "You are a reckless man, but a wise one today. I agree. It will be much cooler tonight, and the horses will make better time."

"Time?" grinned Thunder Bow. "Time has little to do with it. It is just more comfortable, little brother. You act like a man who is about to be struck by lightning."

Green Fire Mouse returned the smile, but it was feeble. The strange feeling still persisted within him and he felt weak because of it. He fitted the string to his bow and tested it. The touch of it eased his tension.

"Come then!" Green Fire Mouse grinned broadly, throwing off the feeling completely. "Let us go hunt for our meal, crazy one."

There are Rainbows in the Mountains of Sweet Medicine, the Place of Seven Arrows. These Circles of Color Reflect in the Twin Paintings of the Medicine Lakes. There are Four and Seven of them Within the Lodge of the Buffalo Child.

White Rabbit was enjoying her comfortable lodge and its warm fire, which served to give light as well as warmth. She was combing and braiding the hair of her sister, Moves From Your Sight Little Red Star. Red Star felt her sister's fingers moving smoothly through her locks. She paused in her beading now and then, lifting her head and closing her eyes to enjoy White Rabbit's gentle touch.

"Did you know that Spirit Woman is pregnant?" Red Star asked, turning to look into White Rabbit's face. Her sister smiled and turned the younger girl's head back around to finish her work.

"Yes, I had heard of this," answered White Rabbit. "She is a gentle and very beautiful little She-Wolf, and that big shaggy Buffalo she walks with loves her very much."

Red Star turned around again to face White Rabbit. She frowned and searched White Rabbit's face intently, looking deep into her sister's eyes.

"If Spirit Woman's Medicine is that of the Wolf, would not the man she walks with who is of the Buffalo Medicine then feel threatened or hunted by her Wolf Medicine?" asked Red Star, still searching.

"You must have lived in an empty lodge, little sister, if you ask that," White Rabbit answered with a smile. "Have you not been taught the Ways of the Beginning Medicines?"

Red Star looked down at her hands. All expression left her face. "When I was little we lived near the forts of the whitemen. The only teachings I received from my mother were those of the stinging water. Then one day my uncle took me from her. But he raised me for a short time. Then our camps were split, and he left me to follow the path of war against the whitemen."

"Do you remember very much of your mother?" White Rabbit asked, pretending to find a fault in her braiding. She recombed Red Star's hair, looking at the girl who sat in front of her and trying to imagine her mother.

"Yes," Red Star answered. "She was so very beautiful. And I was happy to be with her, even at the times when her spirit seemed to be gone from her because of the stinging water. But sometimes it was very bad."

"We can talk of this later if you wish," White Rabbit broke in.

"No," answered Red Star. "It is all right. I can speak of it without hurt now. It has been almost two years since I last saw her. She made love to many whitemen, but the men who slept with her treated her cruelly. Once one of them even beat her. She cried for a very long time after he left. I hated them and I wanted her to go away, but when I told her this she would only hug me tightly. She would never answer."

"Your mother understood that the whitemen did not know of the Medicine Way," White Rabbit answered, now loosening Red Star's other braid and beginning to do it over again.

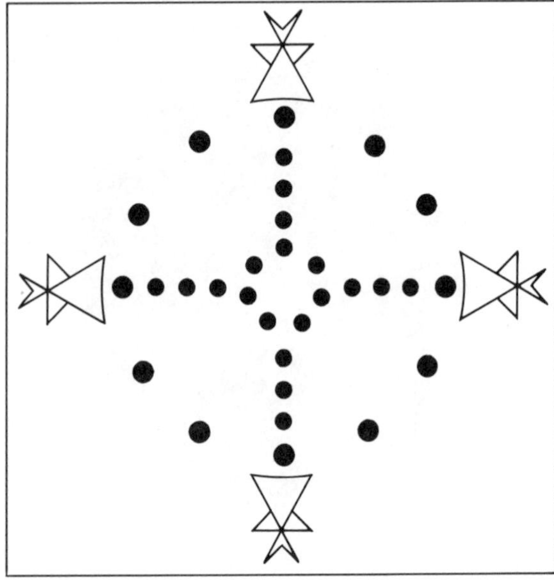

"Then tell me about this Way, because I wish to understand," Red Star said, turning to look in the woman's face again.

"First, I will draw you this Medicine Wheel," White Rabbit began.

"As you see, I have drawn Eagle Lodges at all Four of the Directions," explained White Rabbit, "one to the North, one to the South, one to the East, and one to the West. When we are born into this world, we always enter into it from one of these Ways.

"Of course there are many Ways and many Medicines. I will begin with the example of the Eagle first. Some people are born with the Medicine of the Eagle. When they reach adulthood, at about nine years of age, they begin to experience this Medicine. If a person was born Yellow Eagle, he would wear the Yellow Robe of the East. This would be his Gift of Perceiving. He would be able to See Far in the things of Illumination. If this Eagle were instead to wear the Green Robe, he would still Perceive Far, but from within the Innocence of Heart of the South. If he were to wear the Black Robe, he would Perceive Far from the West, from Looks-Within. If he wore the White Robe, he would Perceive Far in the things of Knowledge. Each one of these people would be given the Beginning Medicine of the Eagle, but each one would be different. Each one would Perceive Far from whatever point he was Given as his starting Gift on the Medicine Wheel. But no person should be content with Perceiving from only One Way. It is for each person to seek the Other Ways in all that he does. It is through this seeking that he then will Grow."

"Then within these Ways are found the Names of the People!" Red Star exclaimed.

"Yes," answered White Rabbit. "We are given our beginning names almost at birth. But these are only our beginning names, and they are always names from our Clan. For instance, a man or woman may be born into the Clan of Water, or Rattling Hoof, or even Kit Fox, and they will be given a beginning name of this Clan. But this name will not be who they truly are. They must then seek their true Name. This is done through the Vision Quest and the Sun Dance. Through the Ways of the Brotherhood."

"Then," Red Star broke in, "the man who visited our camp who was called Night Bear had another beginning name."

"Yes, he did," White Rabbit answered. "His Clan beginning name was Bull Looks Around. He was born in the Brotherhood of the Buffalo Clan, and his uncles were all those men born into this same Clan. I spoke to him about this and discovered that he was one of my Clan uncles. Even though his language was both that of the Little Black Crow and also that of the Painted Arrow, I never knew which of these was his first tongue. He was my Clan uncle, even though I was from the People of another tongue. I was as you are, born of the Little Medicine Bird People."

"Then that handsome one was my uncle, too?" Red Star asked excitedly.

White Rabbit laughed. "I cannot know this of you, little sister. I do not know to which of the Clans your mother belonged. If your mother was of the Clan of the Buffalo, then he was your uncle."

"But then how was he given the Name of Night Bear?" asked Red Star, frowning again.

"He learned of his Name through the Vision Quest," White Rabbit answered as she began

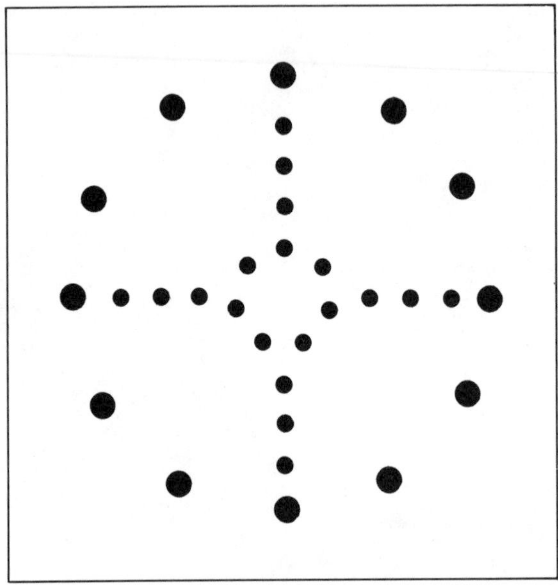

beading on some moccasins. "He spoke with the Power and was taught by Seven Arrows. He not only discovered that his Name was Bear, but he discovered that he was the Looks-Within Bear of the Four Star Colors."

"Then are his uncles of the Buffalo still his uncles?" asked Red Star.

"Yes," answered the woman, smiling. "This will never change. But what is more important is this. He discovered his Perceiving and his Brotherhood."

"Brotherhood?" asked Red Star. "Is this Brotherhood of which you speak the one of the Shields?"

"Yes," White Rabbit answered. "Now not only does he have uncles of many tongues, but he has Brothers of many tongues. His Brothers are of the Four Stars."

"Is there more?" asked Red Star.

"Yes, there is much more," answered White Rabbit. "This is only the beginning. The next Teaching is of the *Masuam,* or Animal Dance. The Animal Dance is the Give-Away. Let me draw you another of these Wheels for explanation.

"Each dot I have made with my finger in the dirt is an animal," said White Rabbit. "There is no one of any of the animals in this world that can do without the next. Each whole tribe of animals is a Medicine Wheel, in that it is the One Mind. Each dot on the Great Wheel is a tribe of animals. And parts of these tribes must Give-Away in order that they all might grow. The animal tribes all know of this. It is only the tribes of People who are the ones who must learn it. It is this Way because the People were placed here upon the Earth to learn. The Power gave each person a Beginning Way to learn.

That is his Medicine. And the Medicine is given to us from one of the animal tribes, because we too are animals."

"How is it you say that we are animals?" asked Red Star. "That is hard for me to believe."

"No," White Rabbit laughed. "We are not really animals. But we are of this Earth and therefore we are Medicine Animals. It is an Understanding, this Medicine Way. Those of the People who are Buffalo wish to Give-Away. That is their nature. Your own mother was one of these Medicine Gifts. The shame is that the whitemen never understood this. They used her, instead of receiving her as a Gift. It is a pity."

"Then why did she not stop giving?" Red Star asked. "Why did she take such punishment?"

"Why does one person feel almost no desire?" answered White Rabbit. "And why do others have great desire? These questions are the same with everything, and are equal. Why does one person eat more than another? Why is one more frightened? Another more greedy? Still another more shy? These questions are equal and are the same. What we must each ask ourselves is, who am I? What is my Medicine? In what Way do I Perceive? Why? Because some of us are given the Gift of Perceiving as Mice, some as Buffalo, some as Eagles, some as Foxes, and on and on and on. Each person is born with a different animal Medicine, from which he receives his own Medicine Way. But often, even when two people are of the same animal Medicine, they may still Perceive differently. This depends upon where they were born on the Medicine Wheel, to the East, the South, the North, or the West. Within these many Medi-

cine Ways we must seek our Name and our Perceiving. Now naturally, a person born with the Medicine of Wolf will not eat his brother or sister who is Buffalo. No! That would be silly. It is the Understanding that is the Gift."

"Then the girl who is a little She-Wolf is able to receive the same things Buffalo wishes to give?" Red Star asked.

"Yes," White Rabbit answered. "These people who are Buffalo have an overwhelming desire to give. If a Buffalo had married me, I no doubt would have loved him. But there is not much a Buffalo can offer to me, a Rabbit. Our Understandings are different. It is the little She-Wolf who is Hungry for Buffalo. And this little Wolf is the one who can accept her Buffalo's Gifts."

"But then how is it that the Buffalo too can be Full?" asked Red Star.

"Those who walk together are like the Twin Medicine Lakes. They are Two Mirrors. She-Wolf is Hungry for Buffalo, and Buffalo Hungers to Give-Away to the She-Wolf. They both Give in this manner. It is a Way of Understanding. It is the perfect Circle. It is a Way for all People to come together in Brotherhood, Wolves with Rabbits, Birds, Mice, and Weasels. All are beautiful and all are equal in the great Give-Away Dance. This Dance is the Sun Dance. There we learn of our Perceiving, and also of the Ways of our brothers and sisters. This Brotherhood is found among all the tongues of the People. The most powerful Sign of these things is the Understanding of the Medicines. Whenever you hear a Story, my little sister, all the Names you hear within it are Signs. These Signs are of the Medicine Wheel and its Growing. Each one is a part of the Universe. Each one is Sweet Medicine."

"The rain has stopped," Red Star said, getting to her feet. She opened the lodge flap and peered outside. High Silver Pine, Red Star's closest friend, was coming toward the lodge. She was holding her moccasins in one hand and the fringes of her dress in the other, keeping them both out of reach of the tall wet grass. The minute she reached the lodge, she grabbed Red Star's hand and began to talk excitedly.

"Standing Fox has just visited me with gifts!" She laughed as she told the news. "And I," she searched for words, "I just cannot believe it."

"No!" squeaked Red Star, her face reflecting Silver Pine's happiness. The two girls sat down together upon one of the sleeping beds. Their knees were touching, and they were holding

each other's hands.

"Yes," Silver Pine laughed again.

"No," Red Star giggled, hugging her sister.

"Of all times to bring the Gifts!" Silver Pine laughed. "You should have seen him!" She laughed again. "I was talking with Black Eagle Feather, my father, when he came into the lodge. He was dripping wet."

"You mean he brought the Give-Away horse in all that rain?" White Rabbit laughed.

"Yes!" Silver Pine laughed. "You should have seen Black Eagle Feather's face!" Tears streamed from her eyes as she went on. "I never saw anything so wet and so beautiful as Standing Fox in all my life."

For some time the three laughed again and again, as Silver Pine told them more of what had happened. Finally, when she was through, Silver Pine touched Red Star's hand. "We are going to leave this camp tomorrow morning," she said. "And I would be made happy if you were to come with us. Do you wish to do so?"

"Yes, I do!" Red Star answered quickly. "To which camp will we go?"

"We shall go across the mountains of the Curved Horn and Eagle," Silver Pine smiled, "to the lodges of the Perfect Bow. There is a man living there who is called Mirror Seeing. He is my husband's father."

It was a long time before the three happy girls fell asleep, but then they slept soundly.

Suddenly, early the next morning, an alarm was shouted throughout the camp. A band of riders, all of them warriors, had been seen moving directly toward the village.

The women were put onto ponies with their children, and scattered into hiding. All of the young men also mounted and swiftly prepared

themselves for battle. Four bowmen concealed themselves along the trail leading to the camp. Everyone waited tensely.

Braided Grass soon appeared far down the valley, riding hard for the camp. He had been the farthest away of the two men who had been posted as lookouts. He jerked his pony to a stop in front of the half moon of mounted men.

"Those who come are People of the Perfect Bow, and Green Fire Mouse is with them," Braided Grass shouted to the group. "There is also a Man of the Shield with them."

"Then we should have nothing to fear from them," Teaching Rock said.

"It appears to be that way," answered Pretty Weasel.

It was only a short time before Green Fire Mouse came into sight, riding hard at the head of the large group of warriors.

"Green Fire Mouse is in a race with our visitors," Pretty Weasel smiled.

A chorus of whoops went up as the people from the camp rode out to meet Green Fire Mouse.

"Who are our visitors?" Pretty Weasel asked him as they rode back to the camp.

"They are People of the Perfect Bow," answered Green Fire Mouse. "Night Bear and I met them as we were traveling to the camp of Morning Star. They are from a large camp that is at the River of the Shields, near the Yellow Stone Medicine River."

Soon after the visitors arrived, the women of the camp returned and began making dinner around their camp fires. After everyone had eaten, the visiting began. Thunder Bow was walking with White Rabbit and Red Star. He was teasing Red Star, when he became aware of

a far away sound so small that it almost defied hearing.

"Listen!" he yelled as loudly as he could to the whole camp. All talking ceased and everyone waited for Thunder Bow to speak. He was about to apologize for his interruption when the faint sound came again. This time, unmistakably, he recognized it to be the distant roaring of a thunder iron.

No one wasted any time as the men raced for their ponies. The camp was again emptied of people almost immediately. Where moments before the camp had been full of the sounds of laughter and talking, now there was only the faint crackling of abandoned camp fires to be heard.

Green Fire Mouse ran his horse as hard and as long as everyone else, slowing him to a trot at times only to let him get another wind. The pounding of the other horses' hooves all around made it impossible for him to hear if there were any more sounds of firing.

Soon the valley they were riding through split into two low ravines, before smoothing out again farther ahead into a small plain. A knot of men had already halted at the divide, undecided as to which fork to take. Green Fire Mouse rode into the throng of milling horses, straining his ears for a sound that would decide their direction. But he could hear only the hooves of the milling animals and their heavy breathing.

All during the ride down the valley, a longing for battle had been growing within Green Fire Mouse. The closer he had ridden to what he believed to be certainly a small war, the more determined he had become that he would fight. Thoughts of ending forever the threat to his

wife and children had been flowing in Green Fire Mouse's mind like poisoned water. These thoughts had grown until now they had turned into a strange lust. He had been aware of the fork in the valley, but now that he was there the two directions from which he had to choose became things to thwart him. His mind was driven into a confusion that swirled as madly as the dust the horses raised around him. He was about to end his desperation with a blind kick to his pony's ribs, sending it at random down whichever of the two valleys it might have chosen, when suddenly Pretty Weasel rode into the melee.

Wait! Pretty Weasel waved his signs. *We have no idea what we may be riding into. Let us trot our horses, so that they may keep their wind. There may be too many enemies for us. These two small valleys open onto a grazing place only a short distance from here. Let us stay together and move more cautiously.*

Pretty Weasel then turned his horse into the valley to his right, letting his horse walk. Green Fire Mouse's pony felt the tension in his rider, and lunged again and again, trying to run. Each time, Green Fire Mouse pulled hard on the pony's head, keeping him from obeying his first instinct. The horse danced and bucked, fighting for its head. Finally he calmed when Green Fire Mouse began to pat him, easing the tension in both himself and his mount. As he did this, Green Fire Mouse suddenly became aware again of the other men around him.

Pretty Weasel and Thunder Bow rode at the head of the small column of men, signing to one of the young warriors of the Perfect Bow People, who rode between them. The others in the band were either riding quietly or were busy

adjusting their weapons. Green Fire Mouse was amazed at everyone's calmness. It did not seem real to him. Even the small sounds of the grasshoppers and birds seemed unreal.

One of the men of the Perfect Bow was riding almost at Green Fire Mouse's elbow. He appeared to be about forty years old, and had a face that was unmistakably kind.

Maybe you had better string your bow, the man signed to him. *You young people amaze me with your calmness.*

"By all the Power of the Medicine Wheel!" thought Green Fire Mouse. "What an utter fool I am! Running off to a war with my bow unstrung!" He almost laughed out loud at himself, smiling instead to hide his embarrassment.

This is indeed a mad world at times, the man signed again. *Do you know the Man of Peace who rides with us?*

Yes, I have come to know him quite well, Green Fire Mouse signed. *And I also feel what you say about the world's madness. You thought I was calm, but in truth I was so confused within my own feelings I forgot to string my bow. And the Man of the Shield who carries no weapons at all?* Green Fire Mouse swept his hands in the violent sign of an explosion. *This Peace Man carries no weapons at all, and yet I tell you I know him and should understand him? Yes, my brother, it is a mad world at times.*

We are here! Thunder Bow signed, turning around to face the massed riders. *And it is a good day either to die, or to learn.*

But the sight that greeted the party was not the whiteman's army that Green Fire Mouse had expected, nor was it the hunting party that Thunder Bow had expected to find. Standing in the middle of the high grassy knoll were three horses. One was a pony which had belonged to one of the People of the Plains, and the other two were whitemen's ponies. Three men were lying on the prairie near where the horses were grazing, and all three men were dead.

They have killed each other, Green Fire Mouse signed, taking the reins of one of the ponies. Other men in the party quickly dismounted and began stripping the dead of their thunder irons, and of anything else that appeared usable.

One of the men suddenly stooped and held up an object that shone brilliantly in the sun. Everyone gathered around the man who had found it, marveling at its beauty and wondering what it possibly could be.

It is alive! the man signed who held it. *Listen, you can hear its heart beat!* The object was then passed around from hand to hand, everyone listening to it and examining it carefully.

"It is indeed alive!" Green Fire Mouse said out loud to Thunder Bow. "It is iron that has a heartbeat."

Amazing! signed Thunder Bow, who now was holding it. *The wonder and greatness of these whitemen's Gifts bewilders my mind.*

That evening, everything that had been found was distributed evenly among the People. Half was given to the People of the Perfect Bow, and the other half to the People of the camp. The amazing object with the heartbeat was left with the People of the Perfect Bow.

The next morning, the young man who had ridden between Thunder Bow and Pretty Weasel the day before came to Green Fire Mouse's lodge.

My brothers, I have news, the man began his signs. *The amazing object died early this morning. Its heart beats no more.*

What will your People do with it now? signed White Rabbit.

"I do not know, the Perfect Bow signed in answer. *We are leaving today to join our main camp at the river. Your brother, Standing Fox, will be leaving with us.*

Yes, we know, signed Green Fire Mouse. *My wife speaks the same tongue as the wife of Standing Fox. His leaving with you will no doubt mean that others of our People will go with you also. But it is my own plan to find the camp of Medicine Water, the Painted Arrow.*

Will you then ride with us? the Perfect Bow then signed to Thunder Bow.

Yes, Thunder Bow signed. *I will travel with the lodge of Hides On The Wind. There are many things I wish to learn from him.*

Four days later, Green Fire Mouse, White Rabbit, and a girl named Dancing Moon were on their way to Medicine Water's camp. Their trip had been extremely slow and difficult. The summer heat was oppressive, and it had forced the small caravan to stop three or four times a day for rest and shade.

Green Fire Mouse had been searching for three days for a place to descend from the mountain range they had been following. Medicine Water's camp was north and to the east of a place named Ten Sleeps, on the Greasy Grass River. Green Fire Mouse knew that he could save several days of difficult riding if he could find a short cut, but this hope vanished little by little with each false trail. Soon they were forced to turn back along the trail they had come on, to find the long way around to the Greasy Grass.

"Well, here we are right back again almost to where we started," Green Fire Mouse said, scowling into the fire. "I have been leading us like a blind mole running around on a rock."

White Rabbit laughed.

"What is it that you find so funny?" Green Fire Mouse snorted. "My stupidity?"

"No," White Rabbit laughed again. "I was

not finding humor in your hard work. It was the Owl expression you had on your face."

"Nuuuuueh!" Dancing Moon said softly. "Look at him. Maybe he really is an Owl. I think we should throw him into the creek."

Both women grabbed him at the same time, and began dragging him toward the creek. Green Fire Mouse pulled White Rabbit and Dancing Moon down into a tangled heap and ran to escape them. White Rabbit jumped to her feet and began chasing him around the lodge. Then Dancing Moon took the buffalo-skin water bag from its place and threw it over Green Fire Mouse, just as he had grabbed White Rabbit and was about to pin her to the ground.

"Yaaaaaeergah!" Green Fire Mouse yelled. "I am wounded! Now I will probably even die."

"Anyway, I hope that your sour old Owl is dead," Dancing Moon laughed.

They set out again the next day with the first light and stopped only twice, both times to care for the children, until midday. The heat then was stifling even in what little shade they could find to rest in, but everyone's temper was better now than when they had first begun.

The remainder of their journey was uneventful, though it seemingly grew hotter with each day. The thought of the cool valley of the Greasy Grass became more beautiful with each step that the horses took nearer to it.

Twelve days later they reached the valley. They remained there bathing in the river, resting, gathering sweet berries, and enjoying the cool evenings.

Their camp was well hidden in a place Green Fire Mouse had chosen immediately after they had arrived. The lodge had been set up within a cut in the bluffs. Anyone coming down upon the camp from above would signal his arrival with falling stones and gravel. Anyone coming from either up or down the river would be unable to see the camp, because of the trees that grew to either side of it. The open ground between Green Fire Mouse's camp and the river was the only path to it likely to be taken either by riders or by men on foot, and because of this they would be seen long before they reached the lodge. It was a perfect place, and its security brought even more joy to their stay.

It was mid-afternoon one day when Green Fire Mouse saw a rider approaching. White Rabbit had just settled the children down for a rest. She was about to go for a swim with Dancing Moon, when Green Fire Mouse suddenly announced that they would soon have a visitor.

"It is an old man who is coming," Green Fire Mouse said as he gathered more leather for the rope he was braiding. "And I am certain that he is alone. I have been watching him for some time. He is riding a horse that is nearly as old as he is, so it will still be a while more before he gets here."

"As always, I notice that old Lightning Nose is as yet unaware of our invasion," Dancing Moon smiled as she petted the camp dog. The old dog opened one of his eyes when the girl touched him, and wiggled closer for more attention. "Do you not know we have a visitor coming," Dancing Moon addressed the dog, smoothing his hair, "and that you should be out barking and scaring him away?"

"Wheyeahsheee!" Green Fire Mouse teased as he went back to his watching. "A prairie dog would be more fierce."

"Well," White Rabbit said, sitting down, "I guess our swim will have to wait. I will feed the old man first, and then we can have our bath."

"I wish it was a handsome young warrior who was coming, instead of just an old man," Dancing Moon said dreamily.

White Rabbit was about to answer, when they were interrupted by the sound of Green Fire Mouse's voice calling out a greeting to the old man.

"He must be a thousand years old!" Dancing Moon whispered to White Rabbit when the old man came into sight.

Yes, White Rabbit signed as she rose to her feet.

The old man's thin grey horse was as stretched and ancient as the weathered skin on an old discarded drum. The man who rode him blended with the animal rib for rib, with the exception of the new buffalo headdress he was wearing.

"Greetings, Daughters," the Old Man signed, Sliding from his Horse and Sitting Down almost where he Dismounted. "It is my Guess that the Youngest One would Rather I had been a Powerful Young Warrior Instead of Only this Dry Leaf, but I will Make Up for her Disappointment." He Smiled. "I will Tell Hand Drum Songs, and Paint Dreams for my Beautiful Daughters."

"That would be Wonderful!" Dancing Moon signed. Then she Handed the Old Man a Bowl of Food, and added, "What Camp are you Going to?"

"Camp?" the Old Man signed, his Face suddenly Turning Mysterious. "Why, this Camp of course! Is this not the Camp of Touches the Rainbow? The Maiden Stolen from her People? The One Destined to bear the Child of the Sun Warrior?"

"It is the Same Maiden!" White Rabbit signed. "We Found her Lost Upon the Prairie. And she Told us her Name was Dancing Moon."

"And she has Unbelievable Powers!" Green Fire Mouse joined with his signing. "She almost Drowned me!"

"Zahuah!" the Old Man signed, his Eyes Growing Wide. "Did you Know that she is the Daughter of the Lightning Elk Woman?"

"No! No!" White Rabbit signed. "What is the Story? She has Told us Nothing."

"Well," the Old Man Began, "it all Began when One of my Grandmothers Sent me for Fire Wood. I was Playing Beside a small Stream with my Brothers and Sisters when the Old Woman Called.

"Will One of my Grandsons Bring me Fire Wood?" she Called.

No One Seemed Able to Hear her, because Everyone Continued their Play Without any Notice.

"Will Little No Name Carry me some Wood?" she Called.

"Can you not Hear our Grandmother Call?" I asked my Brothers.

"No," they answered. "Whose Grandmother is Calling?"

"She is Calling for her Grandson who is Named Little No Name," I answered.

"Then it is not I," one of my Brothers answered.

"And not I," answered Another.

"Not I either," One Other answered.

"Is it you?" All of the Children asked me.

I Thought and Thought, but I could Find No Name.

"It must be me she is Calling," I answered, "because I do not Know my Name. I do not Know who I am."

I Left the Tiny Stream where I was Playing, and Went to the Old Woman.

"Here I am, Grandmother," I said when I Reached the Lodge of the Old Woman.

"You?" she said Looking at me Closely. "What is your Name?"

"I am the One you Called," I answered,

Looking Down so as not to Make her Angry. "I am No Name."

"You are a very Strange Little Boy," the Old Woman said, Squinting Hard at me. "Who was it who Gave you the Name of No Name?"

"I Thought because I had No Name that this then was my Name," I answered.

"You are Making a Joke of me!" the Old Woman Suddenly said, still Squinting Hard. "If I call No Name then there is No One Named No Name, and Now you Confuse a Simple thing by Telling this Old Woman that you have No Name, and because of this you are No Name. Is that not Simple enough?"

I was very Perplexed and could only Shuffle my Feet.

"Where is my Wood?" she asked.

"I am very Sorry, Grandmother!" I said, "but I Forgot."

"How very Strange!" the Old Woman said, now Looking at me even more Closely.

By this time many People had Gathered Around and were Listening. Each One was Crowding In for a Closer Look.

"Does Anyone here Know this Boy?" asked the Old Woman of the People.

No One Answered. Not even the Mother and Father who had Raised me.

"What is it you are Doing here?" the Old Woman asked.

But I could not Think of an Answer.

"Can you Do Anything?" asked the Old Woman.

"I can Play," I answered, "and I can Run Among the Lodges. And, and I can Make Up things, and I can Pretend!"

"Those are Useless things!" the Old Woman Scolded, and her Eyes Grew very Large. "What will we Do with him?" she said, Turning to the People who Stood there.

"Give him to me," one of the Men who was Standing there said, "and I will have him Make Bows."

"No!" answered Another. "Give him to me, and I will have him Learn from me."

"No!" yelled Another. "He should Learn my things, not yours."

Pretty soon Everyone was Yelling. And I Slunk Down Close to the Ground and Crawled Away, because I was Frightened. I Ran and Ran until I could not Hear them Anymore.

Then the Old Man Lit his Pipe and Offered a Smoke in this Way. "The Western Sky, the Father, Became the River Rainbow, Reflecting the Sacred Mountains and its Lakes, and Mirroring itself Within the Evening Sky Robe. This Way Reached Out with Hands that Gently Held the East and West. The Grass and the Trees of the Prairie Heard because they Too were Touched. The Third Mirror Sung of the Colors of the Heavens, Blending their Paintings of Green, White, Gold, and Black Into its Endless Robe. It was the Warm Robe of Earth, the Mother. The Little Boy, Alone and Lost, was the Fourth and Final Touching, because these Gifts are Made for those who are of this Heart."

Then he Continued his Story.

Tired, the Child Searched for a Place to Rest and Found One. It was a Place on the Top of a small Hill, Soft and Warm with Sweet Grass. It was the Place a Mother Deer had Prepared the Night Before. The Boy was Lonely, but not Frightened. Stars by the millions Warmed the Night Sky, Easing his Eyes Into Sleep. And he Slept as Only Children can Sleep.

The Next Morning he was Awakened by a Meadow Lark's Sun Song. He Sat Up and Rubbed his Eyes, Letting his Surroundings Become a Part of him. Remembering his Lodges, he Looked very Hard in the Direction he Thought he had Come from, but Saw Nothing. He Turned Slowly in a Circle, Straining his Eyes to their Utmost, and could see Only the Endless Prairie. He was just about to Complete his Circle when he Saw the funniest Little Man he had ever Seen in his Life. He was Sitting on the Ground in Front of a tiny Fire, Roasting some Meat. The Man's tiny Figure, Standing Up as Straight as he Could, was not Tall Enough to Reach the Boy's Waist. His Hair was Silver-White, and Hung in Braids Almost to the Ground. He was Dressed in a tiny Vest and had Leggings to Match. And on the very Tip of his Nose was a small Red Wart. The Little Boy was Unable to speak.

"Is he Real, or is he not?" Thought the Boy.

"Yes, I am Real!" the Little Man answered in Almost a Scolding Voice, "and I am Hungry. You are the Slowest Guest I have ever Had. I Thought you would Never Wake Up!"

"You Mean that I can Eat with you?" the Boy asked, Sitting Down Immediately and Taking One of the Pieces of Meat. He Hardly Finished his Sentence before he had Taken his First Bite.

"Zahuah!" the Little Man said, his Eyes Growing Wide. "I Foolishly Thought I would have to Ask you Twice."

The Boy Ate Quickly, Paying little Attention to the Old Man until he Finally Began to Slow Down. Only then did he Begin to Remember his Host.

"Hummmmmmm, what? hummmm." The Boy Started to Speak, Hesitated, then Began again. "Hummmmm, where ummmmm."

"What? Where? Hummmmmm?" the Old Man answered Looking Quizzically at the Little Boy. "Am I to Understand that this Means the Food was Good?"

"Hummmm, yes!" the Boy answered, Looking very much as the Old Man had. "But, I Guess, hummmm." He Hesitated again, then Blurted

Out, "Why are you so Small?"

"Why are you so Big?" the Old Man Smiled.

"Me?" the Boy answered with Surprise. "Me, Big?" Then he Laughed. "I am not Big." He Stopped again and Looked Around himself Quickly. "I do not Think I am, I Think . . . I do not Know why I am so Big. Do you Suppose I Grew Overnight?"

The Little Old Man Leaned Over and Studied the Boy Carefully before answering. "I Guess you did Grow, at least just a Little Overnight. But it is my Understanding that you Came here to Learn of your Name. Is that not So?"

"Me?" the Boy answered Thoughtfully. "Yes, I Think you are Right. Do you Know my Name?"

"No, I do not," answered the tiny Man. "But I Know where it is."

"You Do?" the Boy asked. He was Intensely Interested. "Where is it?"

"It is in the Sacred Mountains," answered the Old Man, "and I will Take you there."

"Zahuah!" the Boy said Excitedly, "but How will we Go there?"

"We will Walk there, of course," the tiny Man answered. "We will Walk there Together."

"Can we Leave Right Away?" asked the Boy, Clapping his Hands Together.

"Yes!" answered the Old Man. "Let us Go right Now!"

"But," the Boy said Suddenly, still Sitting there even though the Old Man was On his Feet Ready for the Walk, "Which Way will we Go?"

"This Way!" the tiny Man said as he Started to Walk.

The Boy Jumped to his Feet and Began to Follow. It did not Take him Long to Catch Up, because of his Longer Legs.

As they Walked, the tiny Old Man would Stop every Now and Then to Look at something that Grew Upon the Prairie or something that Moved there. One time it would be a Flower, and Another Time it would be to Watch a small Rabbit or other Being.

"Look," the Old Man said, Stopping a short Distance from a Herd of Buffalo. "See how Beautiful our Brothers are? Would you Like to Meet them?"

"Yes!" answered the Boy. "I would very much Like to Visit with them. But is this Possible?"

The Old Man Winked. "Certainly!" he answered. "Here, Let me Introduce you. But you will have to Touch the One you Wish to Speak with."

"But they are so Big!" the Boy said, Slowing his Walk. "Their Horns are so Big!"

"Do not be Afraid," the tiny Man Laughed. "They are your Brothers. These Buffalo will Never Hurt you."

So the Boy Walked Up to the First Buffalo he Saw in the Herd, very Cautiously of course, and Timidly Touched her.

"Greetings," the Buffalo said to the Boy. "Thank you for Touching me, for Now I can Speak."

"It is True!" the Boy said in Delight. "You can Speak!"

"I see that my Brother, Seven Arrows, is Walking with you to the Sacred Mountains," said the Buffalo.

"Seven Arrows!" the Boy said in Surprise, Turning to the tiny Man. "Are you Seven Arrows?"

"Yes," Seven Arrows said, Dancing Around in a small Circle. "Yes, I am."

"But," the Boy said in Dismay. "I Thought . . . hummmm, I Thought . . ."

"Yes. We Know," the Buffalo said. "Some See him as One Thing, and still Others as Another. Look at him Now."

The Little Boy Looked but where Once Stood a

tiny Man Now Stood a Great Buffalo Bull.

"Amazing!" the Boy said, Unable to Believe his Eyes. "I would Never Believe it, but for his Eyes! And those Eyes can Only be those of Seven Arrows."

"But Look at yourself!" the Great Buffalo Bull laughed. "Look at yourself!"

The Boy Looked Into a small Pool of Water that was Near By, and Received the Surprise of his Life. For Now he too was a Buffalo.

"I am a Buffalo!" the Boy laughed, Kicking Up his Heels and Running Around in a small Circle. "I am a Buffalo! I am a Buffalo," he Sang.

"Come," the Buffalo Bull said. "Let us Continue our Journey to the Mountains." And he Loped Off Across the Rolling Green Prairie. The Boy, who was Now a Smaller Bull, Kicked Up his Heels Once again and Raced after him.

They Traveled for a long time, Stopping every Once in a While to Enjoy the Abundant Sweet Grass, Eating all they Wanted. Then Suddenly, Out of Nowhere, Came a Song.

"Do you Hear that Song?" the Smaller Bull said, Stopping.

"Yes," answered the Great Bull. "It is Wolf, and he Wishes to Speak with us."

It was not Long before Wolf Came Over a small Rise and Came Up to the Two Buffalo.

"Greetings, Brothers," the Wolf said, Sitting On his Haunches. "There is a Camp Near By, and the People there are very Hungry. They are Starving, and the Children are Growing very Weak."

"Thank you very much for Telling us," the Great Bull answered, "for Now we can Give-Away."

"That is Good," the Wolf said, Getting to his Feet. "And Now I will be On my Way." And he Left.

"But!" the Smaller Bull said with a Great Deal of Apprehension in his Voice, "if we Give-Away, we will Become the Food for the People. And we will Never Get to the Sacred Mountains!"

"It is your Decision," the Great Bull said After a Time.

"We will Continue On to the Sacred Mountains," the Smaller Bull answered.

"They are this Way," the Great Bull said, Changing Directions. "Come, Follow me."

"But Wait," the Smaller Bull said, Stopping again. "I Hear the Children Crying. Even if it Means my Death, I Cannot See my little Brothers and Sisters Starve. I Want to Give-Away."

The Smaller Bull had hardly Finished Speaking when they were Surrounded by the People of the Camp. And their Arrows Touched the Two Buffalo, and they Fell Down. And they Slept.

Then the Boy Woke Up. He was very Surprised to Discover that he was Alive, but he was even more Surprised to Discover that he was Now Another Being of the Prairie. And Standing not Two Arms Lengths Away was a Small Wolverine. Frightened, the Boy Jumped to All his New Four Legs and Ran Toward the River.

"Wait!" the Small Wolverine Called, Running After him. "Wait for me!"

But he would not Wait, and Ran as Fast as he Could, Straight to the River. When he Got to the Bank of the River he Looked Hurriedly for a Place to Jump In and Swim Across. But when he Looked Down, he Received his Next Surprise. For the Reflection that Looked Back at him from the Surface of the Water was that of a Wolverine.

"Ooohhh, Trouble, Trouble," the Boy said, Looking at his Reflection. "I am in Serious Trouble Now. Look! I am a Wolverine."

"Do not be Troubled," the Other Wolverine

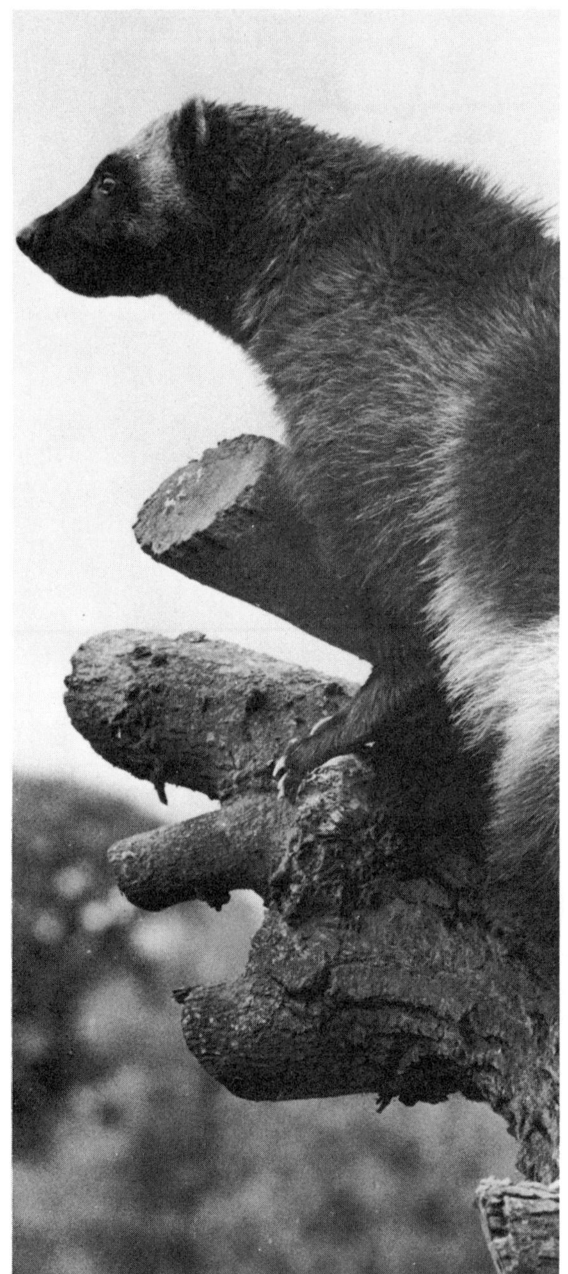

said, Coming to the Larger Wolverine's Side. "We now Can Continue our Journey to the Sacred Mountains."

"Is that you?" asked the Larger Wolverine of the Smaller. "Are you Seven Arrows?"

"Yes," the Smaller Wolverine answered. "It is I, but Come, Let us be On our Way."

"This is Terrible," the Larger Wolverine mumbled to himself as they Started on their Way again. "This is simply Terrible."

They had not Gone very Far when they Came Upon Two very large Bears Locked in a Life and Death Struggle.

"Look!" the Larger Wolverine called to the Smaller. "They will Kill Each Other if we do not Do something. One Brother will Kill the Other!"

"This is Terrible!" mumbled the Smaller Wolverine. "This is simply Terrible."

"We Cannot just Stand here," the Larger

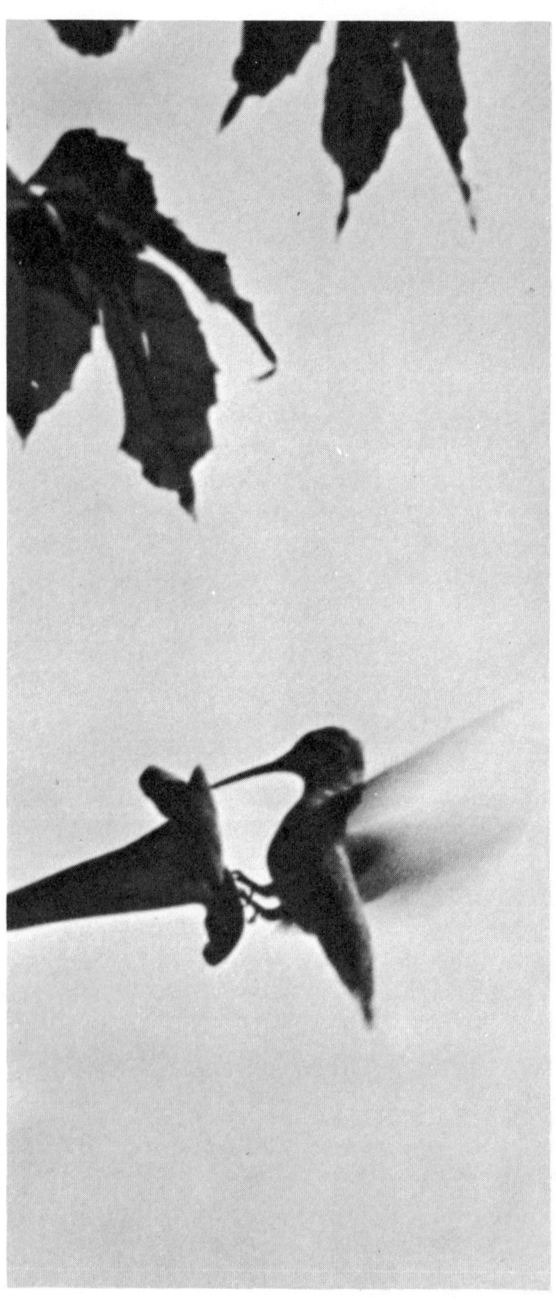

Wolverine said. "We must Do something!"

"This is Terrible," the Smaller Wolverine mumbled again. "Just Terrible."

The Larger Wolverine could Stand it No Longer. He Threw all Caution Away, and Ran Between the Two Bears.

"Stop it!" the Larger Wolverine Ordered. "Stop your Fighting at Once!"

"Yes! Yes!" Both Bears said, Backing Away Frightened. "Anything you Say!" Then they Both Turned and Ran just as Fast as they Could.

"Well!" the Larger Wolverine said, Puffing Up his Shoulders, "I Guess they Knew I Meant it." The Power of what he had just Accomplished Felt very Good.

"Yes," answered the Smaller Wolverine. "I Guess they Did."

Indeed, the Bears must have been very Impressed by what had Happened, because they Told a great many of the Beings about it. And many of the Other Beings Came to the Larger Wolverine to Resolve their Differences. Rabbits, Skunks, Elk, Deer, Weasels, and many more Came to the Larger Wolverine to Settle their Problems, and Every Time, the Larger Wolverine would Tell the Smaller Wolverine to Wait. He was the Center of Attention, and he Enjoyed a very Powerful Position. But After a While All the Beings Left him and He was Alone.

"Where is the Smaller Wolverine?" the Larger Wolverine asked a Rabbit.

"I do not Know," answered the Rabbit, "but I have Come to you to Say that the Beings of this Prairie are Building you a Special Lodge, and you will be Given a Special Place."

But the Larger Wolverine said, "Tell All the Beings of this Part of the Prairie I am Thankful, but I Wish to Find my Brother, the Smaller Wolverine."

The Larger Wolverine Searched and Searched,

but could not Find his Brother, the Smaller Wolverine. One Day he was so Heartbroken he Sat Down and Began to Cry. And as he Sat there Crying, a very tiny Yellow Hummingbird Flew Down and Sat Next to him.

"Come," the Yellow Hummingbird said. "Let us Continue our Journey. Come and Test your Wings."

The Little Boy could hardly Believe his New Fortune. Now he was a light, fragile, Blue Hummingbird.

"Well, what are you Waiting for?" asked Yellow Hummingbird.

"I Think I am Afraid to Fly," answered Blue Hummingbird.

"Jump Up," coaxed Yellow Hummingbird.

Little Blue Hummingbird Took One tiny Hop, Flapping his Wings. Just a Little, he Lifted Lightly from the Ground, ever so Little. But even this was too Much, and he Fluttered Back to Earth, Frightened. He Tried again and again, a New Way each Time. One Time he even Held his Breath. But After probably his millionth Try, or anyway that is what the Little Boy Thought, he Finally could Fly. Of course he could not Fly too High, because these Hummingbird Beings Live with the Flowers.

Near this Place was a Dry River Bed where Flowers Grew, a great River of Flowers that Flowed from the Mountains. Within this Gentle Flow of Color was a Whole New World of Beings.

"This is a Beautiful and Strange River," Blue Hummingbird said, Flying Closer for a Better Look. "Do we have Brothers here?"

"Yes, we Do," answered Yellow Hummingbird, Hovering Above a Honeyed Flower. "There are many Lodges just Below the Surface of this Wonderful River, and in Each One are our Brothers."

Blue Hummingbird Floated Up Stream just Above the Moving Color, when quite Unexpectedly a small Furry Head Bobbed Above the Flower Surface. It was a soft and very Friendly Baby Brown Rabbit.

"Greetings," said Brown Rabbit. "Will you Deliver a Message for me?"

"I would be very Glad to Deliver a Message for you," answered Little Blue Hummingbird. "Tell me and I will Take it for you."

The small Brown Rabbit had just Taken a large Bite from an especially Delicious Flower, and he had to Wait for a Moment before he could Speak again. "There is an Old Man who Lives near here, and he is Asking the Wind for Help."

"Good!" Yellow Hummingbird said, Flying in a Small Dance Circle. "We will Bring the Message for the Man."

"I do not Understand," Blue Hummingbird said, Flying Near By. "That is no Message."

"I Know," answered Yellow Hummingbird, "but Let us Fly to the Old Man and Learn."

They Flew a little Way from the Living River of Flowers and Found a Hunting Camp. Tending the Fire at that Camp was an Old Man.

Blue Hummingbird Watched Curiously as Yellow Hummingbird Darted here and there Near the Old Man. Then he Flew in a Quick Circle Around his Head, and the most Amazing of things Happened. The Old Man, who had been Haggard and Bent with Despair, now Straightened and Smiled. Blue Hummingbird even Detected a tiny Tear Under each Old Eye, a Tear of Joy. Yellow Hummingbird must have Seen the Question Upon Blue Hummingbird's Face, because he Immediately Began to Explain just at the very time Blue Hummingbird Began to Speak.

"The Old Man had Asked for a Sign," Yellow Hummingbird Hummed.

"A Sign?" said Blue Hummingbird, Blinking. "What do you Mean?"

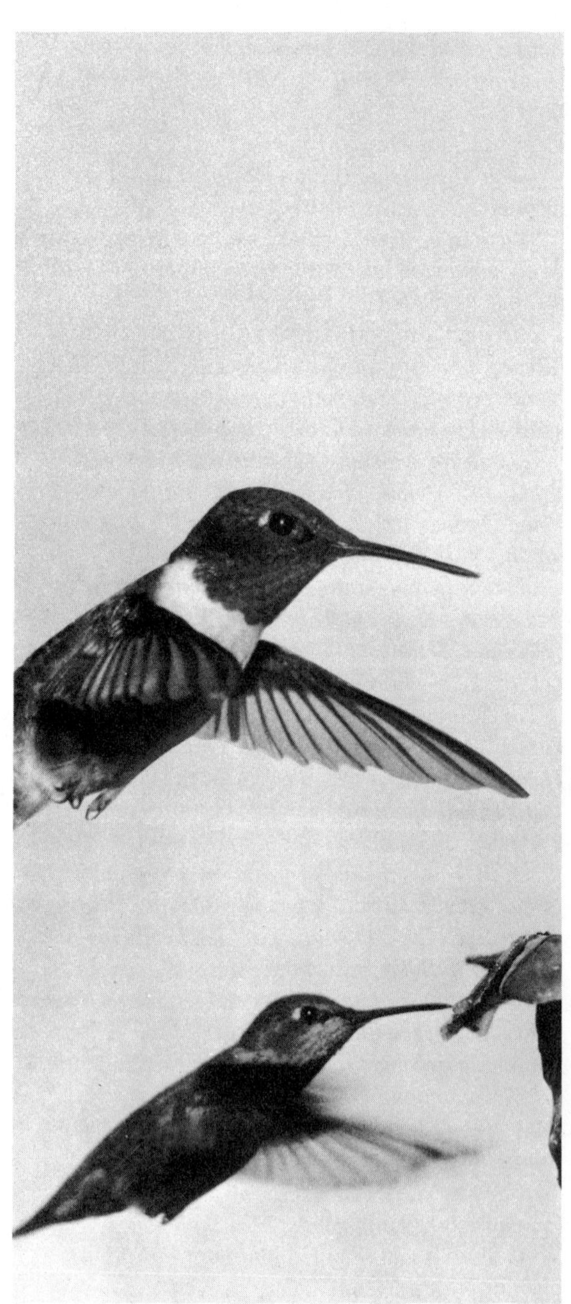

"Many times there is Doubt Among the Old," Yellow Hummingbird answered, Tasting a Bright Blue Flower. "And Many times there are those of the Old who Ask for a Gentle Sign. Fly Near the Old One as I did, and Circle his Head, and you will Understand."

Blue Hummingbird Did as he was Instructed, and Darted here and there as Yellow Hummingbird had. Then he Circled the Old Man's Head.

"Thank you," Blue Hummingbird Heard the Old Man Whisper, and his Eyes Explained the Rest.

"It is Magic," Blue Hummingbird Hummed when he Returned.

"Yes, it is," answered Yellow Hummingbird. "It is Magic to those who Seek a Sign."

The Blue and Yellow Hummingbirds Flew and Flew that Day, Until the Night Came Once again.

"We will Sleep here Tonight," Yellow Hummingbird said, Settling himself Within the Sweet Grass.

Only a Yawn Humm was Heard in Reply from Blue Hummingbird as he Snuggled Within the Warm Sweet Grass, and the Little Boy Slept.

The Next Morning the Little Boy Sat Up and Rubbed his Eyes. It was a Beautiful Morning, and One he Knew would be Full of New Adventures. He Looked Around Quickly for Seven Arrows, and Found a Surprise even more Beautiful than Seven Arrows. It was the Little Boy's Father.

"Come, my son," the Little Boy's Father said, as he Hugged him. "Come and Tell us of your Name."

That Evening, Green Fire Mouse Went for a Swim with White Rabbit and Dancing Moon. The Old Man Sat at the Edge of the River and Watched White Rabbit's Two Children. The Three Young People Swam Until the Moon was Bright and Full Overhead. Then, Tired and Refreshed at the Same Time, they Warmed themselves by the Fire at the Lodge. They Ate Fresh Berries White Rabbit had Gathered and Enjoyed the Meat Dancing Moon had Boiled in Preparation for the Evening. It was an Evening that would be Remembered Forever.

"Where are you taking the children?" White Rabbit asked as she busied herself with the lunch she was packing.

"Buffalo hunting," Green Fire Mouse answered without looking up from the book he had been reading.

"Buffalo?" White Rabbit frowned, turning around to face her husband. "Have you got something up your sleeve?"

Green Fire Mouse only smiled his answer as two children suddenly burst in through the door.

"You commin or aintcha?" one of the children said as he took his grandfather's hand.

"You won't get very far without me," the old man said, pretending to scowl. "I've got the keys."

The old man walked as steadily as he could out to where a young man was waiting for him by an old truck. The two children clung and almost swung from the old man's hands as they pulled him toward the waiting pickup.

"Can I drive, Grandpaw?" the young man asked as he reached for the door handle.

"Sure," the old man answered as he slid into the seat.

"We're gonna fish again at Owl Creek, right?" the young man said as he started the truck.

"Nope," Green Fire Mouse answered as he lit a cigarette. "We're going to the Little Horn this time. Up to the mountains."

"You kids sit down!" the young man bawled out the window to his brother and sister who were in the back of the pickup. "And don't jump around!"

Rocky put the truck in gear and pointed it toward the mountains. As he drove along his mind became deep in thought.

"Hey, Grandpaw," Rocky said turning to Green Fire Mouse, who by this time appeared to be almost asleep. "What do you think about this school business anyway? You know they fill your head with one hell of a lotta junk."

"You don't like school?" Green Fire Mouse answered from under his reservation hat, still not looking up.

"No, it isn't that," Rocky said quietly, still thinking. "I really like the sports and stuff. Actually, I guess what really bugs me is their religion, if you know what I mean. I mean it's really a mess, man. Original sin and everything."

"They haven't understood about the seven arrows yet," Green Fire Mouse answered from under his hat.

"The seven arrows!" Rocky almost laughed. "Wow, Grandpaw, you gotta be kidding. Nobody talks about the seven arrows any more. And what's that got to do with all of that other stuff?"

"Green and red apples," Green Fire Mouse said from the hat. "You know that's the symbol of original sin, don't you?"

"Apples?" Rocky frowned. "Yeah, I guess it is, but . . ."

"And," the voice continued from under the hat, "what's happened to Christianity is that it has become an old woman, a wicked witch. You see, the child of this old woman's marriage was poisoned by the apple, and has been asleep. She is a beautiful young maiden waiting for the spirit of peace that is in each of us to kiss her. Then she will awaken. And the paradox, my son, is this. This symbol of the young maiden is multiple. The young maiden is every woman. And she is the symbol of the way, the new lodge, like in the story of the buffalo wives."

"Wow! Grandpaw, you gotta be kidding with all that old time talk!" Rocky almost laughed out loud.

"No, I'm not," the voice from under the hat answered. "It's a teaching. And there are seven arrows in the story too. They are called dwarfs. They give away the gems of wisdom of the north to all those who understand. And their hair is white, these seven dwarfs."

"Tell me the story, Grandpaw," Rocky said. "What's the name of the story?"

"The name of the story is Snow White," Green Fire Mouse answered, as he sat up and began his story. "You see, once upon a time . . ."

Finally they arrived at the river. The kids scrambled from the pickup and soon everyone was fishing.

"What was the symbol of the mirror in the story, Grandpaw?" Rocky asked as they fished.

"It is the people. It is the circle, and it is the shield," answered Green Fire Mouse. "But it is more than that. It is also the law."

"Are there more teachings, Grandpaw?" Rocky asked.

"Sure," the voice again answered him from under the hat. "There is the entire world and everything in it that can teach you much, much more. There are the songs, the bibles, the cities, and the dreams. Everything upon the earth and in the heavens is a mirror for the people. It is a total gift. Jump up! And you will see the Medicine Wheel."

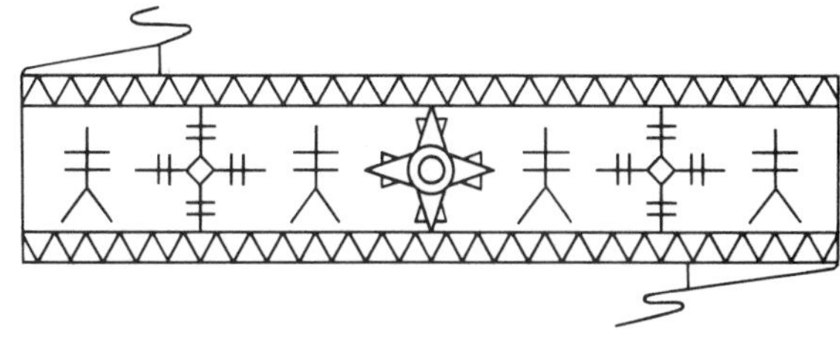

Picture credits

Shields
designed by Hyemeyohsts Storm and Karen Harris, painted by Karen Harris

Medicine Belts
designed and drawn by Sandra Storm

The American Museum of Natural History
45, 115, 128–129.

Bettmann
346

Black Star
Lornig; 72.

Courtesy of The Brooklyn Museum
32–33, 46–47, 106–107, 130–131, 198–199, 228–229.

Brown Brothers
38–39.

Culver
197.

Richard Erdoes
237, 268, 329

FPG
Kent, 52–53; Photoworld, 252–253

Courtesy of Lowie Museum of Anthropology, University of California, Berkeley: 98–99, 119, 332.

Monkmeyer
Falk, 102–103, 334–335; *Gregor*, 273; *Henle*, 314; *Huffman*, 261; *Sumner*, 84; U.P.R., 86–87.

National Audubon Society
Amber, 78, 95, 317; *Austing*, 232–233, 256, 320, 338–339; *Blood*, 364; *Cesar*, 250–251; *Cruickshank*, 48–49, 79, 150–151, 174–175, 182–187, 343, 360; *Este*, 204; *Gerard*, 83, 290; *Halliday*, 318; *Hosking*, 74; *Johnson*, 366; *Kestel*, 44; *Maslowski*, 77; *Miller*,

262, 316; *Rue*, 76, 172, 211, 244, 247; *Rush*, 315; *Smith*, 71, 321; *Van Wormer*, 276–277; *Walker*, 366; *Wilson*, 69; *White*, VIII–IX, 68, 178, 208, 362–363.

Courtesy, The New York Public Library Picture Collection
166.

Courtesy, The Pierpont Morgan Library: copyright, E. S. Curtis

157	*Wolf—Apsaroke*
160	*Oksoyapiw—Blackfoot*
162	*A Hopi Man*
165	*Hollow Horn Bear*
171	*Atsina Camp*
190	*Two Strike*
194	*Travaux—Piegan*
216–17	*In Black Canyon—Apsaroke*
219	*Atsina Chiefs*
223	*Medicine Crow—Apsaroke*
226–7	*The Chief and his Staff—Apsaroke*
235	*Spotted Bull—Mandan*
238	*Assinboin Boy—Atsina*
241	*No Bear—Atsina*
249	*Lone Flag—Atsina*
255	*Yellow Kidney—Piegan*
259	*White Calf—Piegan*
265	*Apsaroke War Group*
271	*Four Horns—Arikara*
280–1	*The Piegan*
283	*In the Land of the Sioux*
284	*A Cheyenne Chief*
293	*New Chest—Piegan*
294	*Arikara Girl*
297	*Apsaroke Medicine Tipi*
298	*Little Wolf—Cheyenne*
301	*Black Belly—Cheyene*
304	*Left Hand—Comanche*
307	*Sioux Chiefs*
308	*Painted Lodges—Piegan*
310	*Head Dress—Atsina*
313	*Mosa—Mohave*
323	*High Hawk*
324-5	*Arikara Medicine Fraternity—The Prayer*
330–1	*An offering at the Waterfall—Nambe*
348–9	*The Land of the Atsina*
350	*Watching for the Signal—Apsaroke*
352	*Cheyenne Warriors*
355	*Tearing Lodge—Piegan*
357	*The Scout—Atsina*

Rapho-Guillumette
Bauer, 209; *Henderson*, 368–369.